HIGH SOCIETY

ALSO BY JOSEPH A. CALIFANO, JR.

The Student Revolution:
  A Global Confrontation (1970)

A Presidential Nation (1975)

The Media and the Law (1976)
  (with Howard Simons)

The Media and Business (1979)
  (with Howard Simons)

Governing America (1981)

The 1982 Report on Drug Abuse and Alcoholism

America's Health Care Revolution:
  Who Lives? Who Dies? Who Pays? (1986)

The Triumph and Tragedy of Lyndon Johnson:
  The White House Years (1991)

Radical Surgery:
  What's Next for America's Health Care (1994)

Inside: A Public and Private Life (2004)

HIGH SOCIETY

HOW SUBSTANCE ABUSE
RAVAGES AMERICA AND WHAT
TO DO ABOUT IT

———

JOSEPH A. CALIFANO, JR.

Founding Chair and President of
The National Center on Addiction and
Substance Abuse (CASA) at Columbia University

PublicAffairs
New York

Published in the United States by PublicAffairs™,
a member of the Perseus Books Group.

Public Affairs books are available at special discounts for bulk purchases
in the U.S. by corporations, institutions, and other organizations.
For more information, please contact the Special Markets
Department at the Perseus Books Group, 11 Cambridge Center,
Cambridge, MA 02142, call (617) 252-5298, or email
special.markets@perseusbooks.com.

A CIP catalog record for this book is available from the Library of Congress.
ISBN-13: 978-1-58648-335-7
ISBN-10: 1-58648-335-8

First Edition

10 9 8 7 6 5 4 3 2 1

This book is dedicated to all those who have experienced the agony of drug and alcohol abuse and addiction and to their families and circles of friends—the mothers and fathers, sons and daughters, brothers and sisters, husbands and wives, grandparents, neighbors, coworkers, and classmates who have shared that suffering. My hope is that this book will show that there is light at the end of the darkest tunnels.

The author is donating all royalties
from sales of this book to
The National Center on Addiction and Substance
Abuse (CASA) at Columbia University.

CONTENTS

PROLOGUE

There was a time in our history—and not so long ago—when smoking was cool, when seat belts were for sissies, and when AIDS was an accepted death sentence for gay sex. Today our attitudes are profoundly different—with powerful and beneficial consequences. Smoking has been cut sharply, and so have the related deaths from lung cancer and heart disease. Auto safety measures have curbed the highway death and injury rate. AIDS is recognized as a serious illness rather than a social curse.

In all three cases, we fundamentally changed our attitudes and, as a result, took actions that greatly improved the quality of life for millions of our people.

This is a book about the pervasive and pernicious role of drug and alcohol abuse in our society. It will show how such abuse causes and aggravates just about every intractable problem our nation faces. And it calls for a fundamental change in our attitude about substance abuse and addiction and a revolution in how we deal with it.

There's ample precedent for such a revolution. In 1978, when, as Secretary of Health, Education, and Welfare, I mounted the nation's antismoking campaign and declared the department's buildings smoke-free, employees demonstrated in opposition and critics called the initiative one of "all smoke and no fire." Yet, today, thirty years later, there is universal acceptance of the dangers of smoking and secondhand smoke. We have moved from a nation where the smoker said, "Would you like a cigarette?" to one where he sheepishly asks, "Do you mind if I smoke?"—and where the common response is "Yes, I do." A generation ago not only auto companies but drivers as well scoffed at the use of seat belts; today the industry sells safety, and just about every driver and most passengers buckle up before the car starts. With an appreciation of the dangers of AIDS and its fierce assault on (and beyond) the gay community, we have mounted an all-fronts medical research and a safe-sex and abstinence-education campaign that in a decade has dramatically changed attitudes about the disease and its victims.

We face many problems in America: entitlement programs that defy reform, rising health care costs, lousy urban schools, prisons bursting at the bars, state family courts and child welfare systems on the cusp of collapse, a bulging federal deficit threatening our economic prosperity and global supremacy, millions of people trapped in pockets of rural and urban poverty, and ample financing for terrorists. To solve these problems, we have passed thousands of laws. We have spent billions of dollars. We have created hundreds of federal, state, and local law enforcement and social service agencies. Parents, children, and spouses have offered endless prayers. We have sent troops to Colombia and tried to stamp out poppy fields in Afghanistan. But these problems persist.

Why?

Because of our attitude about the most sinister and sweeping force that lurks behind them—abuse and addiction involving alcohol, tobacco, and illegal and prescription drugs—and our failure to counter that force.

It is hard to find an American family or circle of friends that substance abuse has not touched directly. Although we are 4 percent of the world's population, we Americans consume 65 percent of the world's illegal drugs.[1] One in four Americans will have an alcohol or drug disorder at some point in his or her life.[2] And most of these people have parents, children, siblings, friends, and colleagues who will suffer collateral damage.

Such is life in the High Society. It doesn't have to be that way. It is so because conservatives, liberals, and moderates alike have become choruses of politicians, stage right, left, and center, each calling for more of their same old programs, chanting in louder and louder voices: "If all the king's horses and all the king's men cannot put Humpty Dumpty back together again, then give us more horses and give us more men!"

This book calls for a revolution in the way all of us—politicians, parents and physicians, teens, schools and universities, clergyman, cops and corporations, judges, lawyers, and journalists—perceive the threat that substance abuse and addiction pose to our people and the obligation to protect our children. It is a call to sober up the High Society, to recognize that substance abuse and addiction is the nation's number one serial killer and crippler, and to acknowledge these fundamental realities:

- Substance abuse and addiction is a chronic disease of epidemic proportions, with physical, psychological, emotional, and spiritual elements that require continuing and holistic care.
- Substance abuse is a culprit implicated in our nation's high health care costs, crime, and social ills, including child abuse and neglect, homelessness, teen pregnancy, the wildfire spread of sexually transmitted diseases, and family breakup.
- There is a statistical and biological (chemical, neurological) relationship between smoking, abusing alcohol, and marijuana use, and between abuse of those drugs and use of cocaine, heroin, prescription drugs, methamphetamines, hallucinogens, and other substances.
- A child who gets through age twenty-one without using illegal drugs, smoking, or abusing alcohol is virtually certain never to do so.
- Girls and boys are likely to use drugs for different reasons, and they exhibit use and abuse in distinct ways.
- Individuals who have become addicts need all the carrots and sticks that can be mustered to motivate them to achieve and maintain recovery—and with the right mix of those carrots and sticks, millions can recover.
- Preventing substance abuse and addiction is a global problem that requires international as well as national leadership by our government.

Accepting those realities leads inexorably to the conclusion that, in terms of public policy, personal and parental conduct and attitudes, medical training and practice, criminal justice and prisons, schools and seminaries, child and maternal welfare systems, family courts, and government programs, it's time to think major surgery and to abandon the iodine and mercurochrome approaches of the past. In the appalling political jargon that has framed prior efforts, it's time to stop waging this "war" with cap pistols and to mobilize all our people and modern science behind a national effort capable of defeating this enemy.

We need a fundamental change in attitude among all our people—parents, politicians, and professionals—about substance abuse and addiction. I'm talking cultural change potent enough to prompt a revolution in the nation's criminal justice, medical, educational, and social service systems, in our foreign policy priorities, and in the exercise of parent power for children and teens.

We must end our denial, stamp out the stigma, rethink our concept of crime and punishment, reshape our medical system, and commit the energy and resources needed to confront this plague. Failure to do so is a decision to continue writing off millions of Americans to lives of debilitating illness, social dysfunction, and crime, and to continue imposing on taxpayers and citizens exorbitant medical, social service, and prison costs.

Though substance abuse has touched most every family and neighborhood, my years of public service and total immersion in this field convince me that few Americans appreciate its complicity in just about every social problem our nation faces—and even fewer believe we can do something about it. The fact is we have never really tried sensibly, creatively, and aggressively to confront substance abuse and addiction across the board. We can do it. The issue is whether we are willing to. This book is my effort to inspire the will and show the way.

We cannot create a Garden of Eden utterly free of drug and alcohol abuse, but we can save millions of lives, untold heartache, and billions of dollars by dramatically reducing this scourge. This book is a call to arms, a manifesto of actions we can take, a cry to fundamentally change the way we view and confront drug and alcohol abuse and addiction.

CHAPTER 1

THE HIGH SOCIETY

What do Judy Garland, Mickey Mantle, President George W. Bush, Snoop Dogg, many mothers on welfare, Elton John, Rush Limbaugh, Natalie Cole, Jamie Lee Curtis, Don Imus, U.S. Supreme Court Justice William Rehnquist, most incarcerated felons and arrested juveniles, Janis Joplin, Frank Sinatra, Mel Gibson, millions of children and teens under twenty-one, Billy Joel, Joe Namath, Robert Downey, Jr., Robin Williams, and former First Lady Betty Ford have in common?

What funds terrorism, spawns crime, drives up health care costs, breaks up families, spreads AIDS, promotes unwanted teen pregnancy, and frustrates so many efforts to eliminate poverty?

What attribute do most victims of cancer, heart disease, emphysema, crippling bronchitis, accidents, and violence share?

What's the culprit in most assaults and homicides, incest, domestic violence, college date rape, and campus racial incidents?

Substance abuse and addiction.

On any given day, 100 million Americans are taking some stimulant, antidepressant, tranquillizer, or painkiller; smoking; inhaling from aerosol cans or glue bottles; or self-medicating with alcohol or illegal substances like marijuana, cocaine, heroin, methamphetamines, hallucinogens, Ecstasy, and other designer drugs.[1]

Chemistry is chasing Christianity as the nation's largest religion. The millions of Americans, who *daily* take some kind of mood-altering, painkilling or mind-bending prescription drug, abuse alcohol and illegal drugs, and smoke cigarettes likely exceeds the number who *weekly* attend religious services.[2] Indeed, millions of Americans who in times of personal crisis and emotional and mental anguish once turned to priests, ministers, and rabbis for keys to the heavenly kingdom now go to physicians and psychiatrists, who hold the keys to the kingdom of pharmaceutical relief, or to drug dealers and liquor stores, as chemicals and alcohol replace the confessional as a source of solace and forgiveness.

We have learned that chemistry makes parenting easier for Mom and Dad and teaching easier for Miss Brooks. Over the decade ending in 2005, the number of kids on Ritalin, Adderall, or some other drug to treat attention deficit disorder exploded.[3] The number of children taking antipsychotic pills has soared since 2001.[4] The age at which children begin to smoke, drink, and use marijuana has dropped below thirteen years.[5] It is no longer surprising to read of nine- or ten-year-olds smoking, drinking, inhaling, swallowing, or even injecting some substance to get high.

From its low point during the last quarter century of 8.5 million in 1992, the number of Americans twelve and older who use illicit drugs more than doubled to 19.7 million in 2005.[6] Similarly, despite some decline since 2002, illegal drug use by twelve- to seventeen-year-olds climbed from its quarter-century low of 1.1 million in 1992 to 2.6 million in 2005.[7]

Athletes thrive on all sorts of stuff: steroids, amphetamines, erythropoietin, bodybuilding creams. The medicine cabinet and chemistry lab are common stops along the expressway to professional stardom. Track stars have for some time been taking erythropoietin to increase their speed and endurance. Baseball players, caught with their steroids showing, have for years swallowed "greenies," amphetamine pills to maintain their energy over the course of the long season. The owners don't care so long as breaking records fill the seats at higher and higher prices. And the fans look at today's athletes the way ancient Romans at the Coliseum viewed Christians fed to the lions: as hunks of fungible flesh served up to entertain with home runs and 325-pound bone-crushing tackles.

Rock stars, high on cocaine, shake the rafters with eardrum-bursting anthems to drug and alcohol abuse. Film and television stars commonly bounce in and out of drug or alcohol rehab. Celebrities fill the pages of *People, US*, the *National Enquirer* and Page Six of the *New York Post* with outrageous alcohol- and drug-fueled antics.

Physicians promiscuously prescribe mood-altering pills to patients, particularly girls and women. The medical profession has pharmaceuticalized the normal stages of female life by prescribing mood-altering drugs for problems related to menstruation, marriage, motherhood, and menopause. Psychiatrists replace the couch with chemistry, pushing pills to squelch patient guilt and anxiety.

Pharmaceutical companies and their Madison Avenue mavens christen new disorders and old ailments with catchy names and hawk pills to treat them. They fill our television screens with happy and comforting images promoting pills that promise uninterrupted hours of serene sleep and clips of frolicking couples who have shed their social anxieties or physical pain thanks to the latest pill. They offer relief from "restless leg syndrome" and "irritable bowel syndrome." In 2006, the Food and Drug Administration approved the first pill specifically to ease wintertime blues, as pharmaceutical promoters branded this condition "SAD—seasonal affective disorder."[8] That same year, psychiatrists dubbed road rage "intermittent explosive disorder" and offered as treatment antidepressant chemicals to target serotonin receptors in the brain.[9] Marketing is so aggressive and the pace of new drug approvals so fast and furious that the American Medical Association has called for a moratorium on direct-to-consumer advertising in order to give doctors a chance to learn about new drugs before patients demand prescriptions to ease their pain, bend their minds, or sleep through the night.[10]

The medications that aim to perfect the human condition are miracles of modern pharmacology. I applaud the scientific geniuses who have discovered them and the health care, marketing, and distribution systems that have made them available to help millions of our people. The fault lies not in these medications, but in ourselves—in how we view these pharmaceuticals and use them. We see them not just as palliative when we, as fallible human beings, overindulge or suffer physical or mental illness despite our best efforts to stay healthy. Rather, they have become a means to allow further abuse of mind and body. We use them to eat, drink, work, play, and perform with abandon, uninhibited by a sense of personal responsibility—as students cramming for exams or partying through the night, Wall Street bankers deal-making around the clock, athletes chasing records, and parents and teachers trying to calm rambunctious children. If Moses were an American at the dawn of the twenty-first century, the tablets he would bring down from the mountain would be Vicodin and Valium, not a set of commandments to guide our conduct.

The anecdotal evidence is everywhere, even among society's most successful members: in the addiction to alcohol and pills of megastars like Elizabeth Taylor and Liza Minelli; in the collapse of the athletic careers of professional superstars like all-pro Lawrence Taylor and Cy Young Award winner Dwight Gooden; in the destructive cocaine and heroin dependence of Eugene Fodor, the first American to win the Tchaikovsky Violin Competition in Moscow; in the problems of teen movie queen Lindsay Lohan and the antics of celebrities like Charlie Sheen and Paris Hilton; in the life-threatening alcohol and drug addiction of Tim Allen and the overdose deaths of John Belushi, Chris Farley, and pop cultural icons Marilyn Monroe and Elvis Presley.

Those who work the halls of national and state legislatures know how treacherous the lure of alcohol and pills can be in the corridors of political success. We've seen this in the political wives, Betty Ford, Kitty Dukakis, Joan Kennedy, and Cindy McCain, and in the long line of alcohol-abusing politicians, including Congressmen Patrick Kennedy, Jim Ramstad, and Mark Foley, and at the peak of their influence two of the most powerful congressional committee chairmen in history, Wilbur Mills and Russell Long, as well as Texas governor Ann Richards, Iowa governor and senator Harold Hughes, D.C. mayor Marion Barry, and Reagan administration cabinet officer Drew Lewis and top White House staffer Michael Deaver. Working as Lyndon Johnson's chief domestic aide, I smoked four packs a day, with regular cigarettes in one pocket and mentholated in another so I could keep getting my nicotine hit even when my throat was raw.

Is there an American without a family member or friend who smoked himself to premature disability and death from emphysema, lung cancer, or heart disease? The celebrity morbidity list here begins with Humphrey Bogart, Joe DiMaggio, and Nat King Cole and gets

longer each day, in 2005 claiming the lives of American comedic icon
Johnny Carson and ABC news anchor Peter Jennings.

The statistical evidence gives substance abuse and addiction its sinister
status as Public Health Enemy Number One:

- 61 million Americans are hooked on cigarettes.[11]
- 16 to 20 million are addicted to alcohol or abuse it regularly.[12]
- More than 15 million abuse prescription opioids, depressants,
  and stimulants each year.[13]
- 15 million smoke marijuana.[14]
- 2.4 million use cocaine; more than 600,000 use crack.[15]
- More than half a million are hooked on heroin.[16]
- More than 500,000 are methamphetamine addicts.[17]
- 1 million regularly use Ecstasy and hallucinogens like LSD
  (lysergic acid diethylamide) and PCP (phencyclidine).[18]
- Almost 2 million of our children have used steroids.[19]
- 4.5 million teens have used controlled prescription drugs like
  OxyContin, Vicodin, Ritalin, and Adderall to get high.[20]

The human misery that addiction and abuse cause can't be calculated—
the broken homes; lives snuffed out in the twenties; teenage mothers
and absent fathers; women victimized by violence and rape; babies de-
formed by a parent's smoking, drinking, or illicit drug use; children mo-
lested by fathers hopped up on beer, pot, or cocaine; old people locking
themselves in urban apartments, afraid of grocery shopping even in day-
time; rural midwesterners wary of exploding methamphetamine labs;
babies neglected, beaten, and sometimes killed by alcohol- and crack-
addicted parents; eight-year-olds sent out to steal or buy drugs for
addicted mothers; children malnourished, wallowing in unsanitary conditions; twelve-year-olds in such agony and despair that they themselves resort to drugs and alcohol for relief; teens committing suicide.
For some children, it may be possible to cauterize the bleeding, but the
scars of drug- and alcohol-spawned parental abuse and neglect are likely
to be permanent.

Substance abuse and addiction visit a special savagery on America's poor and minorities. But they spawn tragedies far beyond the black and Hispanic urban ghettos, migrant workers, and rural pockets of poverty. Three-quarters of illegal drug users work either full or part time.[21] Heroin wrenched life away from Ethel Kennedy's son, David, in a luxurious Palm Beach hotel at age twenty-eight, and alcohol and drug addiction has touched many other members of that royal American family, including Robert Kennedy, Jr., Matthew Kennedy, Michael Kennedy, Patrick Kennedy, Ted Kennedy, Jr., Joan Kennedy, Patricia Kennedy Lawford, and her son Christopher. Alcoholism has devastated the Barrymore family, stunting the careers of patriarch John, his son John, Jr., and threatening the third-generation Barrymore, Hollywood actress Drew. Reality television has brought into American homes the battle with alcohol, drugs, and painkillers of Ozzy Osborne, daughter Kelly, and son Jack.

If we can't calculate the human misery and repair the broken hearts, we can put dollar signs on some costs of substance abuse and addiction. In 2006, the financial bill was moving toward $1 trillion in health care, low productivity, disability, welfare, fires, crime and punishment, property damage from vandalism, interest on the federal debt, legal and court costs, family breakup, child abuse, and the array of social interventions, public and private, to deal with the ravages of this epidemic on addicts and abusers, their families and friends.[22]

Half the beds in many American hospitals hold victims of auto and home accidents, cancers, cardiovascular diseases, liver, kidney and respiratory ailments, AIDS, other illness, and violence caused or exacerbated by tobacco, alcohol, and drug abuse.[23]

Cigarette smoking and alcohol and drug abuse have been pushing up state and local taxes and raiding government coffers for years to pay for rising Medicaid costs. Americans crippled by smoking and alcohol abuse take home billions of dollars in social security and veterans' disability payments.[24]

Drug and alcohol abusers and addicts crowd our prisons and clog our courts. Some 80 percent of adult inmates incarcerated for felonies and of juvenile arrestees are involved in drug- or alcohol-related offenses or have drug and alcohol problems.[25]

Many women remaining on welfare are drug and alcohol abusers and addicts. At least seven of ten abused and neglected children in the nation's family court and child welfare systems are offspring of substance-abusing parents.[26] More than half a million children are in foster care, double the number in the mid-1980s, an increase largely due to parental alcohol, crack cocaine, and methamphetamine addiction.[27]

Alcohol and drugs are the prime suspects in the spread of AIDS and other sexually transmitted diseases.[28] Intravenous drug use is the conventional perpetrator.[29] But abuse of beer, liquor, pot, cocaine, and pills like Ecstasy plays a major role. Young Americans high on such substances are far more likely to have risky sexual relations with many partners.[30]

Every five years, substance abuse and addiction claims some three million Americans—more people than have died in all our wars and auto accidents combined.[31] During the nine years of the Vietnam War, more than 58,000 Americans died in Southeast Asia;[32] during those same years, more than 3.5 million Americans died from smoking-related illnesses, almost 1 million from alcohol abuse and alcoholism, and almost 200,000 from illegal drug abuse. More Americans die in a day from smoking than died in the entire year 2005 in Iraq and Afghanistan.[33]

If there are indications that smoking and marijuana use are leveling off or declining among teens, heavy drinking is rising among high school seniors and college students, particularly girls and women. The number of women who reported drinking to get drunk more than tripled between 1977 and 1993.[34] From 1993 to 2001, the number of women who admitted being drunk three or more times in the past thirty days rose 26 percent.[35] A survey of students visiting the health clinic of a New York City university found that 65 percent had been drunk within the past week.[36] Michael Sovern, when president of Columbia University, told me that he had to move the graduation ceremony from afternoon to morning in order to minimize rampant and unruly drunkenness. Surprised, I mentioned his comment to several other university presidents; most confessed they had done the same. While president of Princeton University, Howard Shapiro called alcohol abuse "the greatest single threat to the university's fulfillment of its mission."

Addiction and abuse have changed the way we educate millions of our elementary and secondary schoolchildren. In many urban centers, teachers are terrorized by drug dealers—some of them students. Those who try to teach find it distracting and intimidating (to say the least) to be ushered, along with their students, through metal detectors as they enter the school building, and, for their own protection, locked in their classrooms while teaching.

America's children are at greatest risk—and not only from illegal drug dealers, but from nicotine pushers in cigarette companies and beer and alcohol merchants as well. They all know that the younger individuals are when they become smokers and regular drinkers, the likelier they are to get hooked on nicotine, booze, and drugs.[37] Drug dealers involve poor children in their street trade and push drugs on teens and preteens. Ninety percent of regular cigarette smokers are hooked in their teens.[38] Children and teens see more alcohol ads in magazines than adults and two television commercials for every three that adults view.[39]

Substance abuse and addiction is the ugly elephant in the living room of American society. Until we appreciate the weight of this elephant and accept its reality, until we end our national and personal denial, until we shed the stigma, we will continue to live with the individual and family tragedies spawned by tobacco, alcohol, and illegal and prescription drug abuse, to suffer the failures that have limited the effectiveness of well-intentioned public and private social initiatives, to waste taxpayer money, and to help finance the very terrorism that threatens our nation.

The first steps in curing our self-destructive blindness and eliminating this scourge are to understand how it became the greatest threat our children face and how it has become implicated in just about every social ill our nation confronts.

CHAPTER 2

HOW DID WE BECOME THE HIGH SOCIETY?

Once upon a time in America, people endured pain and adjusted to the changing moods that mark human nature without an endless variety of pharmaceuticals served up by drug companies. Popular musicians performed without snorting cocaine and shooting heroin. Teens partied without smoking pot. College students drank without bingeing from Thursday night until Monday morning. Upper East Side rich kids, Beverly Hills brats, and gays socialized without club drugs. Tobacco didn't kill 450,000 people and make another 8.6 million people seriously ill each year.[1] Crack cocaine didn't turn poor urban neighborhoods into killing fields. Rural garages weren't moonlighting as manufacturing plants for crystal meth. Athletes performed without bulking up on steroids. Young women kept their weight down without smoking. Most all of us stayed awake without amphetamines and got to sleep without sedatives. Rambunctious children were disciplined, not drugged, into correct behavior.

Today, from toddling to the twilight of life, Americans seek a fix for every fret. We're 4 percent of the world's population but consume more than half the world's mood-altering and painkilling pharmaceuticals and two-thirds of the world's illegal drugs.[2] Is it any wonder that, for more than a decade, twelve- to seventeen-year-olds responding to an open-ended question in the annual back-to-school survey of The National Center on Addiction and Substance Abuse (CASA) at Columbia University have named drugs as the number one problem they face?[3]

How and why did we become the High Society?

TOBACCO

Within days of their 1492 landing in the New World, Christopher Columbus and his crew saw how attached American Indians were to tobacco, smoking, snuffing, and chewing it for medicinal and ceremonial purposes.[4] Columbus looked down on these natives, and when his own men began puffing tobacco peace pipes, he reprimanded and disciplined them for sinking to the level of the "red savages."

But he couldn't stop them. With unwitting public health prescience, Columbus sensed the addictive nature of nicotine. "It was not within their power to refrain from indulging in the habit," he said.[5]

By the late 1600s, tobacco had become a profitable cash crop for early farmers in Virginia and North Carolina.[6] It was used as currency to pay fines and taxes and even served as collateral against the French loan to the colonies to finance the Revolutionary War.[7] Taxes on tobacco raised money to pay down the war debt.[8]

As the nation expanded westward during the 1700s, pipe smoking became popular on the American frontier, while wealthy easterners, copying British aristocracy, took to snuff.[9] Chewing, however, became the most popular form of tobacco consumption. Easier to consume than snuff and free of the fire hazards of smoking, chewing tobacco allowed men to enjoy their habit while on the job. Manufacturers sweetened, moistened, and packaged their product to make it more palatable, pocketable, and profitable.[10]

With its heftier hit of nicotine and strong masculine scent, the cigar became a favorite of American men during the war against Mexico in the mid-nineteenth century. About this time, cigarettes imported from Europe made their debut on the streets of New York, but they did not capture a significant slice of the tobacco market until the Civil War. That's when soldiers found that inhaling the (once considered effeminate) hand-rolled cigarette delivered a cheaper and quicker nicotine hit than pipes or chewing tobacco.[11] By 1864, Americans were smoking so many cigarettes that President Abraham Lincoln and the Union Congress slapped a federal excise tax on them to help bankroll the War Between the States.[12]

As returning soldiers resumed their everyday lives and went back to chewing and snuffing, cigarette companies scrambled to make brands more appealing. They packaged prerolled cigarettes in attractively labeled boxes with collectible picture cards of famous athletes and actresses. Smoking fathers passed the cards to their children, who lovingly placed the precious items in albums that cigarette companies furnished in what may have been the first industry marketing ploy to set up kids to become smokers.[13]

In 1880 James Bonsack, the eighteen-year-old son of a Virginia plantation owner, patented a machine that produced cigarettes at the same rate as forty hand rollers.[14] The resulting cigarette, cheaper and more solidly packed with tobacco, initially gained popularity among lower-income immigrants from Ireland, Italy, and eastern Europe.[15] Then chewing tobacco became socially unacceptable because spitting was messy and health officials feared it spread infectious diseases at a time when tuberculosis, diphtheria, influenza, and cholera were leading causes of death in America.[16] Cigarettes, on the other hand, were seen to eliminate the health hazards of spitting, produced milder aromas and less smoke than cigars—and were less expensive to boot.

Thus, on the brink of World War I, cigarette smoking was becoming the fashionable and widely acceptable method of tobacco consumption.[17] That war offered a unique opportunity to tobacco companies to enlist cigarette smokers, and they grabbed it. The companies gave the Red Cross and the YMCA, erstwhile smoking opponents, free cigarettes to shower on young soldiers as a reward for risking their lives and a way to relieve the stress of combat. Returning military veterans became a civilian army of paying habitual smokers.[18]

In the 1920s, the intersection of Madison Avenue and Tobacco Road was paved. R. J. Reynolds invested millions of dollars to promote its cigarettes with the slogan "I'd walk a mile for a Camel," and the brand captured 40 percent of the market.[19] Tobacco company advertisements encouraged suffragists to parade with lit cigarettes as symbolic "torches of freedom" and to celebrate their newfound equality by "partaking in this act of leisure, pleasure and sociability without the risks of intoxication."[20] Shrewdly tapping into the glamour of the Roaring Twenties and of the flapper ideal of thin figures, American Tobacco Company bill-boards urged young women to "Reach for a Lucky instead of a sweet." As women lit up, Lucky Strike usurped Camel's spot as the nation's top-selling cigarettes.[21]

As the popularity of cigarettes increased, cigar smoking dipped.[22] To stem that decline, in 1927 the vice president of marketing for Congress Cigar Company of Philadelphia began advertising La Palma cigars on CBS radio. The jump in sales was so enormous that the young execu-tive quit the cigar business and bought the budding radio network.[23] Thus William S. Paley became the founding genius of the CBS net-work and sold untold millions of dollars of advertising to cigarette com-panies to pay for stars like Jack Benny and Fred Allen.*

During World War II, the military and Hollywood joined forces to make smoking a symbol of GI toughness and a practice as American as apple pie for every kid in the nation. The U.S. Army provided young soldiers with cigarettes in their daily C and K rations.[24] In the mid-1940s, when more than 4.3 billion movie tickets were sold each year (four times the number sold in 2005), films set the cultural standards for young Americans.[25] In a familiar war movie scene, brave GIs dying on the battlefield took a final drag off a cigarette held to their lips by foxhole buddies. During the 1940s and 1950s, Hollywood heroes and heroines became the Pied Pipers of cigarette smoking, leading millions of teens to light up in order to be tough, sophisticated, popular, sexily feminine, and ruggedly masculine.

As concerns about the impact of smoking on health—the coughing, sore throats, irritated mouths—percolated and parents discouraged their teens from smoking, tobacco companies paid physicians to en-dorse their brands.[26] Camel touted a nationwide poll in which 113,597 doctors named the cigarette their favorite brand.[27]

In 1950, the *Journal of the American Medical Association* sprinkled the first cold water on the nation's torrid affair with cigarettes in a land-

---

*In 1969, Paley, suffering from emphysema and quitting smoking, would make CBS the first net-work to offer to release cigarette company advertisers from their contracts for radio and television commercials and in effect refuse to accept cigarette advertising. (In 1983, Bill Paley became my father-in-law.)

mark study that linked smoking to lung cancer.[28] Over the next decade, most doctors stopped recommending particular brands (though they continued to smoke), and more than seven thousand articles linked smoking with lung cancer and other life-threatening diseases.[29] In response, even as tobacco companies attacked the articles as junk and scare science, they promoted filtered cigarettes as being healthier* and introduced menthol cigarettes like Kool and Newport to soothe the throat.[30] Cigarette smoking continued to rise, reaching a peak in early 1964, when 42 percent of the population lit up.[31]

That year the first Surgeon General's Report on Smoking and Health linked smoking to lung cancer.[32] The tobacco companies again fired back on two fronts: They disputed the science of the report and began marketing low-tar cigarettes that, they claimed, offered a healthier alternative.[33]

In 1965, as President Lyndon Johnson's assistant for domestic affairs, I urged him to seek a legislative ban on cigarette advertising on television. LBJ himself had quit smoking on doctor's orders after a near fatal heart attack in 1955, and I expected ready approval. As we rode around his ranch together, he stopped the car when I lit a cigarette and turned toward me. "The day you quit smoking, I'll send your bill to Congress," he said, chuckling as he resumed driving. He knew I couldn't quit under the stress of working for him.** When his physician had told him that he had to quit after his heart attack, then Senator Johnson sighed and said, "I'd rather you have my pecker cut off." Though he quit, LBJ often said that one of the first things he would do upon leaving the White House was resume smoking. He did on the flight back to Texas and died four years later of a smoking-related heart attack.

When President Jimmy Carter named me Secretary of Health, Education, and Welfare, I interviewed more than one hundred physicians for top department posts. Without exception they said any serious

---

*In 1952, Lorillard heralded its Kent cigarette "micronite asbestos filter" as safer, and the brand rose to the top of its class. In 1956, that filter was found to increase the likelihood of contracting lung cancer.
**I quit in 1975 at the request of my son Joe, who asked me to do so for his eleventh birthday present. Joe is now a head and neck cancer surgeon and medical researcher at Johns Hopkins University Hospital.

health promotion and disease prevention campaign had to go after smoking. I commissioned a survey and learned two critical facts: Virtually every adult hooked on nicotine had begun smoking as a teenager (or earlier), and most smokers had tried to quit during the past year. That led me in 1978 to mount the government's first major anti-smoking campaign and characterize smoking as "slow-motion suicide" and "Public Health Enemy Number One."[34] In 1979, fifteen years after the first one, we issued a second Surgeon General's Report on Smoking and Health. The scope and accuracy of this three-inch-thick compilation of scientific research marked the beginning of the end of the tobacco industry's claims that smoking was not dangerous to health.

Our report focused on women and children. With lung cancer among women up fivefold since 1955, I wrote, "Women who smoke like men die like men who smoke." For the first time, we pointed out that the percentage of twelve- to fourteen-year-old girls who smoked had increased eightfold in ten years, that six million thirteen- to nineteen-year-olds were regular smokers, and that there were another hundred thousand smokers under thirteen.[35]

Big Tobacco again assailed the science and organized a political effort to silence me. But attitudes in the nation began to shift. President Ronald Reagan's Surgeon General, C. Everett Koop, stepped up the public health attack on smoking and in 1988 found nicotine to be as addictive as heroin or cocaine.[36]

As educated Americans began to shed smoking habits or refused to start, tobacco companies stepped up campaigns targeting women, minorities, and children.[37]

Philip Morris created the women-only cigarette, Virginia Slims. Slogans like "You've come a long way, baby," played to rising feminism.[38] With a newly enacted ban on television advertising, the tobacco industry increased its spending on print ads in women's magazines like *Woman's Day*, *Redbook*, and *McCall's*.[39] As women's incidence of cigarette-related cancer soared, U.S. Surgeon General Antonia Novello snapped, "The Virginia Slims woman is catching up to the Marlboro Man."[40]

In the 1990s, R. J. Reynolds stepped up its assault on the black community with Uptown menthol cigarettes, and Star Tobacco Company introduced "X" cigarettes in the wake of Spike Lee's film about Malcolm X.[41] The industry increased advertising in magazines oriented toward the black community, such as *Jet* and *Ebony*, which receive proportionately more of their revenues from cigarette advertising than magazines with broader audiences, and billboards advertising tobacco products popped up all over black neighborhoods.[42] As the Hispanic community grew, tobacco companies added it to their target list, introducing cigarette brands named Dorado and Rio.[43]

But no pool of potential new smokers is more important to the nicotine pushers than children and teens. They are the tobacco industry's admitted source of "replacement" smokers for those who have been disabled or killed by using its products.[44]

In a shameless effort to seduce children, R. J. Reynolds launched its Joe Camel advertising campaign in 1988.[45]

So ubiquitous was the image of the cartoon character that, by 1991, more than 90 percent of six-year-olds were able to match Joe Camel with a picture of a cigarette, making him as well known as Mickey Mouse; by comparison, only 67 percent of adults recognized Joe Camel.[46] With the advent of the Joe Camel campaign, after years of decline teen smoking rates rose. Threatened with legal action by the Federal Trade Commission, R. J. Reynolds abandoned the campaign nine years—and millions of hooked teens—later.[47]

But the tobacco companies had a hammerlock on the national Congress. Their political contributions gave them veto power over antismoking legislation. With Congress paralyzed by tobacco money, antitobacco forces sought help from the courts with mixed results, and some states and localities banned smoking in public places and increased taxes on cigarettes to make smoking inconvenient and more expensive.[48]

Despite these actions and declines in smoking, sixty-one million Americans still light up cigarettes regularly—most of them were hooked as children and teens.[49]

And each day fifteen hundred children and teens become addicted smokers as the tobacco industry lures four thousand children to take their first puff.[50]

ALCOHOL

Alcohol is the amniotic fluid of the birth of the American nation. During the seventeenth century, Anglo-Saxon and European settlers coming to the New World did not carry water on transatlantic voyages for fear it would spoil and then cause sickness like scurvy and spread deadly infectious diseases. Instead, their vessels were filled with beer, wine, rum, and other alcohol. These beverages, the early explorers believed, would not spoil and become a source of illness and death. When in 1620 the Pilgrims landed at Plymouth Rock, Massachusetts, they stayed because their beer supply was insufficient to take them to their originally targeted destination of Jamestown, Virginia.[51]

Taverns, more than town halls, were political birthing centers for America. There strangers met, merchants cut deals, politicians plotted, and everyone got the latest gossip and news of growing unrest in the colonies.[52]

Thomas Jefferson began writing the Declaration of Independence in Philadelphia's Indian Queen tavern during the summer of 1776. George Washington bid farewell to his officers at New York City's Fraunces Tavern in 1783.[53]

No one thought about age limits. A glass of mulled cider was recommended as "particularly good for infants at bedtime" because "it guaranteed parents a restful night."[54] (This attitude persisted well into the twentieth century, when tired parents dabbed whiskey on the tongues of bawling babies to put them to sleep.) Drinking was taught at home soon after a child learned to hold a cup in order to accustom children to the taste of alcohol and "encourage moderation."[55]

In the early nineteenth century, whiskey was cheaper than coffee or tea, and each year Americans over age fifteen belted down an average of 4 gallons of alcohol per person (nearly twice the 2.2-gallon consumption level in the early twenty-first century).[56] In 1826, incipient concern about the health, social, and moral consequences of such widespread drinking led to the formation of the American Temperance Society, which morphed into the 1.5-million-member American Temperance Union.[57]

Sick of dealing with the drunken men in their lives, women formed the backbone of the temperance movement—not only promoting antidrinking laws, but also lobbying for political power such as the right to vote.[58] In 1851, Maine prohibited the production of alcohol and limited its use to state agencies for medical and industrial purposes. Within four years, thirteen other states went dry.[59] Formed in 1874, the Woman's Christian Temperance Union (WCTU) almost overnight became a political force for temperance and suffrage.[60] While in 1880 the Prohibition Party presidential candidate suffered a devastating defeat at the hands of James Garfield, the WCTU eventually convinced the national Congress and every state legislature except Arizona's to require temperance education in all schools under their control.[61]

In 1893, cities averaged one saloon for every three hundred residents, and the WCTU and the Prohibition Party joined with the Anti-Saloon League to rid American society of its "saloon culture."[62] The group claimed saloons were responsible for producing 80 percent of American criminals, sending sixty thousand girls into prostitution annually, and spawning "more vice, degradation, sorrow, misery, tears, heartaches, and deaths than any other cause tolerated by the government."[63] With the industrial revolution's need for a large, sober workforce, the likes of John D. Rockefeller, William Randolph Hearst, and Henry Ford (who fired any worker who drank alcohol) became allies, cheering on Carry Nation, the WCTU leader who became famous for smashing Kansas saloon bars and windows with her hatchet.[64]

In the midst of World War I (and stoked somewhat by anti-German sentiment directed at brewers), the nation adopted the Eighteenth Amendment to the Constitution, which prohibited the manufacture, sale, or transportation of intoxicating liquors within the United States. In 1919, the Volstead Act criminalized violations of the ban.[65] Because of women's defining role in the prohibition movement, suffrage and prohibition became political peas in a pod, and the Nineteenth Amendment giving women the right to vote was ratified in 1920.[66]

With Prohibition, American drinking slid to less than one gallon per person a year, and the incidence of alcohol-related diseases like cirrhosis of the liver plummeted.[67] However, speakeasies flourished in the

Roaring Twenties, and it became acceptable for women to drink there with men.[68] Widespread violation of prohibition laws, related organized crime and violence, and state and federal government's need for funds in the wake of the Great Depression in 1929 led to repeal of Prohibition in 1933.[69]

The Hollywood films of the 1930s and 1940s did as much to glamorize alcohol as they did smoking. Popular movies, such as *The Thin Man* series in the 1930s and 1940s with William Powell and Myrna Loy playing a sophisticated detective and his even more sophisticated wife, made it socially acceptable for both men and women to do lots of drinking together. Drunkenness was portrayed not only as socially in, but also as great fun—and funny by actors like W. C. Fields.

Amid Hollywood's portrayal of drinking as typical of an affluent and sophisticated lifestyle during the late 1930s, two alcoholics, Bill W. and Dr. Bob, created Alcoholics Anonymous (AA).[70] In 1945, Ray Milland's portrayal of an alcoholic in the movie *The Lost Weekend* graphically and powerfully dramatized the tragedy of alcoholism.

With the exception of taxes, the federal government left alcohol regulation to the states,* which had first introduced age limits in their march to prohibition.[71] When the voting age was lowered from twenty-one to eighteen in 1971, states that had set the minimum legal drinking age at twenty-one lowered it to eighteen.[72]

With the lower age making it easier for teens to buy beer and other alcoholic beverages, the percentage of high school students who admitted being intoxicated at least once a month rose sharply.[73] Though less than 20 percent of the driving population in 1975, drivers between the ages of sixteen and twenty-four were responsible for almost half of all alcohol-related accidents and accounted for six of every ten deaths in alcohol-related crashes.[74] This spike in crippling and fatal car accidents involving teens sparked the creation in 1980 of Mothers Against Drunk Driving (MADD) and similar groups that demanded an increase in the

---

*Though revenue from taxes on alcohol initially helped pay for President Franklin Delano Roosevelt's New Deal programs, as Chapter 11 shows the alcohol industry has been able to block any significant increase in alcohol taxes at the federal and state level, and such taxes fall far short of the costs of alcohol abuse and alcoholism.

legal drinking age. In a report for New York State, I urged Governor Hugh Carey to raise the drinking age to twenty-one, a proposal opposed by the alcohol industry and supermarkets, other retailers, and bars. President Ronald Reagan's Commission on Drunk Driving wanted the drinking age set at twenty-one.[75]

In 1984, Congress required the states to set their age for the purchase and public possession of alcohol at twenty-one or else forfeit federal highway funds.[76] By 1988 all states had complied.

Nevertheless, underage drinkers consume at least 17.5 percent of the alcohol sold in the United States, beer continues to be the drug of choice among teens and subteens, and the age of initiating drinking continues to decline.[77]

There are 16 to 20 million alcoholics and regular alcohol abusers in the United States—and the overwhelming majority of them began drinking well before they reached age twenty-one. Some 100,000 Americans die each year from alcoholism and alcohol abuse.[78]

PRESCRIPTION AND ILLEGAL DRUGS

America's first illicit drug epidemic erupted in the second half of the nineteenth century in the wake of widespread use of morphine during the Civil War and of pharmaceutical companies routinely spiking medications with opiates and cocaine.[79] Blessed "God's own medicine," morphine was dispensed so indiscriminately to wounded Civil War soldiers that many became hooked on the drug, and chronic morphine use became known as "soldiers' disease." The miracle of morphine was also deployed to help "anguished and hopeless wives and mothers, made so by the slaughter of those who were dearest to them."[80] With the advent of the hypodermic needle in the 1850s, "Morphinism" spread like an oil spill among the middle class.[81]

Concern about morphine addiction led in 1898 to the use of heroin, which was thought to be a nonaddictive pain reliever. Touted by pharmaceutical manufacturer Bayer as "the sedative for coughs" at a time when tuberculosis, asthma, and bronchitis were often fatal diseases, heroin depressed respiration and helped produce a good night's sleep. A year after introducing heroin, Bayer was producing a ton of this "wonder drug" annually and exporting it to twenty-three countries.[82] Doctors treated white middle-class women with morphine and heroin for a variety of complaints, including "female problems," serious hiccoughs, and relief of the pain accompanying childbirth.[83]

As the nineteenth century came to a close, cocaine had become the primary ingredient in many elixirs and "restoratives" that claimed to provide relief from depression and a multitude of ailments. Cocaine was also an ingredient in some wines, cigars, cigarettes, chewing gum, teas, and tonics.[84] Pharmaceutical giant Parke-Davis promoted cocaine as a treatment for opium and alcohol addiction.[85] Sigmund Freud hailed it as an aphrodisiac.[86] The drug became the most widely prescribed remedy in the world.[87]

By the turn of the nineteenth century, Americans were spending $100 million a year ($2.3 billion in 2006 dollars) on one or another of fifty thousand patent medicines laced with opiates and cocaine, and the nation had a quarter of a million drug addicts who were largely white middle class housewives and female socialites.[88] Most people had no clue that over-the-counter remedies they used to soothe their ailments were spiked with these drugs. Then in 1905, with Americans consuming eleven tons of cocaine annually, Samuel Hopkins Adams penned a blistering exposé of the pharmaceutical industry in *Collier's Weekly*. His article led to passage of the Pure Food and Drug Act of 1906, which required manufacturers to label the drug content of medicines.[89] Three years later, Congress banned imports of opium for any purpose other than medicinal use.[90]

When these laws proved ineffective in staunching widespread cocaine and opiate abuse, Congress passed the Harrison Narcotic Act of 1914, which made the nonmedical use of narcotics a crime. Anyone producing, importing, selling, or distributing opium, coca leaves, or their derivatives had to register with the government, and physicians were required to record every prescription of such drugs.[91]

As intolerance of illicit drug use rose, in 1930 President Herbert Hoover created the Federal Bureau of Narcotics and named Harry Anslinger its commissioner.[92] Anslinger became the J. Edgar Hoover of drug control. On his watch, Congress passed the Marijuana Tax Act of 1937, which required a sizable transfer tax for all sales of marijuana, effectively criminalizing use of the drug that Mexican farm laborers and American sailors had started smoking in the early 1900s and had spread to the Harlem jazz scene in the Roaring Twenties.[93]

The post–World War II period saw the introduction of mind-altering drugs. Psychiatrists began using hallucinogens, particularly LSD (lysergic acid diethylamide), to treat schizophrenia. During the Cold War, when U.S. military intelligence reported (erroneously) that the Soviet Union had fifty million doses of LSD, the Army Chemical Warfare Service amassed its own stockpile of the hallucinogen for wartime use.[94] In 1959, the military offered $150 to anyone willing to take this new, experimental drug. Among those who accepted were Ken Kesey (whose experience informed his novel *One Flew over the Cuckoo's Nest*) and countercultural poet Allen Ginsberg. The Central Intelligence Agency secretly tested the drug on thousands of unsuspecting individuals.[95]

In the mid-1950s we hailed the arrival of psychotropic drugs to treat mental illness. Wallace Laboratories and Wyeth Laboratories marketed a brand of the central nervous system depressant meprobamate—called Miltown and Equanil—as a safe alternative to anxiety treatments that contained sleep-inducing or potentially lethal sedatives and addictive narcotics. Within a year, 5 percent of Americans were popping these pills, and the wildly popular television comedian Milton Berle was calling himself "Miltown Berle."[96]

In 1963, Hoffman-LaRoche introduced the benzodiazepines Valium and Librium to treat anxiety and depression. Valium promptly became America's most prescribed drug.[97] Two-thirds of Valium and Librium users were white middle-class women, who were four times likelier than any other social or economic group to be prescribed these drugs.[98]

As millions of women found relief in benzodiazepines, others found energy in a group of stimulants known as amphetamines, which the military had used during World War II to alleviate fatigue in pilots and other combat personnel.[99] Students partying or cramming for exams learned that with amphetamines they could stay up all night. So did truckers on long hauls and actors and actresses shooting film scenes from early morning to late night.[100] As thinness became an ultimate value for young women, the pharmaceutical industry promoted amphetamines as appetite suppressants.[101] By the late 1960s, a sizable black market had developed in amphetamines, which became known as "speed."

The dangers of amphetamines and tranquillizers—uppers and downers—made news as they were implicated in the deaths of Marilyn Monroe, Judy Garland, Jimi Hendrix, Elvis Presley, and other celebrities. The "Speed Kills" public health campaign was launched, and many stopped popping amphetamines. But too many switched to what they thought was a safer stimulant: cocaine.[102]

When Harvard professor Timothy Leary urged college students to take LSD in order to "turn on, tune in, and drop out," two million young Americans tried the drug, and his hallucinogenic injunction became part of everyday jargon.[103] The commercial for the soft drink Squirt encouraged consumers to "Turn on to flavor, tune in to sparkle, and drop out of the cola rut." Billy Graham, the preacher to presidents and the nation's premier Christian crusader, asked his congregations to "Turn on Christ, tune in to the Bible, and drop out of sin."

During the late 1960s and the 1970s, marijuana use exploded among college students.[104] With the war in Vietnam, heroin use reached epidemic levels in the U.S. Army. In the early 1970s, 20 to 35 percent of all army troops were using heroin.[105] Meanwhile, at home, the drug changed the character of entire cities like New York and Washington, D.C., as desperate addicts mugged and robbed to get the funds to support their habits.

Widespread marijuana use on college campuses, the glamorization of LSD, the surge in the use of heroin and cocaine, and the abuse of mood-altering pills led Congress to pass the Controlled Substances Act of 1970.

The law classified drugs into five schedules based on their (then perceived) medical benefit and potential for abuse.* I was very much a part of making it easier to take Librium and Valium. In the Senate version of

---

*Schedule I covered drugs such as heroin, marijuana, and LSD, with a high potential for abuse and no accepted medical use; Schedule II, drugs such as morphine, with a high potential for abuse but restricted medical use; Schedule III, drugs such as amphetamines and short-acting barbiturates, with medium potential for abuse and some accepted medical use; Schedule IV, minor tranquillizers such as Librium and Valium, with lower potential for abuse and accepted medical use; and Schedule V, drugs with widely accepted medical use and low abuse potential, such as cough medicine with codeine.

the bill, these drugs were included in Schedule III, which made misuse or unlawful sale, manufacture, distribution, or promotion a felony carrying a five-year sentence. Fearful that this provision would curb use of its most profitable drug by doctors and patients, Hoffman-LaRoche retained me to get Valium and Librium out of that schedule. After convincing the company that some level of control was inevitable in the congressional stampede to stem rising drug use, I set out to persuade the House to create a separate new Schedule IV for Librium and Valium.

We gathered research papers showing that use of Librium and Valium did not lead to dependency and that these pills were prescribed for patients suffering serious stress, anxiety, insomnia, panic attacks, depression, muscle spasms, and back pain. So limited was the knowledge of polydrug abuse at the time that questions of the tranquillizers' use with other drugs, including alcohol, never arose.

I went for help to Carl Albert, the short, affable Democrat from Oklahoma who had just become Speaker of the House. Sitting in the Speaker's office in the spring of 1970, I was making the public health case for a separate schedule for Librium and Valium. "It's just not fair to consign them to the same schedule with bennies and goofballs [amphetamines and barbiturates]."

As I made that remark, Speaker Albert stuck his hand in his pocket and pulled out a plastic container filled with Valium. "You talking about these?"

Hiding my concern about what was to come next, I said, "Yes," and began to explain.

But he interrupted me. "These pills aren't dangerous," Albert said. "They're great. I take 'em all the time. I couldn't get through the day around here without them."

With that I knew we had Albert's support, and the legislation passed by the House in October 1970 had a new Schedule IV for minor tranquillizers like Librium and Valium, with reduced penalties for improper manufacture, distribution, or possession. The Senate accepted the House version.

When a few years later former first lady Betty Ford entered treatment for addiction to alcohol and Valium, we came to realize this tranquillizer's enormous potential for abuse. To this day I wonder how many patients developed problems as a result of my lobbying to keep these tranquillizers free of stricter controls. I remember it as a dark moment in my private practice of law.

Those were the smoking and snorting 1970s, the decade when even future president George W. Bush was a "young and irresponsible" drinker and drug user. The nation was ambivalent about drug use, and Americans in their teens and twenties were smoking and snorting up a storm. Criminal laws had virtually no impact on the cultural acceptability of marijuana (which seventy-five million Americans had smoked by the end of the 1970s), cocaine (which twenty million Americans had used by the end of the decade), and LSD (which two million, largely college students, had tried).[106] At the time we had little appreciation of the dangers of those drugs.

In 1970 Congress repealed tough penalties on marijuana possession and established a maximum punishment of one year of probation for first-time possession. If probation were successfully completed, the proceedings would be dismissed, and for those under twenty-two, records of arrest, indictment, and conviction would be expunged.

In 1971 NORML—the National Organization for the Reform of Marijuana Laws—was formed to press for the legalization of marijuana. In 1973, a national commission appointed by President Richard M. Nixon and chaired by Pennsylvania governor Raymond Shafer recommended that Congress decriminalize the possession of marijuana for personal use, and the cognoscenti of the time applauded the proposal. In 1974 the magazine *High Times* was first published to celebrate the new drug culture. In 1977 President Jimmy Carter asked Congress to eliminate criminal penalties for the possession of less than one ounce of marijuana and replace them with a $100 fine. Over the decade, eleven state legislatures, representing about a third of the nation's population, decriminalized marijuana. The Alaska Supreme Court held that the privacy clause in its state constitution protected the possession of small amounts of the drug in the home for personal use.[107]*

---

*In 2006, at the request of Alaska governor Frank Murkowski, stating that marijuana had evolved into "a dangerous drug," the state legislature restored criminal penalties for the possession of four or more ounces of marijuana.

In 1978, at the Department of Health, Education, and Welfare, we were more concerned about the herbicides used to kill marijuana than about marijuana itself. As HEW Secretary, I opposed the use of paraquat to kill marijuana plants, because the Centers for Disease Control and the National Institute of Environmental Health Sciences indicated "that the smoke of paraquat-contaminated marijuana is likely to cause lung damage when inhaled in sufficient quantities by marijuana users."*

In 1978, one of every five American women and 14 percent of American men were taking Valium. The Rolling Stones' hit song "Mother's Little Helper" underscored the drug's prominence in popular culture—and sent the message to kids that if Mom uses this little yellow pill to feel better and help her through her day, so can you.[108]

By the end of the 1970s, some one hundred million Americans had tried illegal drugs, and marijuana was part of growing up for one in ten high school seniors, who smoked it daily, and nearly four in ten who smoked it at least monthly. Cocaine use was not as common, but the number of regular users in the late 1970s and early 1980s was counted in millions, not thousands, and included a significant number of affluent high school seniors and college students. By the mid-1980s, almost six million Americans were using cocaine regularly.[109] Several physicians, scientists, and sophisticates declared it a nonaddictive recreational drug. Relatively expensive, cocaine was popular among yuppies, entertainers, politicians (it was so widely used among staffers, pages, and some members in the House of Representatives that I was named special counsel to the House Ethics Committee to investigate), and anyone else who could afford to snort it with a rolled up bill.[110]

In 1983, First Lady Nancy Reagan was asked by a child in an Oakland public school she was visiting, "What do I do if someone offers me a joint?" She responded, "You just say no. That's what you do." The story was widely reported, and the president's wife launched her "Just Say No" campaign to encourage young Americans to say no to drugs.

---

*Marijuana use was so common and we knew so little about it that I asked the Institute of Medicine under David Hamburg to conduct a study of the drug. The institute's report, "Marijuana and Health: Report of a Study by the Institute of Medicine, Division of Health Sciences Policy," issued in 1982, was the first to identify the dangers of smoking marijuana.

In 1985 the introduction of crack, a little rock that crackles when heated and smoked, democratized cocaine. Decidedly more addictive than the powdered stuff, crack cocaine was much cheaper (five bucks a pop) and easier to conceal. It flooded inner-city neighborhoods and kicked off a harrowing crack-related crime tsunami.[111]

Then, on June 19, 1986, the cocaine-overdose death of University of Maryland basketball star Len Bias shocked the nation. Heralded as the next National Basketball Association superstar, Bias was to be the draft pick of the champion Boston Celtics.[112] Eighteen days later First Lady Nancy Reagan wrote an op-ed in the *Washington Post* that was widely reprinted, calling for Americans to take personal responsibility in combating drug use. "By accepting drug use," she wrote, "you are accepting a practice that is destroying life—lives like that of Len Bias and of countless kids next door."[113] Bias's death was an earthquake, shaking the nation's eyes open to the devastation drug use was visiting on its children.

All at once we seemed to discover that LSD could fry the brain; that cocaine was indeed addictive (and smoked as crack fiercely so) and could incite paranoia and violence; that those hooked on heroin were likely to die on heroin; and that marijuana might not be as benign as kids and permissive parents thought. We got early clues that kids who abused alcohol and smoked pot might be likelier to use drugs such as cocaine and heroin. The nation turned against drug use, revived and increased criminal penalties, and mounted major public health campaigns to educate our young about the dangers of drug abuse. By 1992 use of illegal drugs like marijuana, cocaine, heroin, and hallucinogens had plummeted.[114]

But the 1990s witnessed the introduction of a host of other substances. Young Americans turned to synthetic drugs like Ecstasy (MDMA) and methamphetamines to heighten their rave- and club-going experiences. Rural America found its children just as involved in drug abuse as the kids in urban ghettos. Teens learned that over-the-counter cold and allergy medicines containing pseudoephedrine could be turned into methamphetamine. Kids discovered they could get high from inhaling aerosol cans and bags of moth balls. Children emulating professional athletes took steroids to bulk up. Middle schoolers learned that the Ritalin prescribed to help kids with attention deficit disorder (ADD) could also be abused to produce a high. Parents, carelessly leaving around the house psychotropic and other addictive drugs they used to treat their own insomnia, anxiety, obesity, depression, and pain, found their kids getting hooked on opioids like Vicodin and central nervous system depressants like Valium and Xanax, as well as stimulants like Adderall and Dexedrine. Children of coal miners who took OxyContin to relieve brutal back pain stole their fathers' pills and crushed and snorted them. Young girls started abusing anabolic-androgenic steroids such as Anadrol and Equipoise for body sculpting.[115] Kids used over-the-counter cough suppressants containing dextromethorphan (DXM) to get high—"Robotripping," they called it, after the popular cough suppressant Robitussin. "Pharming" parties became the rage for many teens.[116]

From 1992 to 2003, the number of people who admitted abusing controlled prescription drugs jumped by 94 percent, from 7.8 million to 15.1 million. That 15.1 million is more than the combined number who admit abusing cocaine, hallucinogens, inhalants, and heroin combined.[117]

These dramatic increases in the abuse of prescription medications have been fueled by unprecedented drug development, indiscriminate physician prescribing, Americans' insatiable appetite for self-medication, and pharmaceutical advertising that promotes directly to consumers an array of mood-altering and painkilling substances. Not surprisingly, in the High Society the average consumption of controlled opioid medications in the United Stated is double that of the world's next largest consumer, Denmark.[118]

Common to our experience with all these substances—tobacco, alcohol, illegal and controlled prescription drugs—is that consumption became acceptable and abuse widespread before we understood the vulnerability of our children and the consequences for our entire society. As a result we have paid a colossal price in private agony and public costs. We need not pay that price or incur those costs if we fundamentally change the way we think about this problem—and understand that the abuse and addiction of all these substances is a disease and that the key to effective prevention is to focus on our children.

CHAPTER 3

THE COMMON DENOMINATOR

Not so long ago kids used to raid their parents' liquor cabinets when they wanted to get high. Today it's their medicine cabinets. Kids gathered in an abandoned Florida warehouse where strobe lights flashed and liquor flowed. Then from purses and pockets the pills appeared: Vicodin, OxyContin, Xanax. It was a "pharming party" where 12 to 17 year old kids washed several pills down with vodka. Two of the kids were school drop-outs—and addicts—at 14.
—CHATTANOOGA TIMES FREE PRESS, *May 9, 2006*

"I started smoking weed when I was 11, and didn't believe what everyone said about it being a gateway drug," 21 year old Robert Dowlen said Friday, admitting marijuana did lead to "harsher drugs" for him.
—LEAF CHRONICLE, *(Clarksville, TN), August 26, 2006*

The methamphetamine problem that has ravaged lives on the west coast is steadily moving east.
—BOSTON GLOBE, *February 14, 2006*

Popular concerns and parental fears about substance abuse, often fanned by sensational media coverage, ricochet from drug to drug. One month the drug of choice in headlines may be Ecstasy, the next Vicodin, another cocaine or marijuana or inhalants or heroin or methamphetamines. The problem is all of the above, and lots of others. The common denominator is the complex combination of physical, psychological, emotional, and spiritual malaise we call substance abuse and addiction.

Alcohol took center stage in the 1960s. Drunkenness was then the nation's number one crime. In 1967 alcohol abuse even captured a prominent place in the first message on crime that any president sent to Congress, when Lyndon Johnson called on the states to treat drunkenness as a disease in the absence of disorderly conduct or some other offense.[1]

By the end of the decade, pot was becoming the hottest high on college campuses, along with hallucinogens like LSD and PCP (phencyclidine). In the mid-1970s, tabloids chronicled the brutal violence of desperate heroin addicts.

A three-hundred-page report on drug and alcohol abuse that I prepared for the governor of New York in 1982 mentioned cocaine only once.[2] But snorting that white powder became the fashion of the well-to-do and the bane of the poor later in the decade. Then cheap rocks of crack cocaine grabbed the headlines as crack addicts and dealers brought Wild West shoot-outs to urban streets. The designer drugs—GHB, MDMA, Ketamine, Rophynol—made news in the 1990s. Ecstasy captured magazine covers at the end of that decade.

At the start of the twenty-first century, teens looking for a high turned to controlled prescription drugs like OxyContin and Vicodin and over-the-counter cold and cough medicines. A survey of thirty New York hospital emergency departments found that, between 2000 and 2002, cases involving the abuse of narcotic pain relievers jumped 79 percent.[3] By 2004, over-the-counter and prescription drugs were involved in a quarter of the nation's 1.3 million drug-related emergency room visits,[4] and in terms of new users, more people abused opioid pain relievers than any other drug, including marijuana. By 2005, prescription drugs were knocked out of first place on the media charts by methamphetamine madness. And binge drinking returned to college campuses with a vengeance.

Drug fashions not only change over time; they vary by geographic area and age. A 2006 *Forbes* analysis based on the number of drinkers, heavy drinkers, binge drinkers, and alcoholics named Milwaukee and Minneapolis–St.Paul as the nation's two drunkest cities.[5] In the West, treatment admission rates for methamphetamine abuse are higher than those for cocaine and heroin.[6] In Idaho in 2002, meth and other amphetamines were reported as the primary drugs of abuse at more than nineteen times the rate for cocaine and more than thirty-eight times the rate for heroin. In Hawaii, 41 percent of those in treatment were meth addicts. But in that same year, in the East, treatment admissions for cocaine and heroin far outpaced those for methamphetamine.[7] Physicians began prescribing methadone as a painkiller, and in Florida, Maine, North Carolina, Texas, and Washington, methadone became, as Florida drug czar James McDonough put it, "the fastest rising killer drug" abused by teens in that state.[8]

In the South and West, abuse of controlled prescription drugs exhibits greater prevalence than in the North and East. The South, with 36 percent of the population, accounts for 44 percent of the nation's abuse of sedatives such as Nembutal and 45 percent of abuse of tranquillizers such as Ativan. The West, with 22 percent of the population, accounts for 31 percent of the abuse of sedatives and 29 percent of the abuse of opioids such as Vicodin.[9]

Drug use also differs among age groups. Teens who abuse drugs favor alcohol and pot. Young girls are likelier to abuse prescription drugs than young boys. For Americans over the age of fifty-five, alcohol remains the drug of choice, but the rates of prescription drug abuse are climbing.[10]

The drug-of-the-month mentality that dominates so much of the popular culture tends to keep the nation and its public policymakers focused on the trees: a pill, a smoke, an illegal drug, a snort, a sniff, an injection, bingeing on beer or vodka, pharming. Congress and state legislatures bounce from substance to substance: one year increasing the penalties for crack cocaine; another, requiring cigarettes to be kept out of the reach of customers; yet another trying to reduce the number of methamphetamine labs by making it harder to buy over-the-counter pharmaceuticals that contain pseudoephedrine; then closing down rave venues where kids congregate and take Ecstasy pills. As a result, it is easy to lose sight of the forest: the common malady of substance abuse and addiction that infects the brain, the psyche, and the soul, whatever the ingredient, time, place, method of ingestion, or age or gender of the user.

Statistics and science reveal the relationship among all these sub-stances. Widespread polydrug abuse underscores the point.

Children and teens who smoke are much likelier than those who don't to use alcohol and drugs.[11] Indeed, the more teens smoke, the likelier they are to drink and drug. In one study, only one in twenty nonsmoking teens used illicit drugs, compared to thirty-nine percent of non-daily smokers and fifty-two percent of those who smoked cigarettes everyday.[12] Teens who smoke nicotine cigarettes are fourteen times likelier to try marijuana than those who don't.[13] Among teens who ad-mit smoking pot, the cigarette smokers are much likelier to be repeat marijuana users; those who don't smoke cigarettes are likelier to have tried marijuana only once.[14]

The statistical relationship of teens' smoking cigarettes and drinking alcohol to their subsequent use of marijuana, and the relationship of their use of cigarettes, alcohol, and marijuana to their subsequent use of drugs like cocaine and heroin, is more than enough to give parents many sleepless nights.[15] While most kids who smoke cigarettes and drink may not use marijuana, and most kids who use all three sub-stances may not go on to cocaine and heroin, for large numbers the use of those gateway substances is a harbinger of entry into a world of even greater drug use. A CASA study in the 1990s found that

- 89 percent of individuals who used cocaine first smoked, drank, and used marijuana—Virtually every cocaine user had first used at least one gateway drug;
- almost 90 percent of children and adults who used marijuana first smoked cigarettes or drank alcohol;
- twelve- to seventeen-year-old children who used marijuana were eighty-five times more likely, those who drank were fifty times more likely, and those who smoked were nineteen times more likely to use cocaine than children who had never used those gateway substances.[16]

The younger children are when they use gateway drugs, and the more often they use them, the likelier they are to use cocaine, heroin, hallucinogens, and other illicit drugs.[17] Heavy teen drinkers are more than twelve times likelier to use illegal drugs than those who don't drink.[18] Of children who smoke pot before age fifteen, 60 percent move on to cocaine; only 20 percent of those who smoke pot after age seventeen use cocaine.[19] Children who are heavy cigarette smokers are thirteen times more likely to use heroin than other children who smoke.[20] Similarly, twelve- to seventeen-year-olds who use marijuana are thirteen times likelier to use harder drugs than those who do not.[21]

CASA then analyzed data from the Centers for Disease Control and Prevention's 1995 Youth Risk Behavior Survey of eleven thousand ninth-through twelfth-graders, and found these compelling correlations:*

- Those who had drunk and smoked cigarettes at least once in the past month were thirty times likelier to smoke marijuana than those who hadn't.
- Those who had drunk, smoked cigarettes, and used marijuana at least once in the past month were more than seventeen times likelier to use another drug like cocaine, heroin or LSD.[22]

The use of gateway drugs in childhood is related to the use of illicit drugs as adults. Children who smoke are three times more likely, who drink are six times more likely, and who use marijuana are seventeen times more likely to use cocaine regularly as adults than children who do not use these substances.[23]

By and large, these statistical relationships hold regardless of the race, sex, ethnicity, or economic status of the individuals involved. They probably understate the risks because they are based on individual admissions of the use of cigarettes, alcohol, and marijuana. Particularly with respect to the use of illegal drugs like marijuana and cocaine, but also with respect to the amount of alcohol consumed and the number of cigarettes smoked, individuals tend to minimize (or deny) the extent of their use.

---

*CASA isolated teen use of tobacco, alcohol, and marijuana, controlling for other problem behaviors, such as fighting, drunk driving, carrying a weapon, attempting suicide, and sexual promiscuity.

To appreciate the power of these statistical correlations, consider the first revealed nexuses between cigarette smoking and lung cancer, cholesterol levels and heart disease, and exposure to asbestos and lung cancer. The 1964 Surgeon General Report on smoking found male smokers nine to ten times likelier to develop lung cancer than non-smokers.[24] The report of the exhaustive Framingham Study found men with high cholesterol to be two to four times likelier to suffer coronary heart disease than men with low cholesterol.[25] In the late 1970s, Dr. Irving Selikoff found the risk of lung cancer to be five times greater for individuals with heavy occupational exposure to asbestos.[26]

Like these other studies, the gateway statistical relationships do not necessarily establish causality. Millions of Americans who smoke and drink never move on to marijuana, cocaine, heroin, or other illegal drugs. Nevertheless, these relationships are so powerful and the risk to America's children and teens is so great that the message to parents, physicians, and policymakers is clear: The younger an individual is and the more often an individual uses gateway drugs (cigarettes, alcohol, marijuana), the likelier she or he is to experiment with cocaine, heroin, and other illicit drugs and to become a regular drug user and addict.

Biomedical research and the brain-imaging work of Dr. Nora Volkow, Director of the National Institute on Drug Abuse (NIDA), help explain why teens who play with the fire of cigarettes, alcohol, and marijuana increase the chance they will get burned by the flames of heroin, cocaine, and hallucinogens. As she said at the CASACONFERENCE, "Up in Smoke: Tobacco and Youth," September 21, 2006, "All drugs of abuse taken by humans whether . . . legal—alcohol or nicotine—or illegal—marijuana, methamphetamine, cocaine, heroin—all of them increase dopamine in the brain, which is considered to be one of the pleasure centers." As dopamine levels rise, an individual's feeling of pleasure increases. A growing body of science is finding that all these substances affect dopamine levels in the brain through similar pathways, and dopamine becomes less active in the brains of addicts who use drugs to trigger its release, a condition that in turn reinforces the need for the drug.[27]

Studies by scientists in Italy reveal that marijuana affects levels of dopamine in the brain in a manner akin to heroin. Gaetano DiChiara, the medical researcher and physician who has led this work at the University of Cagliari, concluded that marijuana may prime the brain to seek substances, such as heroin and cocaine, that act in much the same way through common pathways to the brain.[28] Studies in the United States have found that nicotine and alcohol (as well as cocaine) have a similar effect on dopamine levels through common pathways to the brain.[29] That may explain why some scientists believe that nicotine makes the brain more accommodating to other drugs.

In essence, whatever the substance, the brains of addicts are "rewired," becoming predisposed to cravings.[30] Dr. Joseph Frascella of NIDA points out that "in excessive behaviors such as compulsive drug abuse . . . the brain is changed, reward circuits are disrupted, and the behavior eventually becomes involuntary."[31]

These statistical and biological findings are underscored by the fact that most addicts are polydrug abusers. Alcoholics are likely to abuse tranquillizers, sleeping pills, or other psychotropic drugs.[32] Older teens who abuse prescription drugs are often abusing other drugs as well.[33] A study of Los Angeles emergency rooms found that during the first six months of 2002, 85 percent of marijuana-related admissions represented multidrug episodes.[34] In 2002, two-thirds of methamphetamine-related admissions were multidrug episodes.[35] There are also social elements in the relationship between smoking, drinking, and using various drugs, as well as in polydrug use, particularly among children and teens. Kids who seek the high from marijuana may also want to look for "better" highs from other drugs. As kids start using drugs, they may tend to hang out and share experiences with others who use different drugs. In a sense, these teens end up encouraging each other to use various drugs.

Of special importance is the need to recognize that, for many teens, smoking, drinking, or drug use is often a symptom of incipient depression, anxiety, or some other (usually undiagnosed) mental illness that hikes the youngster's risk of drug abuse.[36]

Mental health problems go hand in hand with smoking, drinking, and drug use for children and adults, and these problems can lead individuals to try a variety of substances to self-medicate. Our current approach to substance abuse does not adequately recognize this reality.

It is easy for parents and public officials to get distracted by the latest chemical peril, to gasp at headlines featuring the coming generation of crack babies, the Ecstasy epidemic, the onslaught of meth madness, or the explosion in addictive prescription drug abuse. Yet these are not islands of illness; they are part of the same landmass: the disease of substance abuse and addiction. Simply chasing each drug as it comes along is pillow public health policy: push down on one chemical substance and another will pop up. With an understanding of the problem, we can turn our attention to the key to preventing it: protecting our children.

CHAPTER 4

IT'S ALL ABOUT KIDS

I'm 27 and I probably had my first cigarette, "just one," when I was 17. If there is one thing in my life that I could take back, one thing that I regret, it is that first cigarette.

—From letter in Boston Globe "Dear Beth" column
from a smoker, June 13, 2006

Mobile County Public Schools in Alabama reported six on-campus pharming parties last year, including one involving a fifth grader.

—ABC News, September 12, 2006

As a tween, Eric Cox got hooked on painkillers he borrowed to relieve an aching wrestling injury. The painkiller made it difficult to concentrate so he got an Adderall from a friend. Getting pills was as easy as asking a friend or classmate. By age 14, Eric was hooked on painkillers and Adderall. At 17 when he became paranoid, he went to his parents for help.

—Indianapolis Star, May 8, 2006

In seventh grade, Lexy Purdum, shopping with friends at the Kalamazoo mall, took Vicodin and methadone. She came home, took more drugs and went to bed around 10:30 p.m. Her mother found her dead in her room shortly after noon on Saturday, a few days before her 15th birthday. It was the second overdose death of an early teen in two weeks in Western Michigan. Merisha Nichols, age 14, died two weeks earlier after "huffing" fumes of a spray air freshener.

—Grand Rapids Press, May 8, 2006

Before graduating high school every American child will be offered the opportunity to smoke, drink, get drunk, and get high on inhalants, marijuana, or other illegal or prescription drugs. Most girls and boys will get such offers many times, from classmates, friends, or older siblings, usually beginning in middle school.[1]

The choice these kids make may be the most important decision of their lives.

Why?

Because a child who gets through age twenty-one without smoking, using illegal drugs, or abusing alcohol is virtually certain never to do so.

All the drug pushers—from illegal street dealers and Colombian cartel bosses to unscrupulous bodega retailers and tobacco and alcohol industry executives—understand this. They've known for decades how important it is to persuade kids to try their stuff. The tragedy is that so many politicians, public health professionals, and parents either don't get it or don't act on it.

Most adults can trace their substance abuse demons to their adolescent years. Two-thirds of patients entering treatment for drug dependency were already abusing illegal drugs in their teens, before they had graduated high school or dropped out.[2] More than nine of ten adult smokers were hooked before reaching twenty-one.[3] Teen drinking is the number one feeder of adult alcoholism, and children who start to drink before age fifteen are four times likelier to become alcoholics than those who don't drink before they turn twenty-one.[4]

Kids are experimenting with illegal drugs at younger ages. Among individuals who entered treatment for marijuana dependency from 1993 to 2003, the initiation of marijuana use prior to age thirteen increased from 20 percent to 23 percent. Among those admitted to emergency rooms for opiate use, the proportion who had begun using drugs before age thirteen rose 25 percent.[5] Teen illicit drug use in 2005 was more than twice its low level in the early 1990s.[6]

From 1992 to 2003, the abuse of controlled prescription drugs by twelve- to seventeen-year-olds more than tripled, rising to 2.3 million.[7] While high school girls are just as likely as boys to drink, smoke, and use inhalants and cocaine, they are even more likely to abuse stimulants, tranquillizers, and painkillers.[8]

The impact of alcohol and drug abuse is devastating on our children. More than 300,000 enter treatment each year,[9] and thousands more should. Beer and other alcoholic beverages are implicated in the three top causes of teen deaths: accidents (notably traffic fatalities and drowning), homicide, and suicide.[10] More than seventeen hundred college students die of alcohol poisoning and alcohol-related injuries each year.[11] Most teen pregnancy occurs when one or both of the partners are high at the time of conception, and teens who become pregnant and drink or use drugs are likelier to have an abortion.[12] In 2004, the Institute of Medicine set the annual costs of underage drinking at $19 billion from traffic accidents and $29 billion from violent crime.[13]

The tragic consequences of teen alcohol and drug abuse can be found in every community. Alcohol was the culprit in the August 2005 car crash in Myrtle Beach that injured three and took the life of fifteen-year-old Erica Wilson; the sixteen-year-old driver was convicted of reckless homicide.[14] In January of 2005, thirteen-year-old Katrina Gonzales shot and killed thirteen-year-old Adrian Urioste after an evening of alcohol and marijuana use in Las Vegas, New Mexico.[15] In September 2005, Patrick Kycia, a nineteen-year-old student in Minnesota, drowned after leaving a fraternity party at which he'd been drinking heavily.[16]

EASY AVAILABILITY

Availability is the mother of use, and today's teens are exposed daily to a dizzying menu of addictive illegal and prescription drugs, beer, wine coolers, fruit-flavored hard liquors, malternatives, candy-flavored chewing tobacco, and inhalants. These substances are usually just a cell phone, school locker, classroom, Internet click, or arm's reach away. Parents stock a wide variety of substances in their homes—from addictive mood-altering pills and opioids in the bathroom medicine cabinet to inhalants in aerosol canisters under the kitchen sink, beer in the refrigerator, and liquor in the living room.

The nation's two legal drugs—nicotine and alcohol—are readily available. Most teens can get cigarettes and beer from their homes, older friends, and careless or inattentive retailers and bartenders, or by using dime-a-dozen phony IDs. Marijuana and addictive mood-altering prescription pills are so much a part of their daily lives that many teens do not consider these drugs illicit substances.

More than 40 percent of America's twelve- to seventeen-year olds (some ten million) can buy marijuana within a day, and 20 percent (some five million) can get it in an hour or less.[17] These kids don't buy pot from some sleazy character in a dirty trench coat; they buy it from their friends and classmates, often in the corridors, classrooms, and play-grounds of our nation's schools.

If teens are swimming in an ocean of illegal drugs, they are riding a tidal wave of controlled prescription drugs. For many, the bathroom med-icine cabinet has become a greater threat than the street drug dealer, as parents who have been prescribed controlled substances leave them around the house and become inadvertent drug pushers. Children con-sider these drugs safe: After all, Mom and Dad use them, and they don't carry the risk of adulteration inherent in street drug purchases.

Then there is the Internet, which has for many kids become a wide-open, easy-access substance supermarket. Its shelves are stacked with opioids like Percocet and Vicodin, stimulants like Ritalin and Adderall, depressants like Valium and Xanax, steroids like Anabol and Masteron, and plenty of alcohol and cigarettes. All the kids need is a credit card. Many of the Internet sites that offer controlled substances such as Vi-codin require no prescription and set no age limits.[18] The number of sites selling such drugs, along with alcohol and cigarettes, has been ris-ing steadily. Web sites offer teens information about hundreds of mind-altering chemicals, herbs, and plants and how to grow marijuana and concoct a host of other drugs including methamphetamine. One such site gets 250,000 hits daily.[19] These Internet sites in the United States and foreign countries are difficult to police.

SCHOOL DAZE

Next to parents, schools—everything about them, including classmates—exert the most influence on teen behavior, and that's bad news for most high school students and lots of middle schoolers.[20] "Drug-free schools," long a popular catchphrase among parents and educators, has become a dangerous oxymoron for millions of these students. Most high school students say that drugs are used, kept, or sold at their schools, and more than a quarter of middle schoolers report similar situations in theirs. That means that more than ten million twelve- to seventeen-year-olds spend several hours each day in drug-infested environments.[21]

As a consequence of the greater availability of drugs at high schools, the biggest jump in the risk of teen drug abuse occurs from age thirteen to age fourteen, typically when a child moves from middle to high school. Fourteen-year-olds are four times likelier than thirteen-year-olds to be offered prescription drugs, three times likelier to be offered marijuana and Ecstasy, and twice as likely to be offered cocaine.[22]

Teens attending schools where drugs are used, kept, or sold are twice as likely as those at drug-free schools to be offered marijuana and three times likelier to try it.[23] The odds are much higher that they will know teenagers who use acid, cocaine, or heroin.[24] Substance abuse at these schools is not limited to "difficult kids" who exhibit discipline problems or are failing or cutting classes. A national survey of high school honor students revealed that drinking beer, smoking, drinking hard liquor, and using marijuana followed only alternative music among the top five "in" things at their schools.[25]

Even more troublesome than the easy availability of drugs in middle and high schools is the attitude of parents. Parental pessimism and despair have led too many mothers and fathers to accept the presence of drugs at their children's schools. Almost half the parents surveyed by CASA in 2005 and 2006 believed that drugs were used, kept, and sold at their children's schools, and most of them accepted this sordid status quo because they believed there was nothing they could do.[26] But they are wrong.

If asbestos is found in a school, parents raise hell and refuse to send their children to class until every speck of the dangerous dust has been removed. But if a school is infested with drugs, parents continue to send their children back day after day. In New York, Boston, Washington, Los Angeles, and other cities, affluent parents spend thousands of dollars a year to send their children to private schools. In return for such hefty payments, ambitious moms and dads demand that the schools get their offspring into colleges like Harvard, Stanford, Georgetown, Holy Cross, Yale, and Princeton. The schools and their well-paid headmasters deliver. When parents make it clear that they care as much about their children's exposure to drugs, alcohol, and cigarettes as they do about their children's exposure to asbestos and College Board test scores, principals and headmasters will clear the fog of tobacco, alcohol, and drugs from their schools.

Many elementary and secondary school administrators and teachers are too quick to press parents and physicians to diagnose rambunctious children as suffering from attention deficit hyperactivity disorder (ADHD). In each month during 2005, prescriptions for ADHD were filled for 3.3 million children, compared to 2.2 million in 2002.[27] Too many teachers and school officials see these pills as a way to quiet schoolchildren who would be better served by being disciplined. There is a serious question of the propriety of teachers and school nurses or counselors pressing such medications on students when they represent the school, not the child.

Moreover, with the explosion in the availability of drugs such as Ritalin and Adderall, which are commonly prescribed for ADHD, prescription drug black markets have sprung up in many schools. Stimulants like Ritalin and Adderall are the top sellers, followed by pain medications such as Vicodin and OxyContin, which are used by 13 percent of students, and by sedatives and tranquillizers, which are used by 10 percent.[28]

In Arizona, Pima County drug court coordinator Sal Calabrese says students know how easy it is to get Adderall: "Indeed it's available. The kids who are prescribed it are often selling it to other kids to make money."[29] In Wisconsin and Minnesota more than a third of eleven- to eighteen-year-old students who had been prescribed Ritalin and other ADHD medications reported being approached to sell or trade their drugs.[30] "If someone breaks their arm, kids will ask them the next day if they have Vicodin or something else they can sell," says Samantha Szelog, a sixteen-year-old junior at Malibu High School.[31]

While students know the score about drugs in schools, many teachers and principals don't even know—or care to know—what inning it is. For more than a decade, responding to an open-ended question, the highest proportion of twelve- to seventeen-year-olds surveyed each year by CASA have consistently listed drugs as their number one concern, far overshadowing social and academic pressures.[32] But fewer than half of high school teachers and only a quarter of middle and high school principals think drugs are used, kept, or sold on their school grounds.[33] Typical of this attitude, Stanley Litow, New York City's deputy school chancellor during the drug-filled years from 1990 to 1993, and later head of a foundation that supports school reading programs, told CASA researchers in 2006 that drugs are not a priority issue in the nation's schools.[34] Even where teachers believe that drugs and alcohol are sold and used at their school, they do not believe that such conduct interferes with their teaching.[35]

Teachers and school principals live in their own antiseptic bubble, tending to ignore warning signals of substance abuse when individual students exhibit sharp declines in grades or fall asleep in class. When pressed to be more proactive, they typically respond that their job is teaching math, English, or science or administering the school. Moreover, they argue, parents are the ostriches with their heads deep in the sands of denial. Teachers who have raised a suspicion of a child's drug use claim they invariably end up in a dispute with angry parents who refuse to believe any such thing about their own child. Further feeding their apprehension, many teachers are doubtful that they will be supported in such situations by school administrators.[36]

These teachers have a point. CASA surveys show that only a relative handful of parents see drugs as their children's top concern. Kevin Schnacknel, an Upstate New York high school student, spoke for most of his contemporaries across the country when he wrote in a letter to the editor of a Syracuse newspaper, "Parents do not know how much of a problem illegal drugs have become in today's schools."[37] Teachers (and principals) should be held accountable not only for passing along subject knowledge in math, history, and English, but also for recognizing conduct that suggests one of their students may be in trouble—and bringing that student to the attention of school counselors and parents.

Many schools claim they fulfill their responsibility by providing a few hours of "drug education" about the dangers of illegal drug use. But alone, this is a one-dimensional policy doomed to failure.

Why?

Because many of the reasons that kids turn to drugs have little or nothing to do with being informed about the dangers of using them. A presentation on the dangers of drug use will have little impact on the likelihood that a child who is experiencing depression, anxiety, learning disabilities, eating or conduct disorders, low self-esteem, or sexual or physical abuse or neglect, or who has no hope for the future, will self-medicate with drugs and alcohol.

The most widely used program, DARE (Drug Abuse Resistance Education), which is taught by cops who are paid to show kids how drugs are used and describe the experiences of those who use them, has been repeatedly found worthless.[38] Extensive research led by Steve West at Virginia Commonwealth University, and published in the *American Journal of Public Health*, concluded that DARE was "ineffective" as a prevention effort and "a huge waste of time and money."[39] The U.S. Department of Education has taken DARE off its list of programs with demonstrated effectiveness.[40] Yet law enforcement lobbies are so strong that Congress, state legislatures, local bodies, corporations, and individuals provide millions of dollars each year to finance the DARE program.[41]

Drug education and prevention should be embedded in elementary, middle, and upper school courses and should address the reasons that kids use drugs. School curricula should be scientifically validated. The best programs—and there are several—provide realistic information to kids in schools; are tailored to the types of schools; recognize gender, age, ethnic, and racial differences; and cover all substances, alcohol and tobacco as well as illegal and prescription drugs.

Many schools resort to "zero tolerance" policies and random drug testing of students. Zero tolerance policies are double-edged swords. Such policies vary: Some hold that any drug use by a student will result in expulsion, others distinguish between use and sale, and still others provide for treatment and counseling and a second (or third) chance for students who accept help and remain drug-free.[42] Zero tolerance policies put enormous pressure on parents to help keep their kids drug-free and give individual students a powerful incentive to say no when offered drugs. But such policies also tend to discourage parents and classmates from reporting drug use of any kind (especially where the punishment is expulsion with no second chance). The unintended consequence may be to let a substance-experimenting teen sink into regular drug use. Policies that offer students a second chance if they take appropriate treatment and counseling and refrain from drug use appear to be the most effective. Such policies do not discourage reporting student drug use, and they offer the opportunity to continue in school to encourage students (and parents) to seek help.

Laws authorizing nonpunitive random drug testing of students are being adopted in several states and communities. These laws permit random testing of children in schools with a view to giving their parents an early warning of their child's drug use. Proponents say they have shown some deterrent power, discouraging kids from using and giving them another reason to decline when offered drugs.[43]

Sensibly executed, these programs may help, but we will never be able to test our way out of the teenage drug problem. Whatever techniques schools employ, as David Hanson (professor emeritus of sociology at the University of North Carolina at Chapel Hill, who has spent a lifetime studying substance abuse and education) stresses, "The overwhelming evidence supports that the modeling that happens at home will still have the greatest effect on how kids ultimately behave."[44]

PARENT POWER

> "Most parents are clueless," said Samantha Tish, 15, who lives in a small town near the Wisconsin border, "they have no idea what goes on at parties . . . or how drugs and alcohol are everywhere."
> —*Orlando Sentinel*, August 17, 2006

Parental conduct is the most potent influence—for better or worse—on a teen's attitude toward substance use.[45] Parental drinking behavior can decisively shape a child's view of drinking. Dr. Stanley Gitlow, one of the nation's premier alcoholism clinicians, told me, "When Dad comes home after work and rushes to pop a couple of martinis, by the time his baby is three years old, that tot sees drinking as the way to relax. Years later, when that child starts bingeing on the weekends in high school, he won't even know what he picked up watching Dad hit the martinis more than a decade before." Jamie Lee Curtis, who lived with the alcohol abuse of her parents Janet Leigh and Tony Curtis and experienced her own alcohol addiction, believes that parents who drink regularly in front of their children are asking for trouble.

Favorable adult attitudes toward smoking and casual attitudes toward alcohol abuse affect children's smoking and drinking habits—whether it's Mom or Dad smoking a pack a day, knocking off a six pack at night, having too many cocktails to relax on the weekends, or getting high at family celebrations. Parents who smoke, get drunk, and drug have sons and daughters who smoke, get drunk, and drug.

Parental sensitivity to the signals of substance abuse is the most important early-warning system to save a child who begins experimenting with drugs. Speaking of his son's death from a drug overdose, venture capitalist James Bildner described his child's "path from innocence to heroin right before our eyes and with a speed that was hard to imagine. Like so many parents we missed the early warning signs: an empty beer bottle in the backyard; the smell of pot on his clothes; a pill in the laundry room we couldn't identify. We chalked them all up to adolescent behavior but we were wrong. The simple truth is that the only defense any kid has are parents who believe it can happen to their kid, that it could be anyone's son. This time it was mine."[46]

When asked what motivated them not to use drugs, the twelve- to seventeen-year-olds whom CASA surveyed in 2005 overwhelmingly replied that it was whether their parents would be "extremely upset" by such conduct.[47] The second strongest motivator was teens' belief that it was immoral for someone their age to use drugs.[48] Kids at those ages acquire their sense of morality from their parents. These motivations far outweighed any others, including knowledge that the conduct was illegal.[49] (Illegality becomes more relevant for college seniors as they approach graduate school or the job market.)

Underage drinking and marijuana use are not just a teen problem. They're a parent problem as well. Many parents are enablers of their children's alcohol and drug abuse. Over the course of a seven-year study of the class of 2005 at Staples High School in the Connecticut gold coast town of Westport, students repeatedly told Columbia University researcher Suniya Luthar that their parents were "way more tolerant of substance abuse" than of behavior such as rudeness, academic failure, and stealing. Too many parents had a "kids will be kids" attitude about their children's drug use, not appreciating how quickly casual use can escalate to addiction. Luthar advised parents to tell their children that there will be serious consequences if they use drugs. Parental disapproval, she stressed, is "the one variable that will make a difference." Almost half the Staples students saw their parents as permissive or uninvolved.[50]

When it comes to alcohol, home is the first stop for many kids to score beer and other booze. A third of sixth- and ninth-graders who drink get alcohol from their own homes.[51] Many times, parents themselves play bartender, serving beer and other alcoholic beverages to teenage children and their pals.

Parents can be blissful palookas, unaware of the teen party scene. Of parents of twelve- to seventeen-year-olds, 80 percent believe that alcohol and marijuana are not available at parties their kids go to; but 50 percent of their children know differently.[52] Teen parties with no parental supervision, as opposed to those with parental supervision, are sixteen times likelier to have alcohol, fifteen times likelier to have illegal and prescription drugs, and twenty-nine times likelier to have pot.[53] Even where parents are present, a third of teen partygoers have attended parties where teens were drinking, smoking marijuana, or using cocaine, Ecstasy, or prescription drugs.[54]

"Of course" parents provide alcohol, said sixteen-year-old Ashley Wentzel, a high school student in Midlands, South Carolina, where two teens were killed in drunk driving accidents: "Then, there's other parents that don't provide it, but they let other teenagers bring it into their house and they don't say anything."[55]

So many parents are acting like the three monkeys—they see no booze, smell no pot, and hear no noise from hopped-up kids in the family room—that more than half the states and hundreds of town councils have enacted laws holding parents civilly and criminally liable when they serve alcohol to underage children or have reason to believe that underage drinking is going on at their houses.[56]

In Scarsdale, New York, Paul and Christine Taxin were arrested and charged with unlawfully dealing to minors after cops busted a New

Year's party at which they were serving alcohol to their eighteen-year-old daughter and her friends.[57] Sixteen-year-old Michael Duni of Huntersville, North Carolina, died of alcohol poisoning after attending a party in December 2005 at the home of Dana Pittsonberger, forty-three, who allowed her own two teenage sons as well as their friends to drink beer and liquor. Pittsonberger was subsequently sentenced to four months in prison after pleading guilty to involuntary manslaughter.[58]

Broadening liability beyond those adults who actually provide alcohol to teens, the town of Gilford, New Hampshire, passed a law in 2004 making it a crime to "facilitate" an underage alcohol or drug party. Susan Hanlon was one of the first charged under the law after she allowed her daughter to hold a sleepover party with alcohol to celebrate her eighteenth birthday.[59] Long Beach, New York, in 2006 enacted a law holding adult hosts of house parties criminally liable if they "know or should have known" that minors are drinking or using illegal drugs on their premises.[60] In North Haledon, New Jersey, parents were found guilty of child endangerment when police found beer and alcohol throughout their house and picked up forty kids, most fourteen- and fifteen-years-old, at their St. Patrick's Day party.[61]

Each spring, thousands of college students go south to Florida, Mexico, and the Caribbean for a break that has become a modern Roman bacchanalia featuring excessive drinking and promiscuous sex. As the 2006 spring break season kicked off, the American Medical Association highlighted the dangers associated with spring break blowouts, warning girls and young women to be cautious for fear of rape, sexually transmitted diseases, and unwanted pregnancy.[62] MTV, the cable channel for teens and subteens, televises the spring break for voyeurs to watch wet T-shirt contests and drunken, sexually suggestive dancing. If parents didn't pick up the tab, most of these students couldn't afford to go south for this week of alcohol-, pill-, and pot-fueled partying. How can these parents expect their kids to "just say no" to alcohol and drugs when they themselves can't "just say no" to children who tell them, "Everyone does it," or "All my friends will be there"?

The permissiveness of parents who want their kids to be popular can lead to tragic consequences: Take Natalie Holloway, who disappeared after a night of drinking and drugging on a high school trip to Aruba;

Steve Saucedo, a University of California (Berkeley) junior who died of alcohol poisoning after vying to win a spring break drinking contest; and Margaret Susan Piton, who choked to death when she passed out in foam at a spring break dance party.[63]

HIGHER EDUCATION

Parents Patty and Rick Spady had no idea about the culture of college drinking when they sent their daughter Sam off to Colorado State University. In high school, Sam was captain of the cheerleading squad, class president, an honor student and homecoming queen. In her sophomore year, 19 years old, Sam was found dead over Labor Day weekend after a night of binge drinking. Investigators believe Sam consumed as many as 40 vanilla flavored vodka drinks that night.

—ABC News, June 12, 2006

This month searchers combing the Mississippi river in La Crosse, Wisconsin, found the body of the eighth college age man in nine years to disappear from one of the taverns and turn up dead in the river. La Crosse officials have debated for years how to keep drunken students safe in a town with three colleges, three rivers and $3 pitchers of beer. The Vibe, where the man was last seen alive, offers an all you can drink special for $5. Shots are a dollar. A sign in the bar's window proclaims, "You're not drunk if you can lie on the floor without holding on."

—New York Times, October 23, 2006

Many colleges have become Meccas of binge drinking for thousands of students, especially freshmen, who on arrival in their dormitories are overnight left to their own devices, free of any parental supervision. Of college freshmen, 25 percent consume more than ten drinks at a sitting; 8 percent consume fifteen or more in a week.[64] These amounts are well above the medically set level of five drinks at one time that constitute binge drinking for men.[65]

University administrators disclaim in loco parentis responsibility, and parents do not appreciate hearing about the escapades of their offspring. When Manuel Pachceco was president of the University of Missouri in the early 2000s, he introduced a policy of notifying parents if their sons or daughters were cited for drunkenness. He expected the students to complain loudly (which they did). What he did not expect were the howls from Pontius Pilate parents who told him they did not want to receive such notices; they considered it the university's responsibility to deal with their children.

Binge drinking has become rampant on and around college campuses. Colleges from the University of Georgia to Yale and Harvard are trying to curb excessive alcohol consumption at athletic events.[66] Tailgate parties before college football games send thousands of drunken students into the stands before the kickoff and many to emergency rooms before halftime.[67] The U.S. Navy has to resort to the Shore Patrol to police excessive drinking by midshipmen in Annapolis.[68] The University of Maryland's college newspaper carries ads from a bar that offers pints of beer for a penny to college women from nine to eleven on Saturday evening as a way to attract them—and men who aren't admitted until after eleven when the women are well lubricated with alcohol.[69]

The sharpest increase in alcohol consumption is among college women, whose rate of drinking to get drunk is many times what their mothers' was.[70] In focus groups to probe the reasons for this sharp increase, women cite stress and their desire to be one of the boys—so they go drink for drink with them (even though it takes less alcohol to get a woman high). They also cite the pressure they are under to have sex—so they use alcohol as a disinhibitor that helps them deal with (accede to) that pressure. Ironically, getting high on alcohol is likely to subject them to even more pressure.[71]

The nexus between heavy drinking on campus and sex is tight. One Ivy League president told me that, during his tenure of more than a decade, every case of rape and date rape at his university involved alcohol abuse. A 1999 CASA report found that up to 75 percent of college rapes involve drinking or drug use by one or both of the parties.

Despite more than a decade of increased attention to substance abuse among college students, about a quarter of them continue to smoke, and their rate of drinking and drug use has risen. From 1993 to 2001, frequent binge drinking was up 16 percent, drinking on ten or more occasions and getting drunk at least three times in the past month were up 25 percent, and drinking for the sole purpose of getting drunk was up almost as much. Marijuana use was up 20 percent. From 1993 to 2005 there was a 52 percent jump in the use of illegal drugs like cocaine and heroin. Abuse of prescription opioids like OxyContin and Vicodin has climbed 342 percent.[72] From 2003 to 2004, the number of alcohol arrests on college campuses jumped 10 percent, more than triple the increase from 2002 to 2003.[73]

Almost one in four (22.2 percent) full-time college students meet the medical diagnostic criteria in the fourth edition of the American Psychiatric Association's *Diagnostic and Statistical Manual* (DSM-IV) for alcohol and drug abuse (10.8 percent for alcohol abuse; 3.3 percent for drug abuse) or alcohol and drug dependence (8 percent for alcohol dependence, 5 percent for drug dependence). This compares to less than one in ten (9.4 percent) in the general population who meet the DSM-IV criteria for alcohol and drug abuse or dependence.[74]

College campuses are littered with (what undergraduates call) "smart pills" like Ritalin and Adderall, which students take to concentrate on their studies.[75] Estimates vary but hover around 1.6 million undergraduates who use what many collegians call "brain steroids."[76] A random survey at the University of Delaware found that 90 percent of the business majors used pills such as Ritalin, Adderall, and Strattera, especially during final exam crunches.[77]

Various incidents of student deaths from alcohol poisoning and drug overdoses and the fact that alcohol is involved in most fatal fires involving college students have moved some colleges to take action on binge drinking.[78] Some have closed down fraternities and sororities where drinking was most excessive.[79] Others provide courses on alcohol abuse and addiction; offer students substance-free dorms, where smoking, drinking, and drug use are prohibited; and provide counseling and treatment for students who become alcohol abusers and alcoholics.[80] Georgetown and the University of California at Berkeley require all incoming freshmen to take an online alcohol education course and pass a written test.[81] The University of Georgia opened an Alcohol Awareness Center in the University Health Center.[82] At Case

Western Reserve University in Ohio, there are "recovery dorms" that help students with drinking and drug problems cope with the permissive university atmosphere.[83] A few colleges have adopted "dry" policies, banning alcohol use everywhere on campus.[84]

What will drive even more aggressive moves by university administrators and trustees to curb alcohol and drug abuse is their potential liability for serious incidents and deaths resulting from their tolerance (facilitation) of excessive underage student drinking and illegal drug use. As courts hold universities liable for deaths, assaults, and rapes of students on campuses related to alcohol and drug abuse, these institutions will have to take more effective measures to curb such abuse and abandon their refusal to accept any *in loco parentis* responsibility.

MUSIC, MOVIES, MUSCLES, AND MADISON AVENUE

> Eric Clapton is playing "Cocaine" in concerts again. The recovering drug addict and alcoholic stopped performing the song when he first got sober. "I thought it might be giving the wrong message to people who were in the same boat as me," Clapton said. "But further investigation proved it's an anti-drug song. It very clearly says in the opening verse, 'If you wanna get down, down on the ground.' That's the focal point of the song." He now performs the song as a reality check on what the drug does.
> —*New York Times*, October 3, 2006

It is difficult for even the most engaged and devoted parents to provide their children with the values and determination to say no when those children are tossed into a world swirling with tobacco, alcohol, and drugs, where substance abuse is often glamorized and its consequences are belittled.

Several of Billboard's greatest hits are rock anthems to the joys of getting drunk or stoned. K's Choice's "I'm Not an Addict" salutes sticking a needle into the veins to feel like a god. Kottonmouth King's song "Where's the Weed At?" is a paean to marijuana. Toby Keith in a hit

CD urges ordinary workers to get drunk on payday. And there's 50 Cent's single "High All the Time."

Girls are besieged with advertising campaigns, models, magazine covers, and celebrities who preach with their words and images, "You can't be too thin." They soon learn that smoking and doping can help achieve the thin ideal. Kate Moss and other supermodels made notorious the term *heroin chic* with their social X-ray physiques and washed-out, drugged-up looks.[85]

Animated films for young children often show good characters smoking and drinking. A review of fifty children's animated films released by the major Hollywood studios from 1937 to 1997 found that twenty-eight portrayed tobacco use by seventy-three characters and twenty-five portrayed alcohol use by sixty-six characters. Most portrayals were favorable. The medical researchers who conducted the review concluded, "Tens of millions of young children are clearly being exposed to a positive portrayal of tobacco and alcohol use in animated films."[86] Another examination of eighty-one G-rated animated films found that in 34 percent of them alcohol use was associated with wealth or luxury, and that 19 percent associated alcohol with pleasurable sexual activity.[87] So concerned are health authorities in Great Britain about the impact of children's animated films that they banned a Tom and Jerry cartoon with scenes that glamorized smoking. As a result, Turner Broadcasting promised to scour fifteen hundred classic cartoons, including those featuring the Flintstones and Scooby-Doo, to edit out such scenes.[88]

A report from the American Legacy Foundation found that, in the spring of 2001, more than half of all teens had seen smoking on television during the week before being interviewed.[89] The G, PG, and PG-13 films released between May 2002 and May 2003 provided 60 percent of youth exposure to smoking in movies.[90] The cinematic example is compelling for kids: 38 percent of ten- to fourteen-year-olds say that they tried smoking because they saw it in the movies.[91]

Twelve- to seventeen-year-olds who frequently watch R-rated films are likelier to smoke, drink, and use drugs.[92] Movies like *40 Year Old Virgin* and *Wedding Crashers* play excessive alcohol use for laughs.

Prime-time television is choreographed with images of alcohol and drugs as either comedic or cool. The teens on Fox's *The O.C.* drop references to "Oxy" as casually as they go for swims.

Liquor is getting increasing face time on television. In *Grey's Anatomy*, characters belt down a few at Joe's Emerald City Bar; in *How I Met Your Mother*, they sip martinis at MacLaren's. There are cameos for alcohol in shows like CBS's *Two and a Half Men* and Fox's *Happy Hour*. The Parents Television Council has expressed its concern because "the shows that depict a lot of partying and drinking are airing early in the evening [when] kids are watching and perhaps not taking away messages about drinking responsibly."[93]

In the television hit *Will and Grace*, the show's character Karen Walker, a frequent drinker, has a closet filled with pills; she is portrayed as an attractive, happy-go-lucky woman who happens to be hooked on Vicodin. The show reveals none of the downside of Vicodin addiction. Dr. David Crausman, director of the outpatient rehabilitation Center for Healthful Living in Beverly Hills, California, points out, "It's no joke at all. [The *Will and Grace* show] depicts a woman who's held hostage to her addiction. They're not showing her when she doesn't get her pain pill, when she doesn't have the alcohol. How she gets diarrhea, how she starts vomiting, how her skin will crawl, her legs will cramp. They don't show that because it's not cute."

In the 1970s, some television shows did portray substance abuse and addiction honestly. *Go Ask Alice* dealt realistically with LSD; *The Morning After*, with alcoholism. And there are some exceptions today. The CBS show *Without a Trace* portrays a key character struggling with addiction to painkillers that a doctor had prescribed to deal with a gun injury. Fox's *House* shows its lead character, a medical diagnostician, wrestling with addiction to painkillers he uses to help with a permanently injured leg.

It is important to portray substance use honestly. Moreover, warning labels should be in all promotional material for films and programs where extensive smoking or drinking is involved.

Surveys indicate that after parents, teens admire as role models—and tend to imitate—not only entertainers, but also professional athletes.[94]

This accounts for much of the explosion in steroid use by high school and college athletes to bulk up for their football, baseball, or basketball teams. Juicing by baseball stars like Barry Bonds and Mark McGwire in order to stoke their home run production, and by many other professional athletes, including track and cycling stars, sets an example that some half a million teens follow.

Steroid use among high school students tripled from 1993 to 2003.[95] Almost 2 million twelve- to seventeen-year-olds have tried steroids at least once.[96] The typical dose of steroids that high school girls take is ten to one hundred times higher than that appropriate for medical purposes.[97] While boys abuse steroids at higher rates than girls, the increase in abuse has been much sharper for girls, rocketing 342 percent from 1991 to 2003.[98] Many teens, who witness the adulation accorded athletes as they shatter records, conclude that juicing is an acceptable avenue to travel in search of their own athletic achievements.

New York Times sports columnist Harvey Araton put it perfectly: "The shame of the steroid era has always been . . . the overriding message of manipulation, the performance-enhancement scourge that worked its way down from the majors to the minors to the colleges and the high schools. Baseball didn't invent steroids, but . . . it . . . used the hugely popular obliteration of its generational links to encourage still-developing young people not to accept what nature bequeathed them. Not to play by the rules because the rewards were certifiably great, and worth the risk."[99]

Tragedies like that of Rob Garibaldi can be the result. Garibaldi was a spectacular baseball player in high school. Only 150 pounds, he injected himself with steroids in order to enhance his weight and strength. A star at the University of Southern California, he was hailed as one of the nation's top 100 college players. The New York Yankees drafted him. Then his life fell apart when he tried to stop using steroids so he would be clean for his major league physical. He became depressed and violent; he suffered wild hallucinations. When Rob's mother and father discovered that he had been using steroids, their son said he was just modeling himself after his heroes, Barry Bonds and Mark McGwire. To make it in pro baseball, he told his parents, he had to take steroids because everybody did. Then, in October 2002, in a spiral of suicidal depression kicked off by his steroid use, at age twenty-four Rob shot himself with a .357 Magnum pistol.[100]

The major professional sports should impose and enforce tough anti-substance-abuse sanctions covering both illicit and performance-enhancing drugs, alcohol abuse, and smoking.

Teens are subjected to an incessant stream of messages from alcohol and tobacco merchants, whose profits depend in good measure on making their products attractive to children. Alcohol and cigarette companies seek to plaster their names wherever the young congregate. Anheuser-Busch puts its brand name above its Sea World and amusement parks.[101] For a one-time payment of $5 million to the University of Colorado, Coors beer bought in perpetuity the name of the university's basketball arena.[102] Teen football and basketball fans in FedEx Field in suburban Washington and the MCI Center in the nation's capital are besieged with signs promoting beer. When Rudy Giuliani demanded that the Philip Morris Company's Marlboro signs come down from the outfield walls at Shea and Yankee Stadiums, the cigarette company and baseball organizations mightily resisted, but they eventually caved.[103]

Underage drinkers are such a large part of its beer sales that Coors Brewing Company mounted a major marketing effort in connection with the teen film *Scary Movie 3*. As it prepared to do the same with *Scary Movie 4*, three California groups launched the "Scary Beer Ad Campaign" against the company's youth-oriented marketing; under intense public pressure, Coors finally backed off.[104]

Alcohol manufacturers spend more than $1.3 billion each year on television, radio, print, and outdoor advertising, much of it, like Budweiser's cartoon characters, sure to capture the attention of kids.[105] In comparison, the entire 2005 budget of the National Institute on Alcohol Abuse and Alcoholism is a third of that amount.[106]

As the beer, wine, and liquor marketers have long known, exposing children and teens to alcohol advertising influences not only how they perceive drinking, but also whether and how much they intend to drink.[107] The more children know of beer brands and slogans, the more positive is their view of drinking and the more frequently they express a desire to quaff beers. Children with a higher recall of brand cartoon characters hold more positive beliefs about the social and ritual uses of beer.[108]

In the late 1980s, Budweiser gained the attention of children with its spokesdog, Spuds MacKenzie, billed by Anheuser-Busch beer company as "The Ultimate Party Animal."[109] A decade later, the company introduced children to an animated trio of appealing Budweiser frogs.[110] The company then added talking lizards to its child-friendly menagerie.[111] American children and teens see on television more ads for beer than for fruit juice, gum, skin care products, cookies, sneakers, or jeans.[112] The U.S. Centers for Disease Control and Prevention found that the alcohol industry routinely violates its own standards by placing 73 percent its alcohol radio advertising on youth-oriented stations. Some 40 percent of radio ads for alcoholic beverages are more likely to be heard by kids than adults, and most of the $1 billion spent on alcohol advertising in magazines between 2001 and 2003 went to publications likelier to be read by children and teens than by adults.[113] Over the years 2001 to 2004, twelve- to twenty-year-olds were exposed to more beer and distilled-spirits advertising in magazines than were adults twenty-one and over.[114]

College students, at least half of whom are underage for buying alcohol, are preferred targets: Beer and alcohol ads have accounted for 35 percent of college newspaper ad revenue.[115] The National Collegiate Athletic Association (NCAA) and the alcohol industry saturate television with beer commercials during the month-long March Madness basketball tournament and fall college football games. In 2002, beer merchants spent $151 million to run more ads during the March basketball tournament than they ran during the Super Bowl, the World Series, Monday Night Football, and college football games combined.[116]

In their relentless effort to attract youngsters to their products, the alcohol merchants introduced wine coolers in the late 1980s.[117] In the 1990s, they added a variety of sweet-tasting and colorfully packaged malt beverages known as *malternatives*, like Smirnoff Ice and Bacardi Silver, and *alcopops*, like Bacardi Rum Refresher, available in flavors like peach, pineapple, and watermelon, and Mike's Hard Lemonade and XS Taquilla Sunrise.[118] A whopping 41 percent of fourteen- to eighteen-year-olds have tried these beverages.[119] Designed to look like soda pop, these sweet, fruity alcohol-spiked drinks have become a favorite of teen girls: An American Medical Association survey found that many more girls than boys swigg alcopops (30 percent vs. 19 percent).[120] Bacardi has even introduced a diet version of its alcopops, Bacardi Breezers, a play to the female teen obsession to be thin.[121] Bacardi touts its Island Breeze liquor as containing half the calories of traditional spirits and half the calories of wine. Marketed as "The Original Lite Spirit," Island Breeze is hawked in print and cable television ads by *Sex and the City* actress Kim Cattrall, whose character on the popular television show "embodied the confidant woman and led a revolution in cocktails."[122] Another product, Cocktails by Jenn (vodka martini four-packs named Blue Lagoon, Appletinis, and Lemon Drop), is designed to appeal to young girls.[123] Anheuser-Busch, the nation's largest beer maker, has introduced Peels, a line of fizzy alcohol drinks flavored as strawberry with passion fruit and cranberry with peach.[124] These products are promoted on cable shows and in magazines like *InStyle*, where underage females comprise a big slice of the viewer and reader demographic.

Individual servings of gelatin and alcohol (packaged to resemble Jell-O but not sold by Jell-O) known as Zippers hold a special appeal to children.[125] Ice pops spiked with liquor (booze-sicles) have been banned in New York state for that reason.[126]

The alcohol industry has singled out African-American and Hispanic children and teens for special attention. Georgetown University's Center on Alcohol Marketing and Youth has found that black teens from twelve to twenty are exposed to 77 percent more alcohol magazine advertising than their white peers, as well as a far greater number of commercials in four of the five largest radio markets. Alcohol advertising appears on every one of the fifteen television programs most popular with African-American teens.[127]

Anheuser-Busch created a new marketing division dedicated to Hispanic advertising and increased its 2006 Hispanic advertising spending by two-thirds; Miller Brewing Company is spending $100 million on three years of advertising with Spanish-language Univision.[128] As a result, Hispanic teens from ages twelve to twenty see 20 percent more alcohol ads in print media and view alcohol advertising during fourteen of the fifteen television shows they most frequently watch.[129] Not surprisingly, Hispanic eighth graders are drinking more and getting drunk at an earlier age than their non-Hispanic peers.[130]

Where the public health community sees these merchandising tactics encouraging the rampant spread of illegal underage drinking, alcohol abuse, and alcoholism, the alcohol industry sees market share and profits. A conservative, peer-reviewed analysis reported in the May 2006 issue of the *Archives of Pediatrics and Adolescent Medicine* found that, in 2001, at least $22.5 million (17.5 percent) of consumer spending on alcohol came from underage drinking and $25.8 billion (20 percent) came from adult pathological drinking that met the clinical criteria for alcohol abuse and dependence. Most disturbing, this analysis reveals that 97 percent of adult pathological drinkers started drinking as teens or even younger. A stunning 25.9 percent of underage drinkers meet the clinical criteria for alcohol abuse and dependence, compared to 9.6 percent of adult drinkers.[131]

Some sixteen million twelve- to seventeen-year-olds—two in five—drink alcohol.[132] The proportion of children who began drinking in eighth grade or earlier jumped 36 percent from 1975 to 1999.[133] More than 11 percent of twelve-year-olds admit drinking alcohol; by age thirteen, that percentage doubles, and by fifteen, it tops 50 percent.[134] Almost half of high school students admit drinking in the past month, and of those who drink, 67 percent of the boys and 61 percent of the girls binge-drink. Of the binge drinkers, 69 percent did so more than once in the past month. Compared to students who don't drink, those who do are more than twice as likely to be sexually active, four times as likely to smoke, and twice as likely to get into physical fights. The binge drinkers were even likelier to engage in such conduct and to use illegal drugs, to be victims of dating violence, and to attempt suicide.[135] Most heavy drinking college students started while in high school.[136] Too many of these kids will pay the piper a fearful price: The younger a child begins to drink, the greater the danger that child will become an alcoholic.[137]

Heavy-drinking teens have frequent blackouts and savage their memory, attention span, and spatial skills. As Dr. Aaron White at

Duke University put it, "There are long term cognitive consequences to excessive drinking of alcohol in adolescence." Recent discoveries about the damage to the teen brain as a result of alcohol consumption are as important, Dr. White says, as the discovery of "what a bad thing it was for pregnant women to drink."[138]

The tobacco industry makes the alcohol industry's ad dollars look like chump change. In 2005, cigarette manufacturers spent more than $9.7 billion—in excess of $26.5 million a day—on advertising,[139] much of it making their products attractive to teens and children. The industry knows what it's doing: Internal documents reveal that major cigarette manufacturers for years studied the smoking habits of children and developed marketing campaigns to influence them. As one industry executive admitted, "The base of our business is the high school student."[140] Tobacco advertising and favorable depiction of tobacco use in films double the odds that children under eighteen will smoke. Of the 1.4 million children under age eighteen who begin smoking cigarettes each year, half do so as a direct result of their exposure to tobacco advertising.[141]

R. J. Reynolds spent a decade seducing American children with the infamous Joe Camel cartoon character until, under threat of legal action by the Federal Trade Commission and the outraged health community, it stopped using the character.[142] Lou Gerstner, who was chairman and CEO of the tobacco company during much of the Joe Camel era,[143] went on to serve as vice chairman of the board of managers of the Memorial Sloan Kettering Cancer Center, which treats patients in beds that he and his fellow tobacco industry colleagues helped to fill.*

Consistent with its Joe Camel heritage, R. J. Reynolds marketed the sweet smell and taste of flavored cigarettes in order to mask the harshness

---

*Gerstner's attitude is typical of the way most corporate executives regard the cigarette business— as selling just another legal product. Before running R. J. Reynolds, Gerstner was president of American Express; after RJR, he became the chairman and CEO of IBM. Jim Burke, the Johnson & Johnson chairman and an IBM board member, headed the board's search committee for a new CEO. In the course of interviewing Gerstner, Burke asked him how he felt about selling cigarettes. Gerstner responded that cigarettes were a legal product. Gerstner has made substantial contributions to the Memorial Sloan Kettering Cancer Center.

of natural tobacco that puts off some first-time smokers, especially children. Packaged in shiny tins with cool names and flashy advertising, these cigarettes offer candy flavors ranging from watermelon ("Beach Breezer") and berry ("Bayou Blast") to pineapple/coconut ("Kauai Kolada"), citrus ("Twista Lime"), and flavored versions of its Kool cigarettes with names like Caribbean Chill, Midnight Berry, Mocha Taboo, and Mintrigue, and alcohol-flavored cigarettes: ScrewDriver Slots, BlackJack Gin, Snake Eyes Scotch, and Back Alley Blend (bourbon-flavored).[144]

R. J. Reynolds—whose internal documents include one titled "Younger Smokers—Ages 14 to 25"—claimed that it flavors cigarettes to give adults an alternative.[145] That claim was belied by the Roswell Park Cancer Institute in Buffalo, which found that, compared with adult smokers over twenty-five, more than three times as many teens who smoke light up flavored cigarettes.[146]

In October 2006, under threat of an investigation by thirty-eight state attorneys general and led by New York's Eliot Spitzer, R. J. Reynolds agreed to a ban of its candy-flavored Camel, Kool, and Salem cigarettes in the United States. The tobacco giant was caught red-handed appealing to children with "scratch-and-sniff" and "lift-and-sniff" promotional cards scented with sweet candy aromas but with none of the scent of tobacco. So concerned was R. J. Reynolds about what must have been in its files about appealing to children that it agreed to the ban before the investigation was even launched.[147] But the problem remains: As cigar smoking is becoming something of a fad among many teens, including girls, manufacturers have introduced cinnamon- and apple-flavored cigars and signed up celebrities to help market them.[148]

As these tobacco companies know, the average age at which kids first try cigarettes has been declining and stands at under thirteen.[149] By masking the regular tobacco flavor and scent, flavored cigarettes made it even more appealing for a ten-, eleven- or twelve-year-old to take that initial puff and keep smoking until he or she gets hooked.

Even more despicable, the tobacco companies secretly increased the nicotine in most cigarettes about 10 percent from 1998 to 2004. The increase, discovered by the Massachusetts Department of Public Health, makes it easier to addict new smokers and harder for regular smokers to quit. Philip Morris and R. J. Reynolds hiked the nicotine content most sharply in so-called "light" versions of brands and those most popular with youngsters and African-Americans.[150] This revelation followed the finding by federal district judge Gladys Kessler that all the defendants in the federal government's racketeering lawsuit against the tobacco industry "continue to fraudulently deny that they manipulate the nicotine delivery of their cigarettes in order to create and sustain addiction."[151]

The most disturbing aspect of these tactics by the nicotine pushers is that, after dropping off for years, smoking among eighth-graders plateaued between 2004 and 2006 for the first time since 1977, and the decline in overall teen smoking, which had dropped sharply from 1979 to 2000, slowed.[152] Is it just a coincidence that this change occurred as flavored cigarettes were introduced at the turn of the century and nicotine levels were increased? Or have the nicotine merchants found a way to counter the effective public health campaigns that had for years discouraged children from lighting up? Is child abuse too harsh a characterization of those who hawk candy-flavored cigarettes with sharply increased addictive power?

Twenty-three percent of high school students currently smoke cigarettes.[153] In 2005, 20 percent of twelve- to thirteen-year-olds had smoked a cigarette at least once in the past month.[154] By eleventh grade, that proportion had risen to 24 percent, and by twelfth grade, to 28 percent.[155] The earlier a person begins to smoke, the greater the likelihood of becoming a long-term nicotine addict.

Not surprisingly, in our High Society, teen substance abusers are just as likely to be girls as boys, eighth-graders as college freshmen, from urban condos as farmhouses, from Brooklyn slums as the Upper East Side, from Los Angeles barrios as Beverly Hills.

Whatever an individual's views about adult conduct, there is universal consensus about society's obligation to protect its children. We are not fulfilling that obligation when we ask them to grow up in a world awash with alcohol and drugs.

Parents are the front line here. They have more power to influence their children than anyone else. Their engagement in their children's lives—eating dinner together, going to their children's events, helping with homework, and listening as well as sending clear messages that the use of alcohol, tobacco, and drugs is unacceptable—greatly reduces the risk of substance abuse.

But parents deserve the support of a broader society, particularly schools, colleges, and the entertainment community, as well as our health care, justice, and social service establishments. The High Society's failure to protect our children and support their parents has seeded a metastasizing cancer throughout our nation, killing and crippling millions of individuals, spawning crime, destroying families, and bequeathing a legacy that affects the way all of us live and most of us die.

It doesn't have to be that way.

CHAPTER 5

AMERICA'S DEADLIEST EPIDEMIC

> Routine substance abuse screening for all injured teenage hospital patients may be the best way to curb drug abuse, concludes a University of Michigan study published in the Journal of Pediatric Surgery which found that 40 percent of pediatric trauma patients in one emergency room tested positive for drugs, including heroin, alcohol, and marijuana.
> —GRAND RAPIDS PRESS, *August 15, 2006*

> The scientific evidence indicates that there is no risk-free level of exposure to secondhand smoke.
> —*The Health Consequences of Involuntary Exposure to Tobacco Smoke, Report of the U.S. Surgeon General*, 2006

> "Meth is the major driver of the HIV epidemic in the United States," said Dr. Staphanis Strathdee of the University of California, San Diego, at a conference presentation.
> —*Reuters Health eLine, August 16, 2006*

The mortality and morbidity toll and personal tragedies from substance abuse and addiction would be regarded as a pandemic if any other illness were involved. Each year, cruel courtesy of America's deadliest epidemic, some six hundred thousand Americans die and forty million suffer debilitating and disabling illnesses and injuries.[1] Substance abuse and addiction is indeed America's deadliest epidemic.

The big-ticket killers and cripplers—the cancers, strokes, heart attacks, respiratory ailments like emphysema and chronic bronchitis, AIDS, accidents, and acts of violence that inflict such pain and suffering and stoke the surge in health care costs—are more often than not caused or exacerbated by tobacco use and alcohol and illicit drug abuse.

Heart disease, cancer, and stroke top the official list of leading causes of death in the United States, but substance abuse and addiction is the chief culprit and tobacco is king of the morbidity and mortality hill. Of the more than 2.4 million deaths each year in the United States, tobacco claims some 450,000; alcohol, more than 100,000; illicit drugs, some 20,000.[2]

In 2003, the federal government named these as the top five causes of death in America:[3]

Heart disease	685,089
Cancer	556,902
Stroke	157,689
Lower respiratory diseases	126,382
Accidents	109,277

But probe the root causes of these leading killers and discover a different deadly pantheon:

Tobacco Use	450,000[4]
Alcohol Abuse	100,000[5]
Infections	90,000[6]
Environmental hazards	60,000[7]
Motor vehicle accidents	43,000[8]
Guns	30,000[9]
Sexual behavior	20,000[10]
Diet/sedentary habits	26,000[11]
Illicit drug use	20,000[12]

Smoking and alcohol and drug abuse are implicated in deaths attributed to all top five official government killers. Substance abuse can also be found lurking in the shadows of poor diet and sedentary habits, gun violence, risky sexual behavior, motor vehicle accidents, weakened immune systems, and the deadly environmental hazard of secondhand smoke.

Cigarettes account for half of all coronary heart disease, are a culprit in most cancers, and double the risk of stroke. Alcohol abuse is the leading cause of chronic liver disease, including cirrhosis, and can lead to serious gastrointestinal problems, including esophageal cancer, pancreatitis, and cardiovascular, neurological, nutritional, and metabolic disorders. Drug abuse is the leading perpetrator in new AIDS cases, with HIV infections as much as three times higher among methamphetamine users than among nonusers, and with intravenous drug users and their sexual partners spreading the disease.[13] Drug and alcohol abuse and addiction are common factors in other sexually transmitted diseases, mental illness, malnutrition, endocarditis, cellulitis, and hepatitis. Other crippling diseases, such as tuberculosis, often result from the unhealthy lifestyles of addicts.

Four of every ten Americans will be involved at some point during their lives in alcohol-related auto accidents that require medical care. About 20,000 people die and another 500,000 are injured each year in alcohol-caused crashes. Marijuana and cocaine also play a deadly role in auto accidents. A 2004 investigation in Baltimore, Maryland, found that most victims admitted to the trauma center who were driving cars when their accidents occurred tested positive for drugs like marijuana and cocaine.[14] A third of those who tested positive for drugs had also been drinking.[15] The drivers in the study with the highest rates of marijuana use were sixteen- to twenty-year-olds, the youngest and least experienced drivers on the road.[16]

Beyond the human tragedy, the annual health care costs of alcohol-related traffic accidents top $7 billion.[17]

THE INNOCENT VICTIMS

Children are innocent victims of parental substance abuse. The damage begins in the womb of mothers who smoke, drink, and drug during pregnancy. Of pregnant women, 17 percent smoke, 9 percent drink alcohol, 4 percent binge-drink, and 3 percent use illicit drugs, commonly marijuana.[18] This substance use is in good measure responsible for the nation's high infant mortality rate, nearly the worst among industrial nations.

Fetal alcohol syndrome is among the top three causes of the birth defects associated with mental retardation, at a yearly health care cost of $2 billion.[19] Babies exposed to illicit drugs in the womb face higher chances of stroke at birth, physical deformity, and mental deficiency.[20] Smoking during pregnancy is responsible for one in ten infant deaths and 14 percent of premature births.[21] Smoking retards fetal growth and doubles the danger of delivering a low-birth-weight baby.[22]

Newborns who have been exposed to cigarette smoke in utero or secondhand smoke after birth are likelier to be victims of sudden infant death syndrome (SIDS) and experience health problems and learning disabilities later in life.[23] Each year exposure to parental smoking racks up three hundred thousand cases of lower-respiratory-tract illness like bronchitis and pneumonia in infants and young children.[24]

One in five children under age eighteen in the United States is exposed to secondhand smoke in the home.[25] Secondhand smoke increases both the number of new asthma cases among children and the frequency and severity of asthma attacks in those already afflicted. No wonder former U.S. Surgeon General C. Everett Koop calls parents who smoke child abusers.[26]

Children are not the only victims of secondhand smoke. In the United States, 60 percent of nonsmokers have biologic evidence of exposure to secondhand smoke.[27] The U.S. Centers for Disease Control and Prevention estimate that exposure to secondhand smoke causes 3,000 lung cancer deaths and more than 35,000 coronary heart disease deaths annually in the United States among adult nonsmokers.[28] Researchers at the University of California (San Francisco) found that eliminating exposure to secondhand smoke could save more than half a million lives and eliminate 850,000 heart attacks over the next quarter century.[29] In 2006, the U.S. Surgeon General concluded that any exposure to secondhand smoke, however slight, was dangerous to health.

TREATMENT: IMPERFECT PRESENT
AND INCREDIBLE POTENTIAL

The cost of treating the substance abuse problems of Americans has sprouted like Jack's beanstalk. In 1966, when I was a White House aide, we proposed and Congress enacted the first federal Drug Rehabilitation

Act.[30] We asked for $15 million to fund the first year of this program (which, among other things, provided for treatment as an alternative to prison). We never imagined that the federal cost of drug rehabilitation would exceed $50 million a year. By 2001, the government was spending $1.3 billion a year for the treatment of drug abusers and addicts under just that program and its progeny—and that's the least of it.[31] Overall, the feds were spending $9 billion on substance abuse treatment.[32] State and local governments were spending another $9 billion, and private insurance and out-of-pocket spending picked up the tab for $6 billion, bringing the national bill to some $24 billion that year.[33]

Despite the billions spent on treatment, services are relatively scarce and often ineffective. The White House Office of National Drug Control Policy (ONDCP) and the U.S. Substance Abuse and Mental Health Services Administration (SAMHSA) have found that only 17 percent of those in need of treatment receive it, and barely more than 10 percent of children and teens who need treatment get any.[34] The treatment gap is especially wide for prison inmates,[35] abused and neglected children,[36] welfare mothers,[37] the mentally ill,[38] and pregnant and old women.[39] Overall, many of those willing to try to shake their habits cannot find space in public treatment programs, and a good number of the programs offered to them are ineffective.

Most troubling is that the available treatment programs, public and private, have low success rates, and so few individuals are able to break free of their addiction to alcohol and drugs on their first try. Moreover, public funds are spent on programs, like acupuncture, which have been found to be of no help to the addict.[40]

For decades, most residential treatment programs operated on a twenty-eight-day cycle, a period established not by medical need, but in response to the reimbursement cap set by commercial insurers. Even blue chip residential programs like the Betty Ford in California and Hazelden in Minnesota, which usually adhered to that limit, experienced success rates of around 30 percent. As financial considerations came to dominate health care coverage generally, many insurance plans cut the period covered to two weeks. The calculation of corporate chief financial officers went like this: If the success rate is 30 percent for a twenty-eight-day program and 20 percent for a two-week program, it's cost-effective to get two-thirds of the success for half the price. Similar approaches have led large employers and insurers in many cases to limit reimbursement to outpatient treatment.

These time and place restrictions ignore the reality that treatment success requires individually tailored lengths of time, often in residence, and depends not only on the program, but also on personal characteristics and situations. Does the patient have a family (spouse, parent, child, other loving relative) and a job (or schooling or other task) to return to? Does the patient have a co-occurring mental health problem or physical ailment? Does the patient with young children have child care available? Success also can depend on the diligence of the patient in attending Alcoholics Anonymous or other support group meetings after completing intensive residential treatment.

Substance abusers and addicts typically experience repeated cycles of abuse and addiction followed by periods of relative abstinence and effective functioning, because addiction is a chronic, relapsing disease, not an acute one.[41] The substance abuse treatment community likes to attribute high dropout and relapse rates not to treatment deficiencies, but to the failure of individual addicts. In fact, problems within existing treatment systems—inadequate certification standards, frequent turnover of staff, erratic program procedures, lack of program performance accountability, absence of professional training—contribute to the discouraging cycle of recovery and relapse.

The field of substance abuse and addiction treatment has never been subjected to the demanding standards of professional preparation for entry and continuing practice that characterize the medical profession: extensive graduate education with academic and clinical components, tough licensing exams, continuing-education requirements, and oversight by professional boards in each state. Medications for substance abuse, such as methadone and naltrexone, have been rigorously evaluated by the Food and Drug Administration. But many methods of treatment for substance abuse have never been systematically subjected to the kind of peer-reviewed, scientifically based outcomes research that has produced high quality in medical and surgical procedures and pharmaceuticals.

In many states, there are essentially no standards for individuals who profess to be treatment counselors. Indeed, the chief qualification often appears to be that the counselor is a drug or alcohol addict now in recovery. In no other disease is there an insistence that those who suffer from it are best qualified to treat it. No one makes the claim that cancer or heart attack victims, or those suffering from mental illness, are the best-qualified oncologists, cardiologists, and psychiatrists.

In the early 1990s, at CASA we sought to evaluate treatment programs in a scientifically sound way. We wished to interview patients as they entered care, to meticulously record the treatment they received, and then to follow the patients for up to five years with random drug testing and periodic interviews. Programs we contacted resisted such a review. The reasons offered were the privacy of the patient (we offered to commit to protect patient privacy, a common component of research protocols) and the fear that such a careful follow-up would be so intrusive that it might hinder the patient's recovery. We believed that sensitive researchers were capable of conducting tests and interviews in a way that would not reduce (and perhaps would even enhance) the patient's chances of maintaining sobriety.

Worse than the failure to subject all treatment protocols to scientifically based outcomes research is how programs calculate success rates. For example, some therapeutic community programs, which normally require patients to stay in residence for eighteen months to two years, claim a 30 percent success rate. They reach that percentage by counting only those patients who complete the entire course of treatment. However, commonly of those who enter therapeutic communities, 80 percent drop out within the first few months. Only 10 percent complete the lengthy program. Of that 10 percent (normally according to their own statements), a third are drug-free a year later, a third are using at lower levels, and a third are back to their pretreatment usage patterns.

Treatment success claims by programs themselves are widely discredited in the research community and by insurers and state and federal legislators. There have been few independent systematic evaluations of substance abuse treatment effectiveness comparable to the kind of assessments that typically precede the widespread adoption of pharmaceuticals and other new medical treatments. The lack of objective evaluations contributes to the skepticism of many elected public officials. Senators and representatives in Washington, and numerous state legislators, are so doubtful of the effectiveness of treatment programs—and the disease is so stigmatized—that they refuse to support additional public funding for such programs and decline to mandate legislatively the same breadth of coverage they provide for medical and surgical procedures.

Health insurers either refuse to cover such treatment or limit their coverage to arbitrary time periods because of the absence of professional standards and scientific studies that establish protocols for effective treatment. Leonard Schaeffer, when he was chairman and chief executive officer of WellPoint in California, and numerous other insurance executives have told me that until they see medically reliable measurements of effectiveness, such as those for other medical procedures and many mental illnesses, they are not likely to provide coverage. The situation is similar to what psychiatry faced in the first half of the twentieth century, until a body of scientific evidence gave insurers a measure of confidence in the efficacy of psychiatric treatment sufficient for them to calculate the odds.

The absence of such objective assessments makes it difficult for those who suffer from addiction to find appropriate treatment. Even individuals as powerful and well connected as Florida governor Jeb Bush and Citigroup chairman Sandy Weill, who in a few phone calls could identify "the best" heart or cancer specialist for any specific condition, find themselves stymied in their search for "the best" appropriate substance abuse treatment for their daughter or son.

Only the federal government has the resources for the kind of treatment research and expensive clinical trials essential to design programs that can confidently produce results. In the absence of such trials, we will continue to have a situation in which insurers, politicians, and even treatment providers pile on the patient for failure to achieve and maintain sobriety. While even the best treatment providers will have patients who relapse, placing all the blame on the addict is camouflage to cover the inadequacies of existing treatment techniques, our failure to do the research needed to improve them, and our refusal to recognize addiction as a chronic and relapsing disease.

Even under present circumstances, where treatment is spotty, the value of treatment compared to the costs of failure to treat is clear. A study at the University of California, Los Angeles, compared the costs of treatment for twenty-five hundred clients in various programs with the resulting reduced costs (less medical treatment, fewer mental health services, and less criminal activity and welfare) and increased earnings. The study found a seven-dollar benefit for each dollar spent on treatment.[42] The finding is similar to those of other studies.[43] That payoff is better than those recorded in many long-shot cancer therapies. An analysis of Medicaid patients who received substance abuse treatment found a 30 percent decrease in their Medicaid costs, from an average of $5,402 per year to an average of $3,627 per year. These reductions were across all areas, including hospital stays, emergency room visits, and outpatient clinic care.[44] With such results even without the professional standards proposed here, imagine how much greater the savings can be with more consistently effective treatment programs.

Immediate, short-term actions can be taken to improve public programs. Delaware pays bonuses to outpatient treatment programs that retain at least 85 percent of their clients for the full course of care. Programs failing to reach that goal receive only 90 percent of the prior year's reimbursement rate. Adopted in 2003, this plan has tripled patient retention rates, an important factor, since retention in treatment is related to success.[45] Beyond financial savings from treatment, the benefit to abusers of their restored lives—family, work, and emotional and mental health—is priceless.

MEDICINE MEN AND WOMEN

The nation's medicine men and women are undereducated and unprepared to spot substance abuse and address it. Presented with a description of the early symptoms of alcohol abuse in an adult patient, 94 percent of primary-care physicians who participated in a national CASA survey failed to include substance abuse among the five diagnoses they offered. Among physicians serving older women, an astounding 99 percent failed to spot the problem. Of the pediatricians surveyed, 41 percent failed to diagnose substance abuse when presented with a classic description of an adolescent patient with symptoms of drug abuse.[46]

In a survey of patients with alcohol or drug problems, 54 percent said their primary-care physician did nothing about their substance abuse.

Of these patients, 43 percent said their physician never diagnosed it; the other 11 percent believe their physician knew about their addiction and ignored it. Less than a third of primary-care physicians carefully screen for substance abuse. Only one in five consider themselves "very prepared" to identify alcoholism or spot illegal drug use, and only three in ten consider themselves "very prepared" to spot prescription drug abuse.

Most patients with alcohol or drug problems agree that physicians do not know how to detect addictions and say that doctors prescribe drugs that could be dangerous to addicted individuals. A third said that, even when aware of their addiction, their physician nevertheless prescribed psychoactive drugs such as sedatives or Valium. The average patient surveyed had been abusing alcohol, pills, and/or illegal drugs for ten years before entering treatment. Of these patients, 75 percent said their primary-care physician was not involved in their decision to seek treatment, and 17 percent said the physician was involved only "a little."[47]

These findings expose a monumental lost opportunity. They also indict the medical profession for its failure at every level—in medical school, residency training, continuing education, and practice—to get up to speed on the nation's number one disease. And since doctors tend to do what they are paid to do, these surveys reveal the devastating impact of the refusal of health insurers and health maintenance organizations to provide coverage for physicians to talk to their patients and for treatment of substance abuse and addiction. The upside-down reimbursement system encourages physicians to give substance abusers mood-altering drugs rather than take the time to find out whether there is an underlying addiction problem and, if there is, refer their patients to appropriate treatment. When a family doctor, facing an overcrowded waiting room every day, finds that a powerful painkiller like OxyContin gets patients off his back, he gives it to them—even though less addictive painkillers will do the job. Doctors often complicate the problems of alcoholic patients by putting them on sleeping pills or tranquillizers because they don't take the time to see the alcohol problem.

Even when spotted, many physicians prefer to ignore substance abuse symptoms and are reluctant to confront patients. These doctors point out that the likely outcome is denial and an argument with their patients, or some kind of extended discussion for which they are not paid. (The matters that patients are likeliest to lie about are their sexual conduct, drinking, drugging and smoking habits, and diet.) How many times have doctors told me, "Insurers don't pay me to talk to patients; they only pay physicians to prescribe pills for them, stick them with needles or cut them with scalpels"? While some physicians consider it fruitless to raise the subject of substance abuse with a patient, others fear they will lose the patient if they do so.

The attitudes of these medicine men and women is particularly disturbing since there is clinical evidence that even the briefest interventions can have a salutary effect on an alcohol- or drug-abusing patient. That's why insurers should be required to reimburse doctors for time spent talking to their patients.

Physicians are behind the scientific curve even with respect to smoking. Virtually all primary-care physicians and heart and cancer specialists ask their patients whether they smoke. But we now know that secondhand smoke kills as many as seventy thousand Americans a year and that there is no safe level of exposure.[48] Yet few physicians ask patients about their exposure to secondhand smoke.

America's medicine men and women must be better trained to identify and deal with substance abuse and addiction, beginning in medical and nursing schools and during residencies. Most medical schools provide only a lecture or two on the subject. Even those that offer an entire course rarely require students to take it.

The medical profession misses important opportunities to deal with substance abuse and addiction, notably in the hospital emergency room. Teens who end up in emergency rooms are likely to have been abusing alcohol or drugs.[49] Some are overdoses, but many are accident victims. Teens in emergency rooms should be routinely drug- and alcohol-tested, and they and their parents should be approached about their problem and encouraged to seek treatment.

Emergency room interventions of a few minutes have been found effective.[50] Dr. Larry M. Gentilello, chairman of the Division of Burns, Trauma, and Critical Care at the University of Texas Southwestern Medical School in Dallas, explains the motivating potential of intoxication-related trauma: "Consider that they had crashed their car, had multiple lines and tubes inserted into them while in the emergency department . . . had . . . various types of injuries . . . . The crisis of trauma represents a 'teachable moment' . . . when patients . . . are very receptive to advice to change their life."[51]

The health insurance industry has played a sinister role here.[52] In 1947, at the urging of the National Association of Insurance Commissioners (NAIC), most states adopted the Uniform Sickness Policy Provision Law, which allows insurers to deny payment of hospital bills if the medical record documents alcohol or drug use. Although in 2001 the NAIC changed its position and supported repeal of these laws, in 2006 thirty-three states still permit insurers to exclude medical services for conditions or injuries related to alcohol and drug use. As a result, hospital administrators discourage trauma doctors from even screening for evidence of alcohol and drug use, for fear that medical care of the patient will not be reimbursed and the hospital will have to absorb the cost. When alcohol and drug use are not diagnosed in the emergency room, the opportunity for a brief intervention to encourage sobriety is lost. State legislatures should repeal these laws and enact ones to encourage hospitals to screen for such use and discourage such use.

There are two sure ways to effect the basic cultural change needed to get the medical profession to accord substance abuse and addiction the appropriate attention as a chronic and relapsing disease. One is to recognize as malpractice the failure of physicians to screen for the disease and diagnose it and, upon such a diagnosis, failure to treat the patient or refer the patient for treatment. The other is to require health insurers to reimburse physicians for time spent talking to patients.

BACK-OF-THE-BUS RESEARCH STATUS

The back-of-the-bus status of substance abuse in America's health care system is reflected in the nation's citadel of medical research, the National Institutes of Health (NIH). NIH supports 90 percent of the nation's basic biomedical research.[53] The focus of that research is lopsidedly on the consequences of substance abuse and addiction: cancers, strokes, cardiovascular ailments, respiratory diseases, and AIDS. NIH spends at least $13 billion a year to research those diseases.[54] Through its National Institute on Drug Abuse and National Institute on Alcohol Abuse and Alcoholism, NIH spends only about 10 percent of that amount to study the largest single cause and exacerbator of that quintet of leading killers and cripplers.[55]

We need a substance abuse Manhattan Project, a massive investment in research into the causes of substance abuse and addiction—neurological, biological, psychological, emotional, spiritual—and the ways to prevent and treat it. Such a complex undertaking requires the assembly of a wide spectrum of scientific specialties, working together.

I believe that we must create a National Institute on Addiction, combining the current Institutes on Alcoholism and Alcohol Abuse (NIAAA) and on Drug Abuse (NIDA), and fund the combined research institute with at least $3 to $4 billion a year.

Our nation's best scientific and medical minds did not serendipitously decide to devote their lives to cancer research. The lure was the commitment of President Richard Nixon, joined by the Congress, and followed by every succeeding president and Congress, to provide enormous resources to cancer research. More recently, presidents and congresses have made and kept similar commitments to AIDS research. Research funds attract scientists the way flames attract moths. Once the finest medical researchers knew that the funds would be there to help them wrestle with these intractable diseases, support them with a full armamentarium of high-tech, costly machinery, and laboratories, and establish clinical networks for their work, they flocked to the effort. In contrast, we offer professionals working to unlock the mysteries of substance abuse slingshots and test tubes.

Substance abuse and addiction is no less intractable, and while the field is filled with dedicated professionals and some talented scientists, we do not have an army of our finest minds working on the ways to prevent and treat it. To enlist the best and the brightest to work on a problem this vexing, we need the kind of research contract the nation has signed with respect to cancer, heart disease, and AIDS.

The research community must be willing to engage in a unique, multifaceted undertaking. This is not simply biomedical research such as molecular biology, neurology, and brain imaging. It is also psychological, emotional, and spiritual research, since this complex disease has elements of dysfunction in all these areas. Co-occurring mental disorders are common where substance abuse is involved. For example, for young teens, cigarette smoking may be a symptom (or an integral part) of an accompanying mental health problem like depression, anorexia, or even ADHD, schizophrenia.[56]

Specialists in these fields must be assembled to work together, something of a revolution for the research community. The traditional wall of separation of "pure" biomedical scientists and "adulterated" social scientists must be torn down, biomedical researchers must abandon their condescending culture about social scientists, and psychiatrists must shed their disdain for the spiritual community.

The need to work together is evident from the increasing number of pharmaceuticals designed to reduce the craving in the brain for drugs. For heroin, there's buprenorphine; for alcoholism, naltrexone, acamprosate and injectable Vivitrol. For cocaine, nicotine, and marijuana, addiction researchers are working on an array of pharmaceuticals to blunt receptors in the brain that produce alluring highs. But chemical manipulation of the brain to reduce craving is not enough. Even as we discover these pharmaceuticals, we must learn how to motivate individuals to take them. After all, we have had Antabuse (which interferes with the metabolism of alcohol and causes drinkers to react with headache, nausea, and vomiting) for more than half a century, and America still has many million alcoholics and alcohol abusers. We have been using methadone since the mid-1960s, but we have not reduced the number of heroin addicts (and, indeed, methadone addiction is a growing problem).

Motivating addicts to take the medicine requires an understanding of their emotional, psychological, genetic, and spiritual situation sufficient to know how to convince them to want to take the giant step of ending alcohol or illegal drug use. It is particularly important to learn more about influencing adolescent substance users. Cope Moyers, a recovering addict, put it well when he spoke of "the other components of this illness," telling scientists that he was "born with a hole in my soul" and "a pain that came from the reality that I just wasn't good enough." John Schwarzlose, head of the Betty Ford Center, cites the millions of addicts and alcoholics that have recovered without any medication, through Twelve Step treatment. Medicines can be a big help, Schwarzlose believes, but the importance of motivation cannot be overemphasized. It is the climate we have created to motivate addicted smokers to quit that has made products such as nicotine patches, pills, and gums so useful.

Moreover, as NIDA director Nora Volkow points out, the horrors of the world of many addicts—depression, sexual abuse, intense anxiety, living in poverty—can override all genetic, biological, and pharmaceutical factors. Research is essential to a better understanding of both the psychological and the biological causes and cures for addiction and abuse. We know precious little about what treatment works best for whom. What helps a teen may not work for an adult; cultural, religious, and racial differences may require nuances in treatment modalities. So, in research as in practice, this disease demands a holistic approach: combining brain-imaging discoveries, genetic markers, and new knowledge about dopamine, serotonin, and chemicals that affect brain receptors with all the psychological, emotional, and spiritual knowledge we can muster, to create a personal-environment antagonistic to drug use and alcohol abuse. Helping addicts requires an analysis not only of their family and neighborhood, but of their cultural petri dish of stress and boredom, entertainment, friends and relatives, economic insecurity, hopelessness, and substance availability.

This is not to dismiss the importance of research in molecular biology, brain imaging, and genetics. Indeed, as is the case with cancers and cardiovascular diseases, if scientists can identify those individuals who are likeliest to become addicted if they smoke, drink, or use illegal drugs, we can warn them in advance and perhaps even create medicines that will counteract their predisposition, just as researchers are trying to identify markers to spot individuals who are virtually certain to get esophageal or lung cancer or have a heart attack if they smoke. Scientists at Yale, working under Dr. Joel Gelernter with the DNA of some four hundred families in which at least two members used the same drugs, have found a location on chromosome 17 that may be complicit in increasing vulnerability to drug addiction; it is similar to genes that have been identified with alcohol abuse. Research like this can spot the individuals at highest risk of becoming addicts.

Combining the two NIH institutes into a single National Institute on Addiction requires not only overcoming the bureaucratic lethargy common to any significant reorganization of government agencies. The alcohol abuse community—with significant support from the beer, liquor, and wine merchants—has opposed such a combination because it does not want its clients tainted by the stigma of drug abuse. Indeed, many alcoholics look down on drug addicts. The illegal drug researchers fear that combining the institutes might reduce their funding because the NIAAA gets less than half the money that NIDA receives. This budget differential—giving so much less to research on the abuse of the substance that accounts for the bulk of dangerous addicts and the most severe consequences of addiction, such as violent crime, child abuse, and family disintegration—has long been attributed to the alcohol industry, which is credited (charged) with holding down the NIAAA budget.

Pressing the combination in Congress is a battle well worth fighting, but many of the benefits need not await the outcome of such a bureaucratically controversial proposal. The Secretary of Health and Human Services and the Director of the National Institutes of Health can view the budgets (and relevant segments of the budgets of other Institutes, such as that of National Institute of Mental Health) as an integrated whole and develop a major research assault on all substance abuse and addiction.

BUSTING THE HEALTH CARE BUDGET

Health care spending in the United States is up 1000 percent since 1980, topping $2 trillion in 2006, rising at twice the pace of the consumer price index and accounting for more than 16 percent of the nation's gross domestic product.[57] That's about $7,000 for each man, woman, and child in the nation.[58] Continuing failure to rein in such costs is likely to condemn more than fifty million Americans to the ranks of the uninsured and set off a chilling system of triage for the elderly.

For more than three decades, in efforts to control health care costs, presidents, senators, governors, and a parade of other public officials, health care professionals, and corporate executives have aimed their guns at doctors, hospitals, pharmaceutical companies, medical equipment manufacturers, nursing homes, and insurance companies. In 1968, President Lyndon Johnson asked the Congress to change the way doctors and hospitals were paid in order to encourage more efficient conduct; Congress refused. In the early 1970s, President Richard Nixon slapped wage and price controls on hospitals and other health care providers for almost three years.[59] As Secretary of Health, Education, and Welfare in 1977, I tried (unsuccessfully) to convince Congress to cap hospital charges. Over the past quarter century, the federal government, states, Fortune 500 companies, and insurers have created bureaucratic behemoths to monitor every physician, prescription, patient, and procedure. Policy wonks and politicians have promoted efforts to close excess hospital beds, curb medical malpractice litigation, eliminate unnecessary procedures, crack down on crooks and cheaters, trim administrative expenses, and increase cost sharing, competition, and regulation.

But these efforts, whatever their rallying cry—managed care, managed competition, free market forces, national health insurance, government price controls—have become tangled in webs of self-protection spun by physicians, hospitals, pharmaceutical companies, medical equipment manufacturers, insurers, health maintenance organizations, and other health care providers, all determined to protect their piece of the health care action.

Amid all this scrambling to attack the rising costs of modern medicine, we have missed the biggest target: substance abuse and addiction, which is responsible for more than 10 percent of what the nation spends on health care, some $230 billion in 2006 and climbing relentlessly.[60] That figure alone explains the grim status of substance abuse and addiction as Public Health Enemy Number One and justifies putting it at the top of the most-wanted list for those seeking to contain costs. And the figure is low, since it does not account for treating the physical and mental suffering of family members and friends that are a consequence of the substance abuse of their loved ones.

The costs attributable to substance abuse and addiction can be found in just about every nook and cranny of the nation's health care system. As many as half the nation's hospital beds are filled with smokers and drug and alcohol abusers,[61] and substance abuse prolongs hospital stays and complicates the treatment of most illnesses.

Substance abuse and addiction cause more than seventy conditions that require hospitalization, or contribute to them: diseases such as lung cancer and low birth weight associated with smoking; accidents and cardiovascular diseases associated with alcohol use; AIDS associated with drug use; and strokes and paranoia associated with the abuse of prescription drugs like stimulants and depressants. The list ranges from spontaneous abortion, asthma, and burns to cervical and colon cancer, seizures, and Crohn's disease.

The substance abuse burden is crushing public health care programs. CASA has traced one of every five dollars of what Medicaid spends on inpatient hospital bills to substance abuse, some $16 billion in 2005.[62] Three-fourths of lung cancer and half of head and neck cancer among Medicaid patients can be traced to tobacco and alcohol use.[63] Medicaid patients with addiction problems have medical costs as much as 60 percent higher than those with no such problems.[64] Medicaid patients with substance abuse as a secondary diagnosis can expect to be hospitalized twice as long as patients who exhibit the same primary diagnosis but have no tobacco, illegal drug, or alcohol problem.[65]

Largely because of the long-term consequences of smoking and drinking, substance abuse exacts an even heftier price from Medicare. Thirty-one billion dollars of Medicare inpatient hospital costs—some 25 percent of all Medicare inpatient hospital spending—are attributable to substance abuse.[66] From 1994 to 2014, Medicare will spend $1 trillion on inpatient care because of substance abuse, most of that amount due to tobacco use.[67]

The Veterans Health Administration spends more than $500 million annually to provide substance abuse treatment and methadone maintenance to veterans. In 2003, the Veterans Health Administration treated seventy thousand veterans for illegal drug abuse. The most commonly abused drug was cocaine (50 percent), followed by heroin, marijuana, and amphetamines. About two-thirds of these veterans were identified as low-income; about a quarter had sustained injuries in combat; four in ten had coexisting psychiatric disorders.[68] Secretary of Veterans Affairs Jim

Nicholson says that the first of the Iraq war veterans began showing up in the homeless population in 2005, very likely as a result of substance abuse. The Veterans Administration (VA) spends many millions more for the increased medical care that substance-abusing veterans require.

The health problems stemming from substance abuse are bringing many of the nation's emergency rooms to conditions of chronic chaos. In 2005, cases stemming from methamphetamine abuse overwhelmed hospital emergency rooms, especially in the rural Midwest.[69] Because meth addicts are often unemployed and uninsured, their treatment places a financial burden on local hospitals so crushing that several have closed their emergency rooms. In a 2005 survey of 200 county hospital-emergency-room officials from thirty-nine states, more than two-thirds reported increases in meth-related visits, noting that there were more visits related to meth than to any other drug.[70]

No health care reform proposal has the potential to yield the kind of savings that come from reductions in smoking and alcohol and drug abuse. Each year, the nation spends $75 billion for treatment for coronary heart disease; for cancer, $69 billion; for hypertension, $48 billion; for stroke, $37 billion; and for HIV/AIDS, $13 billion. More than 52 percent of coronary heart disease, 23 percent of cancers, 11 percent of hypertension cases, 65 percent of strokes, and 32 percent of HIV/AIDS cases are related to substance abuse. Eliminating smoking and alcohol and drug abuse would reduce the total health care bill for these diseases by more than $75 billion annually.[71]

Reducing substance abuse offers savings not only over the long haul, but in the short term as well. Immediate savings will accrue from the reduction in birth complications, injuries resulting from violence and accidents, and strokes among younger people who overdose on drugs. In Pueblo, Colorado, hospital admissions for heart attacks dropped 27 percent within eighteen months after a no-smoking ordinance took effect. Such hospitalizations did not change in the comparison city of Colorado Springs, which had no such ordinance.[72]

We cannot calculate the human misery of children who lose a parent to premature death from smoking or parents whose child dies from a drug overdose, the pain of a smoker suffocating to death from emphysema, or the terror of victims of domestic abuse, child molestation, and rape inflicted by perpetrators high on alcohol and of elderly couples mugged by addicts desperate for money to buy drugs. Nor can we assess with precision the extent to which health problems related to substance abuse intensify the intractability of poverty. We do know that the $230 billion in health care costs directly related to the abuse of drugs, to-bacco, and alcohol is only a portion of the billions the nation spends each year to shovel up the criminal and collateral wreckage that substance abuse and addiction visits on our people.[73]

CHAPTER 6

CRIMINAL HANGOVER

In August 2006, Ricky Jovan Gray, 29, was convicted in Richmond, Virginia, of murdering a musician, his wife, and two daughters. Defense attorneys said Gray was high on PCP when he tied up the family, cut their throats, bashed them in the head with a claw hammer and set their house on fire.

—*Associated Press, August 18, 2006*

An 18-year-old Fayette County man admitted that he was high on crack cocaine when he broke into the home of an elderly woman suffering from multiple sclerosis and raped her.

—Pittsburgh Tribune Review, *July 27, 2006*

In an alcohol-induced rage, Michael O'Connor pummeled his brother and stabbed him with a kitchen knife, killing him. After indictment for murder, O'Connor was picked up twice for drinking alcohol in violation of his bail.

—*Providence Journal, (Providence, RI),*
August 10, 2006

Most violent crimes—murders, assaults, vehicular homicides, domestic violence, child molestations, and rapes—are prompted, abetted, or aggravated by alcohol and illegal drugs. Alcohol abuse is the most-wanted criminal. It is even more tightly linked with violent crime than crack cocaine. In state prisons, 21 percent of violent felons were high on alcohol alone at the time of their offenses; only 3 percent were high on crack or cocaine alone.

Most acts of criminal vandalism can be traced to individuals high on alcohol, cocaine, or methamphetamine.[1] Heroin, cocaine, and methamphetamine addicts who need money to buy drugs account for most robberies and burglaries.[2] The nation's number one crime is driving under the influence (of alcohol, marijuana, methamphetamines, or other drugs).

BEHIND BARS

Thanks largely to alcohol and drug abuse and addiction, in the United States we incarcerate some 2.2 million men and women. That's 1 in every 136 residents, 738 for every 100,000 people.[3] The next highest rate, among western European nations, is in Spain, where one-fifth that proportion—142 people per 100,000—is incarcerated.[4] More of our people live behind bars than in Houston, Texas, the nation's fourth largest city.[5] Most inmates are in state prisons, but the federal prison population, mostly composed of drug offenders, went up more than 500 percent in twenty years, from 36,000 in 1986 to almost 200,000 in 2006.[6]

If we add to the 2.2 million people incarcerated the 4.1 million on probation and the 784,208 on parole, at the end of 2005 a record 7 million of our people—1 of every 32—were caught up in the criminal justice system as inmates, probationers, or parolees.[7]

Some 80 percent of America's inmates—1.8 million—either were high at the time of their crimes, committed their offenses to get money to buy drugs, violated the alcohol or drug laws, have a history of alcohol or drug abuse and addiction, or share some mix of these characteristics. Substance abuse keeps recidivism rates high: The more prior convictions an inmate has, the likelier that inmate is to be hooked on drugs.[8]

While women account for about 155,000 prisoners, their numbers have jumped thirteenfold over the past quarter century, from only 12,000 in 1980.[9] That's twice the rate of increase for male inmates—due almost exclusively to alcohol and drug abuse and addiction and the prostitution and violent and property crime it spawns.[10]

Though blacks are disproportionately represented in prison, the common marker among inmates is not race. It's drug and alcohol abuse. Essentially the same proportion—61 percent to 65 percent—of black, white, and Hispanic inmates are regular drug users.[11]

We are reaping in adult crime and punishment what we are sowing in families and juvenile justice systems. Regularly drug-using inmates are twice as likely as others to have parents who abused drugs and alcohol and family members who served time.[12] Just over a third of adult inmates admit to having been arrested as juveniles; the true number is likely to be more than double that. The adult inmate population is a mirror image of the juvenile offenders who seed it: Some 80 percent of incarcerated juveniles are as involved with drugs and alcohol as adult inmates. Most children and teens in state juvenile justice systems test positive for alcohol or illegal drugs at the time of their arrest. Of ten- to seventeen-year-olds arrested for violent and property crimes, 70 percent are drug and alcohol addicts or abusers. Like adult criminals, juveniles who abuse alcohol and drugs are more likely to be rearrested.[13]

How did our prisons, jails, and juvenile detention centers become holding pens for the nation's alcohol and drug addicts and abusers, many with co-occurring mental and physical health problems?

For decades, we have perpetuated many myths about the nation's prison population. From the 1930s to the 1950s, Hollywood portrayed inmates as swaggering big-time gangsters played by Humphrey Bogart, George Raft, and Edward G. Robinson, or psychopaths like James Cagney in *White Heat*. Since then, the celluloid criminals have been tough guys with hearts of gold (Burt Lancaster in *Birdman of Alcatraz*), charming conmen (Leonardo DiCaprio in Dreamworks' *Catch Me If You Can*, the Frank Sinatra and George Clooney Rat Packs in *Oceans Eleven, Twelve*, and *Thirteen*) or grotesquely insane (Anthony Hopkins in *Silence of the Lambs*).

Politicians have created their own myths about inmates by snorting tough rhetoric. Many have talked and acted as though the only people in prison are violent black (and illegal immigrant) crack and meth addicts and incorrigible psychopaths beyond the reach of any known therapy. As a result, the nation's political dialogue on crime and punishment has been as out of touch with reality as our films. Politicians get reelected by demanding, "Lock 'em up and throw away the key!"—not by proposing treatment, mental and physical health care, and job training for convicted felons. Such proposals don't measure up to the Dirty Harry standard that voters are seen to prefer. As federal district judge John Martin put it, "It is easier to run for Congress by saying that you voted for harsher mandatory sentences for drug dealers than by saying you voted to allocate more money for drug addiction programs."

Treating inmates as incorrigibles who must be kept behind bars serves the interests of private prison corporations, whose profits depend on how many of their beds are filled, and of communities whose economies benefit from the presence of a prison. Large private prisons house almost 10 percent of the nation's convicted felons, and their share is rapidly growing.[14] Like other businesses dependant on government contracts, private prisons thrive on friendly lawmakers. Companies involved in building, financing, and operating private prisons, as well as their lobbyists, gave $3.3 million to candidates for state political offices in the 2002 and 2004 election cycles.[15] Corrections Corporation of America, the largest private prison company (seventy thousand inmates in 2006 and growing), is a major contributor to the American Legislative Exchange Council.[16] This council promotes "tough-on-crime" initiatives that provide a steady flow of inmates into Corrections Corporation's facilities and profits into its pockets.[17] Corrections Corporation also gets political benefits from alliances it has formed with Evangelical Christians, providing them money and franchising their ministries in its facilities.

Communities vie for prison facilities because of the jobs and revenue they generate. One Iowa county estimated that a new prison would bring it an additional three hundred jobs, with a yearly payroll of $11.5 million and economic benefits of $78 million.[18] In Nassau County, New York, in 2005 the Sheriff Officers Association contributed heavily to the County Executive's campaign fund, to express appreciation for the more than $100,000 salaries earned in the prior year by 44 per cent of Nassau jail keepers.[19]

There's another benefit for cities and counties that harbor prisons. For census purposes, inmates are counted as residents of the districts in which they are incarcerated. Since prisoners have no income, they lower the average income levels on census records, which are often the basis for fixing the amount of federal support.[20] Minnesota officials estimate that each inmate provides an additional $200 to $300 annually in federal funding to prison towns.[21] Census demographics are also a basis for drawing legislative districts, so even though felons behind bars can't vote (except in Maine and Vermont), their presence inflates the proportional political power of districts where they're incarcerated.[22]

The most important reason for warehousing drug and alcohol abusers and addicts in the nation's prisons may relate to the reductions in crime that the nation has experienced since the early 1990s. Mayors like Rudy Giuliani and police commissioners like Bill Bratton have spearheaded tougher and more sophisticated law enforcement. The booming economy of the 1990s helped curb property crime. The reduction in drug use since the high-flying 1970s and early 1980s was a significant factor. But the lion's share of crime reduction is likely due to the enormous increase in the number of offenders behind bars. Between 1992 and 2004, as the prison population shot up by 65 percent (from 1,295,150 inmates to 2,131,180), violent crime fell 30 per cent (from 1,932,274 reported incidents to 1,360,088), and property crime fell 17 percent (from 12,505,917 reported incidents to 10,328,255).[23]

Finally, even many state and federal legislators who understand the defining characteristics of today's inmates nevertheless insist on warehousing this population because they lack confidence in the effectiveness of substance abuse treatment for them. As a result, they are reluctant to provide treatment in prison, since they believe that prisoners with a history of alcohol and drug abuse are prime candidates to resume their criminal activity upon release, regardless of any treatment such prisoners receive. Even legislators who believe treatment can help are reluctant to fund it for inmates when law-abiding constituents are demanding more resources for schools, roads, sewer systems, and the like.

After years studying the relationship between crime and substance abuse, I am convinced that this jumble of warehousing and punishment-only prison systems is public policy crafted in the theater of the absurd. Despite all the political rhetoric, get-tough laws and mandatory sentences, the average felony inmate (excluding murderers) is set free in less than five years.[24] Temporarily housing such prisoners, and then returning them to society just as we found them, is a profligate use of public funds and the greatest missed opportunity for further dramatic—and cost-effective—reductions in crime. Releasing drug and alcohol addicts and abusers without treatment or training is tantamount to visiting criminals on society and a government price-support program for illegal drug dealers.

The 250,000 inmates who dealt drugs but didn't use them belong in prison—and for a long time. So do those drug- and alcohol-involved inmates who would have committed their felonies regardless of their substance abuse. But it is just as much in the interest of public safety to rehabilitate those who can be redeemed as it is to keep incorrigibles incarcerated. For hundreds of thousands of inmates, likely more than a million, the hard-core problem is substance abuse and addiction, often complicated by mental illness, illiteracy, and lack of any job skills—a poisonous combination that led to their criminal conduct. With treatment for substance abuse and mental illness, and (as needed) literacy and job training, these inmates could become law-abiding, taxpaying citizens and responsible parents.

Although most inmates are alcohol and drug abusers and addicts, treatment programs receive a negligible fraction of prison funding. The federal system spends less than one cent of every such dollar on treatment.[25] States aren't much better. Only a third of juvenile correctional facilities claim to provide any substance abuse treatment.[26] In many cases, the treatment offered adults and juveniles is merely an admonition or four-page pamphlet suggesting that substance-involved inmates go to Alcoholics Anonymous (AA) or Narcotics Anonymous (NA) meetings. Some prisons do not even have such meetings.[27] Bizarrely, as the number of adult inmates in need of treatment has grown, the proportion receiving treatment has declined. In 1991, one in four state inmates who needed treatment received any; by 1997, it was down to one in ten; in federal prisons the rate dropped from one in six to less than one in ten.[28]

The original rehabilitative purpose for establishing the nation's fifty-one juvenile justice systems (in each state and the District of Columbia) has fallen victim to the punishment-only penchant of politicians who demand that juveniles be treated as adult criminals. In some situations—premeditated murder, aggravated assaults, and other calculated acts of brutality—such treatment may well be appropriate. But for most juvenile offenders the central problems are drug and alcohol abuse and addiction and related mental illness and lack of education and job skills. Yet, juvenile justice systems provide precious little substance abuse treatment, or literacy or job training or education, to help reshape the lives of kids hooked on drugs and alcohol. Juvenile offenders should, of course, be held accountable for their conduct. But if we demand accountability from children and teens, we should give them the tools to be accountable.

In 2004 American taxpayers forked over more than $60 billion in taxes to construct and operate jails and prisons.[29] The cost of maintaining an inmate in prison can run as high as $45,000 a year.[30] Those costs keep rising as prisons are required to treat inmates with substance-abuse-related ailments like AIDS and other sexually transmitted diseases, cirrhosis, and liver, lung, kidney, esophageal, and other cancers. In 2004, the Sampson County, North Carolina, sheriff's office was $15,000 over its dental budget, four months into the fiscal year, because of the cost of treating "meth mouth," rotting teeth caused by use of the drug, a condition that has busted many state prison dental budgets in recent years.[31]

Add to the incarceration expense the costs of social service systems to care for the children of substance-abusing inmates and welfare and Medicaid for inmates' spouses.[32] And there is the bill for law enforcement, damage to the victims, and court systems clogged with the drug cases of repeat offenders. One exasperated Oregon judge expressed his frustration: "[Alcohol and drug abusers and addicts are] the ones who commit the crimes. They are the repeat offenders. They are the ones costing our county to incarcerate, prosecute, release, re-incarcerate, re-prosecute . . ."[33]

The cost of substance abuse to juvenile justice programs is at least $14.4 billion annually, including $4.6 billion for the construction and operation of juvenile detention and correctional facilities. This amount does not include the taxpayer dollars spent on probation, physical and mental health services, child welfare, family services, and schooling, which easily bring the total to $25 billion.[34]

Yet, as these costs keep climbing, each year the government builds more adult prisons and juvenile detention centers and hires more prison guards to warehouse more inmates with drug and alcohol problems. In the words of the Pete Seeger's folk song of the 1960s, "When will they ever learn?"

CRIMINAL JUSTICE REVOLUTION

It's time for a top-to-bottom restructuring of the nation's criminal justice systems and for a revolution in the way we view crime and punishment, judges, prosecutors and police, corrections, probation and parole officers, and all those associated with juvenile justice systems. Such a revolution holds the potential for the greatest reduction in criminal activity the nation has ever experienced.

We must take steps to ensure that the offenders who are likeliest to become sober citizens enter treatment, that they stay there long enough, and that they maintain their sobriety.

How?

By enlisting substance abuse experts in psychiatry, psychology, and treatment counseling to identify those likeliest to benefit from treatment, and then deploying the criminal and juvenile justice systems to provide the combination of rewards and punishments necessary to motivate such offenders to seek treatment and sustain their sobriety. The National Institute on Drug Abuse estimates that each dollar spent on treatment saves the nation four dollars in crime costs.[35]

America's punishment-only prison systems are as anachronistic and inane as the debtor prisons of nineteenth-century England so effectively ridiculed and condemned in Charles Dickens's classics *David Copperfield* and *The Pickwick Papers*. It's time to open a second front in the war on crime in the nation's prisons by offering treatment to all inmates who need it, with incentives to encourage them to accept the offer and stay clean. We need to view incarceration of these inmates as an opportunity to get addicts into effective treatment.

Drug courts and a comparable use of prosecutorial discretion can craft a potent combination of the carrots and sticks needed to get young drug offenders and addicts into treatment and back on track. These courts and the creative exercise of prosecutorial discretion should become the rule for nonviolent drug crimes, and perhaps even for some violent crimes, such as assault and battery, when committed under the influence of alcohol or illegal drugs.

The judicial system can lead the way by combining the threat of incarceration with the promise of a self-sufficient future in order to motivate drug-abusing and -addicted offenders to seek treatment and training. In 1989, Miami federal district judge Herbert Klein grew exasperated by the endless line of repeat drug offenders circling his courtroom. "There must be a better way," he said as he worked with Florida chief federal district judge Gerald Wetherington, then State Attorney Janet Reno and Public Defender Bennett Brummer, to try something new. Why not offer indicted nonviolent drug- and alcohol-abusing offenders an opportunity to avoid incarceration if they enter treatment and remain sober for two years?

To test their idea, they convinced Judge Stanley Goldstein to create the nation's first drug court.[36] Judge Goldstein began offering substance-abusing offenders a chance to avoid prison if they entered and completed treatment. During treatment, he regularly called them to his court and subjected them to random drug testing, with immediate sanctions and rewards. In 2000, CASA did an analysis of nine drug courts in several states and found that the participants were far more likely than nonparticipants to maintain their sobriety and far less likely to be reincarcerated. The federal government began supporting drug courts, and the results have been so successful that courts across the nation have followed suit. In New York, Dallas, and Chester County, Pennsylvania, drug court graduates are at least a third less likely to be rearrested than those who go through the usual state systems.[37] Utah has begun screening each criminal defendant for drug use in order to determine whether treatment should be recommended instead of (or in addition to) incarceration.[38] By 2006, more than seventeen hundred drug courts were serving at least seventy thousand clients—and most judges wanted to increase their capacity but lacked the funds.[39]

In Brooklyn, New York, District Attorney Charles J. Hynes was even more frustrated than the judges in Florida as he saw young offenders convicted, incarcerated, released, and promptly rearrested, reprosecuted, and sent back to prison. Many were addicts who also sold drugs. The Rocke-feller drug laws, passed during New York's heroin crime epidemic in the 1970s, curbed judicial discretion by requiring judges to impose a variety of stiff mandatory sentences.[40]

Hynes decided to use his prosecutorial discretion to offer offenders a chance to avoid prison if they entered treatment and straightened out their lives. The Hynes Drug Treatment Alternative to Prison (DTAP) initiative sends repeat nonviolent felons to residential treatment for in-tensive drug treatment and vocational training closely monitored by the prosecutor. Hynes made this program available not only to addicts arrested for possession but also to addicted illegal drug sellers.* In its initial phase, from 1990 to 1998, the DTAP program deferred prosecu-tion: A DTAP-eligible defendant was given the opportunity to enter treatment after indictment but before trial. A defendant who failed the program would be tried and, if found guilty, convicted and sentenced to prison. In 1998, Hynes changed the program to require offenders to plead guilty to their offense so that failure to complete treatment and vocational training resulted in immediate sentencing and imprison-ment. That certainty of prompt punishment led a much higher per-centage of DTAP offenders to stick with the treatment program.[41] DTAP graduates have rearrest, reconviction, and reimprisonment rates far lower than a matched comparison group who go through the cus-tomary criminal justice process. These graduates are three-and-one-half times likelier to be employed than they were before arrest, and nine out of ten are working a year after graduation.[42]

The persuasive power of certain punishment can also be seen in the experience with Proposition 36 in California, which mandates treatment in lieu of incarceration for nonviolent drug offenders. It has fallen short of its full potential because there is no accountability (punishment) for offenders who drop out of treatment.[43]

Drug courts and programs such as DTAP provide a return on invest-ment that would toast Ebenezer Scrooge's cold heart. The Judicial Coun-

---

*The DTAP program is also directed at other drug-addicted felony offenders who have not previ-ously been convicted of a violent crime.

cil of California found that drug courts could save state taxpayers $90 million annually, just from the reduced costs of victimization and criminal justice system agencies. For an investment of $3,000 for a participant, the Council found that the average savings from fewer arrests alone was $11,000; the average rearrest rate of drug court graduates was 17 percent compared to 41 percent for those in the usual criminal justice process.[44] The state of Washington got a return, typical of these programs, of $1.74 for every dollar spent on its drug courts.[45]

The most expensive aspects of any residential substance abuse treatment program are the costs of housing, medical care, and food. For inmates, taxpayers are already picking up those tabs. CASA has estimated the cost of providing all inmates in the United States with drug and alcohol problems intensive treatment, education, and job training and has assumed that, upon release, only 10 percent of them (in the study, 120,000) become sober citizens working at the average wage of a high school graduate. CASA's analysis demonstrates that investment in such programs would pay for itself within a year in reduced criminal activity; savings on the costs of rearrest, prosecution, incarceration, and health care; and benefit to the economy. For each subsequent year that these ex-inmates remain employed and drug- and crime-free, CASA estimates that the nation would receive an economic benefit approaching $10 billion.[46]

A comparable investment to provide substance abuse treatment and comprehensive services and training for each substance-involved juvenile who would otherwise be incarcerated would break even in the first year if only 12 percent stayed in school and remained drug- and crime-free, according to a similar CASA analysis. If those 12 percent remain crime-free as adults, there would be at least sixty thousand fewer adult inmates and fewer felonies, as well as enormous economic benefits from employment and reduced criminal justice, health care, and social service costs.[47]

The potential crime reduction of such programs is big league. Expert estimates of crimes committed by a drug addict range from 89 to 191 a year.[48] Successfully treating and training inmates could deliver the greatest reduction in criminal activity in the nation's history.

To achieve these returns, drug- and alcohol-abusing inmates should be offered treatment, education, and literacy and job training, with an array of effective incentives to get them into these programs. The training should be for jobs that will sustain self-sufficiency upon release, not for five-dollar-an-hour jobs in a twenty-dollar-an-hour economy.

The difficulties of recovering from drug or alcohol addiction are enormous even for middle- and upper-class addicts. For those with family histories of substance abuse, living in poverty, with limited education and vocational skills and mental and physical health problems, the treatment process is exponentially more complex and challenging, and self-esteem can be as important as coercion. Employment can be critical to building the self-esteem essential to maintain sobriety. Student loans for vocational training and higher education should be available to recovering alcoholics and addicts who are trying to improve their situation with better jobs. Holding out the right to vote, a marker of the return to full citizenship, can nourish their motivation to maintain sobriety. Allowing them to become full-fledged citizens will help them shed the lingering stigma associated with their substance abuse and will contribute to their self-esteem.

The relationship of religion and spirituality to effective substance abuse treatment among inmates has received little systematic analysis and merits further study. Much evidence suggests that spirituality and participation in religious groups can play a significant role in the rehabilitation of many inmates. Inmates and treatment providers often cite spirituality (God or a Higher Power) as a factor in getting and staying sober, coping with prison life, successfully reentering the community, and ending criminal conduct.

Religion—notably Christian and Muslim—appears to be an important part of the lives of a substantial number of inmates: 33 percent of state inmates and 38 percent of federal inmates participate in religious activities, Bible clubs, or other religious study groups. Several studies suggest a link between religion and reductions in deviant behavior. For example, a study of New York state inmates in the Prison Fellowship programs founded by Charles Colson showed that inmates who were very active in Bible studies were significantly less likely to be rearrested during a one-year follow-up period than those who were less active in the program and those in a matched comparison group who did not participate in the program.[49] Although the inmates who participated in the Bible studies were a self-selected group, this finding highlights the potential of religion as a factor in reducing recidivism.

Upon release, all substance-abusing offenders should be required to enter aftercare programs like AA and NA. This requirement can be enforced by including a period of parole in each sentence, so that failure to enter and remain in aftercare is a violation of parole that results in an immediate return to prison.

We should measure the success of private companies that operate prisons not simply on the basis of how cost-effectively they incarcerate, but on the relapse and recidivism rates of those they incarcerate. These companies should be obliged to offer drug and alcohol treatment as well as mental and physical health services and literacy and job training. Why not set target goals in their contracts and offer them bonuses based on their ability to reduce recidivism rates of their inmates?

Illinois provides an example of how dramatically we must rethink our concept of prison. The state has established one of the nation's first prisons dedicated to drug and alcohol treatment. The Sheridan Correctional Center, a neatly groomed ninety-five acres about seventy miles southwest of Chicago, provides treatment and job training to about fifteen hundred repeat offenders who are addicted to heroin, cocaine, marijuana, alcohol, or some combination of those drugs. In early assessments, it appears that those who complete the course of treatment and job training, and who enter appropriate aftercare upon release, are half as likely to be rearrested or reincarcerated as those in the state's regular prison system. Providing community-based aftercare services that include assistance with housing, education, employment, and health care has been a critical component of this initiative. Its success has led the state to establish a second such institution and has inspired California governor Arnold Schwarzenegger to propose similar prisons in California, whose 70 percent recidivism rate is among the highest in the nation.[50]

It is also essential to get tougher and smarter with punishment and law enforcement. Selling illegal drugs to teens and helping teens acquire such drugs should be serious felonies with long sentences. We should calibrate sentence severity to the age of the child to whom the drug is offered—the younger the child, the greater the penalty—rather than simply to the amount or type of illegal drugs in the possession of the seller. A similar system of stiff punishments should be adopted for sales of alcohol to minors. This approach recognizes not only the greater vulnerability of the younger teen, but also the fact that the earlier a child begins to use drugs or alcohol, the likelier it is that child will become an addict or alcoholic. It also takes into account the far more extensive role that alcohol abuse plays in violent crime.

Law enforcement should be stepped up across the board in urban centers. Local police forces should enforce drug laws with equal vigor throughout their jurisdiction and put an end to tolerating open drug bazaars in poor neighborhoods like South Central Los Angeles, Northeast Washington, and Harlem, which would be eliminated within minutes in affluent enclaves like Beverly Hills, Georgetown, and the Upper East Side.

If the objective is to provide incentives to reduce recidivism and reform those prisoners who can be turned into productive citizens (and thus enhance public safety), there is no more irrational criminal justice policy than mandatory sentences. Drug addicts and alcoholics need every carrot and stick that can be mustered to help them get and stay sober. Requiring inmates with substance abuse problems to serve their entire sentences takes away the carrot of early release to encourage them to enter treatment while in prison. It also means that released inmates will not be on parole, thus removing the stick of an immediate return to prison if they fail to enter aftercare programs.*

What I am suggesting here is thoroughly recasting the way we view crime and criminals in America and the way we operate our court, prison, and probation and parole systems. Prosecutors and judges need to strengthen their staffs with professionals in the substance abuse field. A U.S. attorney or federal district judge with a complicated antitrust

---

*Moreover, mandatory minimums are a counterproductive tactic. The Rand Corporation found that every $1 million spent to extend the sentences of dealers resulted in a decrease of cocaine *distribution* by 13 kilograms, whereas the same $1 million applied to provide substance abuse treatment to heavy cocaine users would reduce cocaine *consumption* by 100 kilograms.

case seeks economists and industry experts to help negotiate the complexities of prosecution and shape appropriate relief. But prosecutors and judges swamped with criminal cases involving drug and alcohol addicts and abusers do not routinely seek expert help to identify those likeliest to benefit from treatment and training.

Corrections and probation and parole officers need training in substance abuse and addiction to help them deal with inmates and those released from prison in ways that will reduce relapse and recidivism. They also need caseloads commensurate with the responsibility to help substance abusers. Probation and parole have become standing jokes in many large cities, where individual officers often carry caseloads in the high hundreds.[51]

For juveniles, we should return to the original intent of establishing a separate corrections system: rehabilitation. Indeed, a generation ago, we called juvenile facilities *reformatories* and *reform* schools. Reasserting that goal for today's juvenile justice population requires a significant investment in substance abuse and mental health treatment, education, and job training. The entire juvenile justice system staff—law enforcement, juvenile court judges, administrative personnel, social workers, corrections officers—should be trained to recognize substance-involved kids and know how to deal with them. Juvenile offenders who are drug and alcohol abusers and addicts should be given an opportunity to enter treatment and receive other appropriate services in custody and detention, during incarceration or other out-of-home placement, while on probation and in aftercare. We must also provide comprehensive in-home services, juvenile drug courts, and other drug treatment alternatives to incarceration.

Federal funding of state and local prison, criminal court, and police systems should be conditioned on their adopting sensible policies to deal with drug and alcohol abusers. Federal funds should be granted to state prison systems only if they provide treatment and training for all inmates who need it.

I recognize that many offenders would commit their crimes whether they were alcohol and drug abusers and addicts. But hundreds of thousands would be law-abiding, taxpaying citizens if it weren't for their alcohol or drug abuse. In the long term, treating, educating, and training these offenders will reduce taxes and enhance public safety by ending the irrational current policies that release drug-abusing prisoners after serving their term without any effort to break their habit. Those policies maintain demand for illegal drugs and ensure continued criminal activity, since virtually every addicted inmate released from prison without treatment or training will revert to the drug and alcohol habit on the day of release. Such was the experience of a CASA five-site demonstration called OPS (Opportunity for Success), which found that unless substance-involved inmates were greeted at the gate as they exited prison and taken into residential treatment programs, they immediately reverted to drug and alcohol abuse.

We know what doesn't work: same-old-same-old policies that keep alcohol and drug abusers and addicts in prison for a few years and release them without any treatment. The plateauing of declines in crime since 2000, as well as the recent surge in violent crime, reveal that we have exhausted our ability to incarcerate our way out of crime. The FBI reported a 4 percent increase in violent crime (robberies, homicides, aggravated assaults, forcible rapes) in the first six months of 2006 over the same period in 2005. The 2005 numbers were an increase of 2.5 percent over the prior year. Robberies, which many criminologists consider a leading indicator of future trends, shot up 10 percent in 2006. These trends indicate that we have reached the limit of increased incarceration to keep crime rates down.[52] With prisons overcrowded and states forced (by judges or lack of funds) to release untreated drug and alcohol abusers and addicts, we are likely to see the crime rate continue its recent rise.

The pressure for change is building, and there's ample evidence of the effectiveness of drug courts, DTAP, and similar programs in reducing crime, and of the effectiveness of the treatment and training of inmates in reducing recidivism, to support politicians with the courage to make the case for revolutionary change. Exploding costs of the current criminal justice systems across the nation—corrections costs alone jumped almost 1000 percent from 1982 to 2006—and high recidivism rates are driving states to seek new methods of handling offenders whose core problem is alcohol and drug abuse and addiction.[53] The

Reentry Policy Council, an assembly of 100 policymakers and elected officials established by the Council of State Governments, has called for reinvention of the nation's corrections systems, including treatment for substance-abusing offenders to reduce recidivism.[54] A blue ribbon Oklahoma panel established by the state's governor and attorney general advocates a system to identify early in the criminal justice process individuals with mental illness and alcohol and drug problems in order to divert them to treatment.[55] Two-thirds of Maryland voters view drug treatment as more effective than simply incarceration.[56]

If we open this second front in the war on crime in the nation's courts, prosecutorial offices, prisons, and probation offices, the streets will be safer, the cost of law enforcement will be lower, and millions of children and adults will become productive citizens rather than criminal predators. Failure to do so will be the nation's greatest missed opportunity for enhancing public safety while at the same time reducing public costs.

CHAPTER 7

COLLATERAL WRECKAGE

The children had been left alone for days, were physically abused, forced to get high, told to steal from loved ones and to lie to authorities, and they had seen their parents hyper and delusional. They are the children of methamphetamine users.

—CHILDREN AND YOUTH SERVICES REVIEW, *June 2006*

Illinois, along with ten other states including New York, Pennsylvania, Montana and Minnesota, spend more money on drug abuse related problems like public safety and family assistance than on higher education.

—*Medill News Service, Chicago, January 30, 2001*

The poisonous seeds of substance abuse and addiction produce not only crime and deadly and crippling diseases and accidents, but also a toxic legacy of broken families, spousal violence, child abuse, homelessness, lousy schools, permanent disability, teen pregnancy, and vandalized public housing. The concentration of taxpayer dollars and charitable contributions on these consequences, rather than on the causes of tobacco, alcohol, and drug abuse, is the costliest shortcoming of domestic public policy and private philanthropy over the past half century. The political leadership and public policy establishment have led the nation to burn untold dollars trying to sweep up after the wreckage of nicotine, alcohol, and illicit drug abuse, while fiddling away, by nickel-and-diming research, prevention, and treatment.

Politicians and policymakers exchange sharp, often nasty, partisan barbs over each other's proposals to solve the nation's domestic ills. Those who would repeal or radically recast the social revolutions of the New Deal and the Great Society make their case program by program:

Medicaid and Medicare are too costly so their benefits must be cut back; Social Security disability is out of control; discretionary education funding related to poverty hasn't improved schools, so calibrate dollars to test scores; too many linger on welfare, so arbitrarily limit the years of eligibility. The solution is usually to trim back or eliminate a particular program rather than rework it in a meaningful way.

Those who support the social programs of the New Deal and the Great Society counter that we are not spending enough on them. They call for a host of similar new programs, continuing to insist that scarce public resources be committed to dealing with the consequences rather than the causes of drug and alcohol abuse and addiction.

Thanks to this political parrying of conservatives and liberals, of every state dollar spent on substance abuse, ninety-six cents go to shoveling up the wreckage and only four cents go to preventing and treating the problem.[1] The federal budget is similarly lopsided. It is the politicians, not the people on the ground, who are operating in a fantasy echo chamber, outshouting each other's platitudes and pledges, promising more shoveling-up money—for cops to police the streets, family court judges to deal with divorce and domestic violence, higher-tech hospitals and health care clinics, criminal statutes with harsher sentences, and military and FBI agents to counter terrorism.

But talk to the cop who breaks up a family fight and the county sheriff who picks up reckless drivers, the social worker who tries to help a welfare mother achieve self-sufficiency, the teacher in an urban middle or high school, the family court judge who must decide whether to terminate parental rights, the psychologist who examines an abused child, the Social Security worker who processes disability claims, the priest whose parish sits in a pocket of rural or urban poverty, the parents who discover that their thirteen-year-old daughter is pregnant, the provost of a university where a student is racially attacked or date-raped, the federal law enforcement officer who is tracing the source of funds for terrorists. What do they say?

They'll tell you about the husband high on cocaine, the driver drunk on alcohol, the mother hooked on crack, the classmates dealing drugs in a school corridor, the parental alcoholic or methamphetamine addict sending her children out to pick up booze or drugs, the father hopped up on cocaine, the applicant disabled by smoking-related cancer or heart disease, the easy availability of drugs and alcohol in the parish neighborhood, the thirteen-year-old daughter high on booze or pot at the time of conception, the cluster of college students drunk on beer, or the money terrorists get from the drug trade. As a police captain in Bridgeport, Connecticut, told me about the city's toughest neighborhood, "When my men get a call about disorderly conduct in some East Bridgeport home late at night, they don't know whether they'll face a gun or knife or baseball bat on the other side of the door. But they do know they'll face alcohol or drugs."

FRACTURING THE FAMILY

Substance abuse and addiction lurk just beyond the welcome mat in many homes, a threat to the American family as serious as any. Tobacco-related diseases, like cancer, emphysema, and heart attacks, have left millions of children without a mother or father. Alcohol- and drug-sparked domestic violence destroys families and indelibly scars women and children from the poorest neighborhoods to the most affluent suburbs of Greenwich, Connecticut, and Potomac, Maryland. Rich, poor, black, brown, white, corporate executive, construction worker, college professor, athlete, celebrity, anonymous citizen—the faces bruised by alcohol- and cocaine-related domestic violence appear in many family mirrors.

Alcohol is implicated in most incidents of domestic violence.[2] Cocaine and methamphetamine are not far behind.

Even a nonviolent alcohol- or drug-abusing family member sends shock waves into every corner of the home. Substance abusers are more likely to change jobs regularly, to be unemployed for long periods of time, and to suffer injuries on the job.[3] The uncertainty pollutes the family environment with a smog of fear and financial pressure. Other members of the household shoulder new roles, adapting to the unpredictable, unreliable, and irrationally demanding behavior of the alcoholic or drug addict. In the absence of reform, the marriage often collapses.

The United States has the highest divorce rate in the world, with almost half of all new marriages breaking up.[4] In 2005 the divorced population topped twenty-two million and continues increasing, with more than a million marriages coming apart each year.[5] The direct and indirect costs of divorce top $35 billion a year in legal and court fees, property loss, mental illness, and child welfare assistance.[6]

Sociologists, priests, and policy planners fret over the stubbornly high divorce rate. They write treatises about the fragmentation of cultures, religions, races, and languages, which has left our society with a less cohesive consensus on family, moral and social values, and religious commitment. They note that, before World War II, parents, children, and grandchildren commonly lived in the same neighborhood, often in the same house, but mobility has since separated generations and siblings. They study the atomization of the family and the tensions that complicate relationships in two-career and two religion households. Their weakness is not their lack of passion. It is the blinders that shield their eyes from seeing how alcohol and drug abuse and addiction are corespondents hanging in the closet of so many divorce cases.

Here substance abuse delivers a harsh double whammy: The abuse precipitates the separation and divorce, and the family breakup in turn makes the children more susceptible to alcohol and drug abuse. The dissolution of a marriage can weaken the relationship between children and their parents, leaving children more vulnerable to unhealthy peer pressure. Children of divorced parents confront a change in lifestyle, often including lots more—or lots less—money, a move to a new school or home, and inconsistent support and attention from Mom and Dad. These circumstances hike the risk that children will smoke, drink, and use drugs, especially during the initial separation and early divorce years. [7]

But addicted parents can be equally destructive. Alcoholic men are more prone to aggression, hitting, punching, spitting, pulling hair, smacking, kicking, and spousal raping.[8] A husband with a drinking problem triples the level of marital violence in the home.[9] And the female spouse or partner who binge-drinks is far likelier to be beaten or raped, and to neglect and abuse her children.[10]

The costs go beyond the grueling private agonies. In 2003 the Centers for Disease Prevention and Control calculated the cost of intimate partner rape, physical assault, stalking, and homicide at $6 billion a year. At least $4 billion of that went to medical and mental health care services for the victims.[11]

CRUSHING THE CHILDREN

Nowhere does the failure to grasp the complicity of drug and alcohol abuse create more avoidable and wrenching misery than in the judicial, law enforcement, and social service apparatus that states and localities have cobbled together to protect abused and neglected children.

The cruelest consequences of substance abuse and addiction are on display in the nation's child welfare and protective service systems—which pick up the pieces of families when meth mothers are too high to feed or bathe their children and fathers under the influence treat their kids as punching bags or sexual toys. About three million cases of child abuse are reported each year in the United States, and three out of four involve alcohol- and drug-abusing parents.[12] At least as many more cases go unreported, since some six million children have parents who abuse alcohol or illegal drugs and such parents are almost certain to neglect and abuse their children.[13]

Parental substance abuse and addiction account for 70 percent of the millions spent annually by federal, state, and local governments on child welfare systems and of the related costs such as those for mental and physical health care and the developmental and special-education needs of abused and neglected children, as well as on law enforcement and courts.[14]

This torrent of substance abuse and addiction is drowning the nation's child welfare and family court systems, often forcing them, out of haste, to sacrifice abused and neglected children for lack of time to save them. Cases, one more sickening than the next, with the most severely abused children commonly less than four years old, tumble across the nation's front pages.[15] Governor Jeb Bush is pummeled because Florida's system loses a child.[16] In New York City, children in the system are lost, even killed, because overwhelmed social workers can't keep track of the piles of files scattered all over the desks and floors of their offices.[17] In New Jersey, Governor John Corzine overhauled the system in the face of a lawsuit that sought to put it under federal control.[18] In Michigan, the state supreme court ordered all circuit judges to work with local child welfare agencies in order to find children missing from their court-appointed foster placements.[19]

We have amassed an army of nearly 250,000 caseworkers, judges, lawyers, and child advocates in the nation's one thousand state, local, and private child welfare agencies and twelve hundred family courts.[20] On any given day, thousands more in foster-care and adoption agencies tend to half a million children.[21]

With drugs and alcohol complicating the child abuse and neglect caseload—in some offices, professionals struggle with scores of cases at a time—social workers provide in-home services to a smaller proportion of families, and child welfare professionals are able to investigate only a third of their wards.[22]

Some family court judges hear as many as fifty cases in a single day.[23] A judge with that crowded a docket must assess the circumstances and credibility of the child, parent(s), caseworker, law enforcement officer, and any other witnesses in a mere ten minutes—and this estimate assumes that the judge is working nonstop, only on these cases, for eight hours a day.

Caseworkers and judges are typically thrown into chaotic child welfare systems with little or no training in substance abuse and addiction. For most, it's on-the-job learning. Lacking the expertise to deal with the confounding challenges that addicts and their families pose—denial and dishonesty, blurred lines among use, abuse, and addiction, the difficulty of motivating substance-abusing parents to enter treatment and stick it out, children afraid to "snitch" on parents—many child welfare workers retreat to a "Don't ask, don't tell" bunker. Others burn out from frustration. Still others despair from lack of services for those parents who want to get clean.

Most child welfare cases involve the mothers (the fathers, if known, are long gone).[24] Beyond substance abuse treatment, these women need mental health care and literacy, job, and parenting-skills training.[25] Such services are rarely available at the critical moments of opportunity when a mother is willing to try.

The crack epidemic of the 1980s and the methamphetamine explosion at the turn of the twenty-first century slammed social workers with the one-two punch of parental abuse and addiction. These drugs not only threatened the lives of children. They also shattered the basic tenet that had inspired generations of compassionate individuals to devote their lives to child welfare: Keep the child with the biological parents. Indeed, most considered themselves failures when they were unable to hold the biological family together.[26]

The addictive tenacity of drugs like crack and meth and the erratic and violent behavior they spark, paints in blinding colors the clash between the rapidly ticking clock of a child's cognitive and physical development and the slow-motion timepiece of recovery for the addicted parent. In the earliest years, the clock of child development runs at supersonic speed—intellectually, physically, emotionally, and spiritually. Weeks are windows of early life that can never be reopened. For the addicted parent, the clock of recovery runs slowly: It takes time—months, often years—and relapse, especially during the initial weeks and months, is common. Quick fixes and cold-turkey turnarounds are the rare exception to the usual rule of two steps forward and one back. Alcohol and drug abuse slap caseworkers in the face with this anguishing question every day: Is the time needed by addicted parents to achieve stable sobriety so long that their children will be permanently damaged during their own phase of rapid development?

The tenacious grip of addiction has sabotaged the basic motivation that child welfare workers traditionally relied on to reform neglectful and abusive parents: the maternal (paternal) instinct. While regaining child custody is a powerful incentive for many women, those addicted to drugs like crack cocaine, meth, and alcohol are often more driven to get their next fix or drink than to recover their children. The experience of Brooke Byers, a volunteer attorney in the nation's capital representing mothers whose drug use had cost them their children, is typical. She was repeatedly stood up by clients who failed to show for appointments or family court hearings to try to get their children back from the child welfare system.

Further discouraging these mothers is the inclination of many public officials to use child welfare as an adjunct to the criminal justice system.

Caseworkers who receive reports of maltreatment are conscripted into service as criminal investigators in order to avoid any situation that might embarrass political appointees in the local media. Decisions to terminate parental rights become driven more by the desire to avoid a politically embarrassing tabloid story than by a professional assessment of the capacity of parents to conquer their substance abuse in a timely manner. This environment has led many parents and children in child welfare systems to fear their caseworkers, rather than to confide in them.

The need to remove more children from their biological parents has put a premium on adoption and foster-care agencies, which have found themselves ill prepared for the rush of children of addicted parents. Overall only one in four available children is adopted, and children of substance-abusing parents stand at the end of the line.[27] These children have been raised in chaos by their biological parents. They are likelier to do poorly in school, to exhibit disciplinary and social problems, and to experience clinical anxiety and depression.[28] The sexual and physical abuse that many have experienced increases the chance they will self-medicate with alcohol and drugs: They are ten times likelier then their nonabused peers to use illicit drugs.[29]

Most foster-care and adoption agencies lack resources and trained personnel to help these children. Desperate to place them in homes, many agencies tend to look the other way for fear of scaring off potential foster and adoptive parents. Instead of providing funds to train social workers, who in turn could prepare foster and adoptive parents to deal with the vexing challenges of raising children of substance-abusing parents, the federal government in 1980 spit in the wind, passing a law that simply decreed that, in cases of child abuse and neglect, family preservation was preferable to public intervention, foster care, and adoption.[30]

A few child welfare agencies have revamped their systems to face the reality that substance abuse and addiction drives the explosion in the number of cases. The director of the Sacramento County Department of Health and Human Services required all employees to be trained in substance abuse and addiction.[31] Connecticut has enlisted specialists in drug and alcohol addiction to screen and assess parents, place them with treatment providers, and monitor their progress.

Family court judges in Reno, Pensacola, and New York's Suffolk County have reorganized their courts to push parents into treatment, follow them closely, and make timely decisions about their children.[32] In Pottawattamie County, Oklahoma, judges have been testing a new system, CASA Safe Haven, which brings together all the relevant players: child welfare, attorneys for parents and children, foster care and adoption agencies, and substance abuse and health care agencies. Working together, they try to decide more quickly where the child should live.[33]

These are important steps, but the overwhelming majority of child welfare systems lack effective substance abuse screening and assessment practices, caseworkers and judges trained in substance abuse, timely access to appropriate treatment and related services, and adoption and foster-care agencies with the capacity to help children of alcohol- and drug-abusing parents and to prepare prospective foster and adoptive parents for the needs of such children.[34] Without such capacities, asking the child welfare system to deal effectively and compassionately with substance-abusing parents and their abused and neglected children is like asking them to shovel sand with a pitchfork.

WASTING ON WELFARE

Since the mid-1990s, politicians from both parties have touted the success of welfare reform in getting women "off the dole and back to work." In 1995, more than ten million people were on the welfare rolls. By 2001 that number was cut in half.[35]

But the number of women on welfare has held around the same for several years.[36] Welfare reform and a booming economy have removed the low-hanging fruit—the women who needed only the economic incentive, largely the reality of no longer being eligible for benefits and the availability of jobs, to move to self-sufficiency. Most of these women were literate and only temporarily on the rolls; a good number had job skills and work experience.

Many remaining welfare mothers, perhaps most, are drug and alcohol abusers and addicts who also suffer from serious mental illness and other ailments.[37] The failure to confront this problem, and to provide funds for their treatment and training, has consigned many women and children on welfare to a cruel Catch-22: They are being forced off the rolls "to stand on their own two feet" while being denied the tools they need for self-sufficiency. Without treatment (and for most, literacy, job and parenting-skills training as well), many of these women won't be able to hold down a job and become responsible parents. Cutting off the benefits for thousands of women and children without offering them treatment and training will only scatter more homeless individuals on our streets and produce more crime and more abused and neglected children.

Too many of these women spent their formative years in a culture scarred by poverty, family chaos, and substance abuse. Illiteracy and inadequate housing were their norm. Their own substance abuse began at a young age. Teen pregnancies were common: More than 75 percent of all unwed teen mothers began receiving welfare within five years of giving birth.[38] And not surprisingly, many (if not most) teens report that they are usually drunk or high when they have unprotected sex.[39] Churches preach abstinence and public schools teach safe sex, but such words of wisdom are unlikely to take hold in minds clouded by alcohol and drugs.

If we attack the root cause of the problem, drug and alcohol abuse, with prevention, treatment, and related social services, the potential cost savings are enormous. For each unemployed substance-abusing woman on welfare who becomes self-supporting and maintains sobriety, the annual benefit to society is about fifty thousand dollars.[40]

Why haven't our politicians and government bureaucrats tackled this problem publicly? In 1977, I called welfare reform the "Middle East of domestic politics." Today, I would say that the substance-abusing women on welfare are the dirty little secret of welfare reform.

Conservative politicians find it easier to pander to resentment by invoking the (discredited) "welfare queen" imagery of Ronald Reagan. Liberal politicians and social workers in and out of government hesitate to disclose how widespread drug and alcohol abuse is among the women remaining on welfare. They fear prompting even more Draconian steps "to throw the bums off the rolls" in order to stop substance-abusing welfare recipients from using public funds to buy alcohol, marijuana, heroin, cocaine, and meth.

We need to recognize and address all the debilitating characteristics of this population. Appropriate treatment, mental and physical health care, and literacy, job, and parenting-skills training should be made available. The necessary incentives should be put in place to motivate women to take advantage of these services, including a requirement that, as a condition of eligibility for welfare benefits, addicted individuals must enter and complete substance abuse treatment.

Providing such services can make a difference. In June 1998, CASA piloted CASAWORKS for Families to provide women on welfare treatment, literacy, job and parenting-skills training, mental and physical health services, and a gradual move to work. The services were concentrated and offered at the same time and place. Program participants experienced dramatic reductions in alcohol and drug use, increases in income from legitimate employment, and a return to responsible parenting.[41] Their acquisition of literacy, job training, and parenting skills and their movement to work, even part time, increased the effectiveness of the treatment. Some one thousand families were served. More than half the women remained in treatment at least six months. After a year, there was a 60 percent reduction in drinking and a 34 percent reduction in cocaine use. Three-fourths reported no heavy drinking in the past month. More than 40 percent of the women were employed.[42]

PUMMELING PUBLIC HOUSING

In 1991, when I was considering founding CASA, I went to see Jack Kemp, then Secretary of Housing and Urban Development in the Bush administration. He told me, "The greatest threats to our public housing stock in the United States are drug dealers and the crime, violence, and drug addiction they create."

Public housing complexes were the product of a New Deal public works program under the U.S. Housing Act of 1937.[43] The goal was to provide inexpensive, temporary shelter for the poor. But over the twentieth century, public housing became the permanent housing of last resort for our neediest citizens. Drugs and drug dealers infested the nation's public housing complexes in the 1960s and 1970s, and their destructive power reached magnum force in the 1980s.*

That's when crack cocaine burst like an inferno, engulfing poor urban communities in its flames. Dealers infiltrated the corridors of public housing and spilled over into the courtyards, turning these areas into open drug bazaars. The spread of substance abuse trapped the elderly grandfather in his apartment with scarce food to eat, caused the young boy to peer from the apartment window afraid to play outside, and made the mother run from work to her apartment, dodging drug dealers, drunks, and stray bullets only steps from her doorway. As New York City congressman Charles Rangel has testified, "No segment of the community has suffered as much devastation from the drug crisis as have residents of our public housing projects, especially the housing projects in our major urban centers."

The half-a-loaf government response was atrocious. In 1988, the Congress passed a law to evict drug dealers from the projects but took no action to provide help to the residents who had become drug addicts and abusers.[44] The law requires termination of a tenant's lease if that tenant, or family members or guests, use or sell drugs around public housing projects. But eviction without rehabilitation simply moves the problem up the street to some other public housing complex or neighborhood. As the frustrated New Haven Public Housing Administration director David Echols put it at the time, "All I hear from HUD [the U.S. Department of Housing and Urban Development] is evict, evict, evict."

The eviction-only policy does little or nothing to get at the roots of the problem. It will take a combination of law enforcement, prevention, and treatment to eliminate drugs and alcohol from the stairwells of our housing projects, the shadows of their playgrounds, and the street corners of our most dangerous neighborhoods.

---

*One notable exception has been the Riverbend public housing of 628 duplex apartments in Manhattan, designed by the brilliant architect Lewis Davis and built by developer Richard Ravitch in 1967; the apartments are in mint condition forty years later. Tenants are so proud of their well-designed apartments that they have maintained them and their surroundings beautifully and free of drug dealers.

HAMMERING THE HOMELESS

Over a year, as many as three million homeless men, women, and children are scattered in the streets and shelters of every major city in the nation. They transform some neighborhoods and alleyways into American Calcuttas.[45] Most are alcohol and drug addicts and abusers, commonly suffering from related mental illness.

Among the homeless adults in shelters, almost 90 percent are alcoholics and alcohol abusers; more than 60 percent are drug addicts and abusers.[46] The numbers are strikingly similar for homeless children: A 2003 study of 198 thirteen- to nineteen-year-olds found that 8 out of 10 met the medical criteria for dependence on or abuse of at least one substance such as alcohol, marijuana, and cocaine.[47]

New York City is typical of large urban centers. A random sample of 150 homeless men and women in the city's Riverside Park found that 95 percent abused drugs and alcohol. In parks lining the East River, including Carl Schurz Park, home of Gracie Mansion, the mayor's official residence, outreach workers found that at least three-fourths of one hundred homeless individuals were alcoholics or drug addicts.[48] Father John Adams, who for more than thirty years has been running SOME (So Others May Eat), a program to feed and house the homeless in Washington, D.C., tells me that more than 90 percent of his clients are drug and alcohol addicts. Since the Vietnam War, combat veterans with substance abuse and related mental health problems can often be found among the homeless.

For decades, co-occurring substance abuse and mental health disorders have characterized the homeless. Governments, private agencies, and churches provide shelter and meals, but they lack the trained personnel and resources to move this population off the streets; away from needles, powders, pills, and cheap wine and liquor; and into stable living environments.

The U.S. Substance Abuse and Mental Health Services Administration (SAMHSA) has found that homeless people with serious mental illness or substance abuse disorders can be helped by programs that provide "outreach and engagement, housing with appropriate supports, multidisciplinary treatment teams, integrated treatment for co-occurring disorders, motivational interventions, modified therapeutic communities, and self-help programs."[49] A survey of six model programs reached the same conclusion. Although the programs differed from each other in size and style, all gave housing a high priority early in the treatment process and located various services under one roof (or as near each other as possible).[50] Homeless substance abusers who are provided housing have been found twice as likely as those without it to remain drug- and alcohol-free after twenty-five weeks.[51] Shelter-based treatment with psychiatric care has also been found effective.[52]

The federal government provides annually more than $1 billion to agencies across the country to help the homeless.[53] Yet the population has remained unchanged for years.

Why?

Because so few of those dollars are committed to treatment for the substance abuse and mental illness problems that afflict these men, women, and children. Here again, the nation's refusal to face the reality of the homeless population—or its insistence on denying it—dooms efforts to restore individuals to productive lives. The ineffectiveness of our efforts to get the homeless off the streets is not a failure of programs designed to shelter and feed them; it is a direct consequence of our failure to appreciate and act on the fact that it will take a significant investment in treatment for substance abuse and mental illness to achieve that goal.

SHOVELING UP WITH BLINDERS ON

America's shoveling-up practices have resulted in part from the belief—perhaps hope—of our political and philanthropic establishment in the 1940s and 1950s that the drug problem was *their* problem, not *our* problem. This attitude—which morphed into a public policy assumption—supported punishment-only prison policies and ignored the role of substance abuse in rising health care costs, public assistance, family breakup, child abuse, domestic violence, and other social ills.

Our failure to understand the pervasive culpability of substance abuse and addiction has led to a misconception that the ineffectiveness of many domestic programs in achieving their objectives stems from some inherent flaw or (as some contend) the inability of government ever to get it right. In fact, the limited effectiveness of many well-intentioned initiatives stems from our refusal to recognize how substance abuse and addiction infect the social problems we are trying to solve. Unfortunately, even in situations where substance abuse is seen to be the culprit, we continue to shovel up the consequences, rather than work to stamp out the causes. It's like telling someone whose hand is over a hot cooking flame that we have marvelous lotions to heal burns and miraculous surgical procedures to graft skin, instead of turning off the gas and telling them not to put their hand over the stovetop.

We can sharply cut the numbers of homeless, further reduce welfare dependency, and curb family breakup and child abuse if we accept and act on the reality of the role substance abuse and addiction plays in these problems. Indeed providing treatment to women on welfare is key to the next significant reduction in dependency, a goal all Americans support. An investment of our resources and energies, public and private, to prevent substance abuse and treat those who get hooked offers (including research to improve prevention and treatment) monumental dividends in reduced public costs for maternal and child welfare and hope for the millions of children and families. Such an investment, along with mental health care, is the only way to help the homeless reclaim their lives.

CHAPTER 8

NONMEDICAL MARIJUANA (HEREIN OF LEGALIZATION)

> Matt Bakalar says his parents told him they did not mind if he smoked marijuana as long as he didn't do anything stupid.
> —CHRONICLE OF HIGHER EDUCATION, *June 16, 2006*

> In Gettysburg, Pennsylvania, a woman facing drug charges admitted in court that she smoked marijuana with her 13 year old son, often to reward him for doing his homework.
> — MSNBC.com, *reporting an Associated Press story, September 12, 2006*

> In Bucks County, a 19 year old died last year after crashing into a tree near Oxford Valley Mall. He was under the influence of marijuana, police said.
> —PHILADELPHIA INQUIRER, *May 15, 2006*

One substance merits individual attention because it is the illegal drug most widely used by children and teens. And because there is so much controversy among adults about the danger of using it. That substance is nonmedical marijuana. It is the nation's most widely used illicit drug: More than 95 million Americans have tried it, 25 million in the past year.[1]

The efficacy and safety, benefits and risks, of medical marijuana are matters for doctors, scientists, pharmaceutical manufacturers, the National Institutes of Health and the Food and Drug Administration (FDA), and scientists like those at the Scripps Research Institute who are examining the potential of the drug's active ingredient to stave off Alzheimer's disease.[2] But the potential of nonmedical marijuana as a

119

dangerous, addictive, and gateway drug is a matter of concern for children, parents, physicians, and policymakers.

No drug is more misunderstood. For a variety of reasons, millions of today's adults and teens do not appreciate the sharp edges of smoking marijuana that belie its popular posture as a "soft" drug. Parents who used the drug in the late 1960s and the 1970s often see smoking pot as a benign rite of passage, a phase they passed through on their way to becoming business executives, lawyers, doctors, and teachers.

Those, like billionaire George Soros, the Daddy Warbucks of drug legalization, who have spent millions to promote the legalization of marijuana, underplay the drug's dangers. Their efforts to decriminalize the drug for medicinal purposes through popular referenda in various states have politicized what should be—and otherwise would be—a scientific process. There are numerous dangerous addictive drugs—opioids and central nervous stimulants and depressants—whose ability to safely relieve pain and mental illness has been determined by scientific and clinical analysis through the Food and Drug Administration approval process. That same process has determined that the active ingredient in marijuana—THC (tetrahydrocannabinol)—has medicinal value as an antinausea agent approved for use in the pill Marinol. The claims of terminal AIDS and cancer chemotherapy patients that they smoke pot because they cannot hold the pill down long enough for it to take effect draw sympathetic media and public attention. (Marinol is not yet formulated either as a spray or a suppository.)

Searching for the therapeutic potential of any such substance is appropriate. After all, we have many prescription opioids—some like morphine have been prescribed for decades—and we readily distinguish them from the illegal drug heroin. To the extent that ingredients in marijuana possess properties that can efficaciously and safely relieve individuals suffering from AIDS, chemotherapy nausea, multiple sclerosis, Alzheimer's disease, or other ailments, the FDA should not hesitate to approve them. No currently approved medication is available through smoking, however. It is likely that any new cannabis-based medication would be made available as aerosol or pills, as is the case today with Marinol in the United States and Sativex in Canada.

The government has contributed to the confusion and controversy. The "Reefer Madness" ambiance of the late 1930s, captured in the 1936 Louis Gasnier film, and the early years of drug enforcement, coupled with the establishment's disdain for the pot puffing 1970s, discouraged the Congress from funding scientific studies to assess the medical value of marijuana's ingredients. That failure left the field wide open for others, including some physicians, who felt the drug could help in cases of multiple sclerosis, glaucoma, and nausea, to encourage smoking pot on the sly and to make (scientifically unverified) anecdotal claims for its effectiveness.

The government's failure to conduct timely research has led to a situation reminiscent of the rush to legalize laetrile in the late 1970s. Laetrile was a concoction of crushed apricot pits with cyanide that was touted as a cancer cure. More than half the states legalized its use, and many judges responded to pleas of desperate cancer victims to make laetrile available to them. Though scores of patients and some physicians claimed laetrile purged malignant cancer cells, by all science it was a fool's gold. I was Secretary of Health, Education, and Welfare at the time. Because laetrile was becoming so widely used, I felt we had an obligation to test it even though our scientists considered it ineffective. In 1980, the National Cancer Institute and the FDA worked out an ethically acceptable protocol to conduct such tests and found that laetrile was indeed worthless, and cancer patients stopped using it.

All these missteps and the politicization of the issue of medical marijuana—notably the smoked version—have (intentionally and unintentionally) contributed to the lack of understanding of the drug's properties and have belittled the risk of using it.

Today's teens' pot is not their parents' pot. It is far more potent. As with most other crops, farmers have learned how to grow these plants to produce a far more powerful drug. The average levels of THC jumped from less than 1 percent in the mid–1970s to more than 7 percent in 2005.[3] The potency of sinsemilla (the highly powerful version of marijuana obtained from unpollinated female plants) over the past couple of decades doubled from 6 percent to 13 percent, with some samples hitting THC levels of 33 percent.[4] Antonio Maria Costa, the director of the United Nations Office of Drugs and Crime, in expressing concern about the worldwide rise in marijuana use and the drug's increased potency, said, "Today, the harmful characteristics of cannabis are no longer that different from those of other plant-based drugs such as cocaine and heroin."[5]

Today's marijuana is addictive. Nora Volkow, the director of the National Institute on Drug Abuse (NIDA) puts it bluntly: "There is no question that marijuana can be addictive; that argument is over. The most important thing right now it to understand the vulnerability of young developing brains to these increased concentrations of cannabis."[6]

Even though since 2002 overall marijuana use has been level and teen use has slightly decreased, overall use has doubled to 15 million people from its 1993 low of 7.4 million people, and at 2.6 million, teen use is more than double its 1992 low of 1.1 million. Especially troubling, the number of admissions for treatment for marijuana dependence, largely of teens, hit 300,000 in 2004, more than double the number from a decade earlier, and the number of teen emergency-room admissions in which marijuana is implicated went up almost 50 percent in just five years, from 1999 to 2004.[7] Though alcohol (notably beer) remains far and away their drug of choice, teens are three times likelier to be in treatment for marijuana (partly as a result of drug courts) than for alcohol and five times likelier to be in treatment for marijuana than for all other illegal drugs combined.[8]

The collection of scientific studies in the 2006 book *Cannabis Dependence* makes the case for addiction beyond any reasonable doubt. Of marijuana users, 2 to 3 percent get hooked within two years of inhaling their first joint; 10 percent of those who try it will get hooked at some point in their lives.[9] In the decade ending in 2003, the proportion of admissions with marijuana as the primary drug of abuse more than doubled, jumping from 7 percent to 16 percent.[10] Over this same period, the proportion of admissions citing alcohol or cocaine as the primary drug of abuse fell. In 2003, among illicit drug users, marijuana topped all others (except prescription and nonprescription opiates) as the primary drug of abuse.[11]

The rate of addiction among daily marijuana users, as diagnosed from the fourth edition of the American Psychiatric Association's *Diag-*

nostic and Statistical Manual (DSM-IV), is higher than among daily drinkers.[12] The diagnosis from the DSM-IV, the scientifically defined clinical standard for addiction, occurs when a user experiences at least three of these seven conditions: increased tolerance and diminished impact of same usage, withdrawal syndrome, greater consumption over longer periods, inability to control use, preoccupation with obtaining the drug, important work or recreational activities abandoned, continued use despite the harm it causes.

The addictive nature of marijuana is also revealed by the experience of the university researchers across the country who worked on the *Cannabis Dependence* book. As part of their study, they placed advertisements in papers offering treatment to individuals unable to stop using marijuana. Hundreds responded. (The typical volunteer was a white-collar man in his thirties who smoked pot every day).

A team at the Scripps Research Institute in California and one at Complutense University in Madrid found that rats subjected to immediate cannabis withdrawal exhibited changes in behavior similar to those seen after the withdrawal of cocaine, alcohol, and opiates.[13] *Science* magazine called this "the first neurological basis for marijuana withdrawal syndrome, and one with a strong emotional component that is shared by other drugs."[14] At the 2006 meeting of the American Psychiatric Association (APA), Deborah Hasin, a researcher at the Columbia University School of Public Health, urged that the APA's diagnostic manual and the World Health Organization's disease classifications be updated to include "cannabis withdrawal syndrome." Research shows, she said, that heavy marijuana users who try to stop experience lethargy, insomnia, psychomotor retardation, and clinical anxiety and depression.[15] Staying clean is just as hard for marijuana addicts as it is for heroin addicts, says Robert Stephens, chair of psychology at Virginia Tech University and one of the editors of the *Cannabis Dependence* book.

From the standpoint of protecting children, teens, and the public health, reducing marijuana use merits front-burner attention. As has been true of tobacco since the 1960s, we've learned a lot about the dangers of marijuana since the 1970s. The drug adversely affects short-term memory, the ability to concentrate, emotional development, and motor skills. These consequences are particularly damaging to teens when they are in school learning and their brains and bodies are rapidly developing. Recent studies indicate that marijuana use increases the likelihood of depression, schizophrenia, and other serious mental health problems.[16]

Chapter 3 describes the gateway characteristic of smoking, drinking, and marijuana use and the persuasive statistical and scientific evidence that explains it. The White House Office of National Drug Control Policy has found that adults who were teen marijuana users are eight times likelier than those who were not to use cocaine and fifteen times likelier to use heroin.[17] A study published in the *Journal of the American Medical Association*, which examined 300 sets of fraternal and identical same-sex twins, found that those who smoked pot were four times more likely to use cocaine or crack and five times more likely to use hallucinogens than their twins who did not smoke pot.[18]

The Institute of Medicine report *Marijuana and Medicine: Assessing the Science Base* noted, "In the sense that marijuana use typically precedes rather than follows initiation of other illicit drug use, it is indeed a gateway drug." The report went on to say that "people who enjoy the effects of marijuana are, logically, more likely to be willing to try other mood-altering drugs than are people who are not willing to try marijuana or who dislike its effects. In other words, many of the factors associated with a willingness to use marijuana are, presumably, the same as those associated with a willingness to use other illicit drugs."[19]

The increased potency of today's marijuana, its addictive and gateway potential, and the greater knowledge we have of its dangers justify the attention that law enforcement is giving to illegal possession of the drug. Rudolph Giuliani's success in slashing New York City's crime rate by, among other things, going after low-level street crime such as smoking marijuana and selling small amounts of it inspired many other mayors to follow suit.

But the disappointing reality is that from 1993 to 2005, a 107 percent increase in marijuana arrests was accompanied by a 100 percent increase in marijuana users.[20] Among teens, the number of users over that period more than doubled to 2.6 million. The failure of such a sharp increase in arrests to translate into even a remotely comparable reduction in use of the drug signals that something more is needed.

Like the entire substance abuse problem, the matter of preventing marijuana use is all about kids. Discouraging children and teens from getting involved with the drug begins with understanding the importance of preventing kids from becoming cigarette smokers. Most kids who smoke nicotine cigarettes do not smoke marijuana, but a 2003 survey of twelve- to seventeen-year-olds reveals that teens who smoke cigarettes are much likelier than nonsmokers to try marijuana. They are also likelier to become regular marijuana users.[21]

We should seek to make public policies, including law enforcement approaches, more effective in discouraging teen marijuana use. When five million twelve- to seventeen-year-olds can obtain marijuana in an hour or less and ten million can get it within a day, reducing availability is high on the list.[22] Beyond that—and recognizing that reducing demand is key to that goal—we should use the increased arrest rate as an opportunity to discourage use.

In the mid–1990s, while I was visiting Los Angeles, then Mayor Dick Riordan told me that in his city kids were arrested an average of nine times for possession of marijuana before anything happened to them. I have since discovered that this situation is common in many American communities. Most kids do not even get a slap on the wrist the first few times they're caught smoking a joint. As a result, we let them sink deeper and deeper into drug use, with its dangers to their physical, mental, and emotional development and its risk of addiction and harder drug use.

I am not suggesting that we put kids in jail the first time they get caught smoking pot. But why not treat a teen arrested for marijuana use much the same way we treat someone arrested for drunk driving when no injury occurs? Why not use the arrest as an opportunity and require kids cited for marijuana possession to be screened psychologically and referred for help if appropriate, and to attend sessions to learn about the dangers of marijuana use and how to decline the next time they are offered a joint? The incentive to be screened and attend such classes would be the threat of the alternative: for the first couple of arrests, loss of a driver's license or a fine stiff enough to sting that has to be paid by the teen or worked off; for continued use, intensive treatment, including random testing and staying clean to avoid jail time. Getting kids to attend sessions designed to discourage their marijuana use would give some practical meaning to increased law enforcement and would bring reductions in drug use more in line with increased arrest rates. The certainty of swift punishment can not only discourage use but can also be a powerful incentive for these kids to attend classes or get needed treatment.

These steps will help, but we will never be able to arrest our way out of the teen marijuana problem. Parents are the first line of defense. Parents must understand that the drug available today is far more potent and dangerous than what they might have smoked thirty years ago.[23] For their children, smoking marijuana is not a harmless lark but a dangerous experiment that can bring serious harm and may end up destroying their lives. When parents understand that and make it clear to their children that they strongly disapprove of any marijuana use, that will discourage their kids from using the drug.

The controlling context of the legalization debate is our children, and the central question is: What would it mean for our children if we were to legalize drugs?

The argument that legalized drugs would be for adults only and would not be available to children does not hold water. Nothing in the American experience with alcohol and tobacco gives any credence to our ability to keep legal drugs out of the hands of children. It is illegal for them to purchase cigarettes, beer, and liquor. Nevertheless, three million adolescents smoke, an average of half a pack a day, constituting a $1-billion-a-year market.[24] Millions more children and teens drink, accounting for more than $22 billion—almost 20 percent—of alcohol sales in 2001.[25] Moreover, few people first try drugs when they are adults; virtually all addicts began using as children and teens.[26]

Legal status increases use in three ways: economic availability (cost), physical availability (e.g., liquor and drug stores), and psychological availability (perceived social approval).

Legal drugs would presumably be less expensive than the prices addicts now pay on the street for cocaine and heroin. By all the laws of economics, reducing the price of drugs would increase consumption. Prices of illegal drugs are as much as ten times what they would cost to produce and sell at a profit legally.[27] The price of a legally produced dose of cocaine, for instance, would fall well within the range of most children's lunch money. Efforts to increase the price of legal drugs by taxing them heavily in order to discourage consumption would be likely to meet the same resistance by well-heeled industry opposition that attempts to increase taxes on beer and cigarettes have faced. Only a few communities have been able to increase taxes on cigarettes sufficiently to reduce teen smoking significantly. The U.S. Congress has been unable to enact taxes on cigarettes or alcohol high enough to discourage use.

Recent historical evidence demonstrates the impact on usage levels of the widespread acceptability and availability of drugs. In the 1970s, the United States de facto decriminalized marijuana. The Presidential Commission appointed by President Richard Nixon recommended decriminalization, as did President Jimmy Carter. The result was a soaring increase in marijuana use, particularly among youngsters. Physicians, and even a Harvard Medical School professor, touted cocaine as a non-addictive high, and its use exploded.

Legal acceptability would usher in an era of widespread experimentation. Few individuals foresee their addiction when they start using; most believe they can control their consumption. Not only are young people in particular convinced that nothing can harm them, but recent studies have shown that the part of the brain involved in impulse control is not fully developed until the early twenties. Legalization for adults would lead more teenagers to smoke, snort, and inject those substances at a stage in life when the brain is developing, habits are formed, and the social, academic, and physical skills needed for a satisfying and independent life are acquired, thereby heightening the risk of psychological dependence and physical addiction.

Some proponents of drug legalization contend that such a move might reduce the number of users, arguing that there would be no pushers to lure new users, and that drugs would lose the "forbidden-fruit" allure of illegality. But virtually no one advocates legalization for kids. Thus the forbidden-fruit allure would remain and be joined by the badge of adulthood, a combination that has made it so difficult to keep cigarette and alcohol out of the hands of kids. In any event, these proponents conveniently ignore the first rule of substance abuse: availability. Moreover, not only would legalized drugs be more openly available, as beer and cigarettes are today, but of even greater damage to our children would be the commercial reality that Madison Avenue marketers would be free to glamorize substances like marijuana and cocaine. Do we want to create a Philip Morris for weed? An R. J. Reynolds or Anheuser-Busch for cocaine? Under such circumstances, can anyone doubt that drug use would explode not only among adults, but also among children? Do we want college students bingeing on cocaine as well as beer?

Laws define acceptable conduct in a society. Criminal laws make a stronger statement than civil laws, but even the latter can discourage individual consumption. Studies have found that the greater the perceived likelihood of getting caught and swiftly punished for using drugs, the less likely individuals are to use them. In separate studies, 60 to 70 percent of New Jersey and California students reported that fear of getting in trouble with the authorities was a major reason they did not use drugs.[28] Any move toward legalization would decrease the perception of the risks and costs of drug use and would thus lead to wider experimentation. Enacting such laws would also undercut critical support for parents, teachers, and others attempting to steer kids away from drugs.

Today, the nation has some sixty million regular smokers, sixteen to twenty million alcoholics and alcohol abusers, and about six million illegal drug addicts.[29] It is logical to conclude that, if drugs are easier to obtain, less expensive, and socially acceptable, more individuals will use them. Experts such as Columbia University's Dr. Herbert Kleber believe that, with legalization, the number of cocaine addicts alone could leapfrog beyond the number of alcoholics.

It is possible that, in the short term, legalization would reduce crime. But any short-term reduction in arrests resulting from repealing criminal drug laws would evaporate quickly as use increased and, with it, the criminal conduct—assault, murder, child molestation, vandalism, and other violence—that drugs like cocaine and methamphetamine spawn. The U.S. Department of Justice reports that criminals commit six times as many homicides, four times as many assaults, and almost one-and-a-half times as many robberies under the influence of drugs as they do in order to get money to buy drugs.[30] Moreover, while legalization might temporarily take some of the burden off the criminal justice system, such a policy would impose heavy additional costs on the health care and social service systems, schools, and workplaces.

The reduction-in-crime argument is founded on a misreading of the American experience with the prohibition of alcohol. There are two important distinctions between prohibiting the possession of illegal drugs and alcohol prohibition: Possession of alcohol for personal consumption was never illegal, and alcohol, unlike illegal drugs such as heroin and cocaine, has a long history of broad social acceptance dating back to the Old Testament and ancient Greece. Largely because of this history, the public and political consensus favoring Prohibition was short-lived. By the early 1930s, most Americans no longer supported it. Today, though, the public overwhelmingly favors keeping illegal drugs illegal.[31]

Despite these differences, which made Prohibition more difficult to enforce than the current drug laws, alcohol consumption dropped from 1.96 gallons per person just before Prohibition to .97 gallons per person in 1934, the first full year after Prohibition ended.[32] Death rates from cirrhosis among men came down from 29.5 per 100,000 in 1911 to 10.7 per 100,000 in 1929.[33] During Prohibition, admission to mental health institutions for alcohol psychosis dropped 60 percent; arrests for drunk and disorderly conduct went down 50 percent; welfare agencies reported significant declines in cases due to alcohol-related family problems; and the death rate from impure alcohol did not rise.[34]

Nor did Prohibition generate a crime wave. Homicide increased at a higher rate between 1900 and 1910 than during Prohibition, and organized crime was well established in the cities before 1920.[35]

I put these facts on the record not to support a return to Prohibition, something I strongly oppose, but to set the historical record straight.

Like advocates of legalization today, opponents of alcohol prohibition claimed that taxes on the legal sale of alcohol would increase revenues dramatically and help erase the national deficit. The real-world result has been quite different. Indeed, the U.S. Congress has demonstrated a distinct distaste for increases in taxes on cigarettes and alcohol, even though such increases have been demonstrated to reduce teen smoking and drinking and despite the costs that smoking and excessive drinking impose on our society.

Harlem Congressman and House Ways and Means Committee Chairman Charles Rangel made the practical case against legalization when New York City Mayor John Lindsay was thinking of an experiment to legalize heroin. Disgusted, Rangel, who knew firsthand the drug's savagery in his Harlem district, asked Lindsay, "Under your plan can anyone get heroin?"

"No, you'd have to be an adult, eighteen years old."

"So if a sixteen-year-old comes in and asks for it, you'll tell him he has to wait two years?" Rangel cracked, and then asked, "Can any adult get it?"

"No," Lindsay replied. "You'd have to be addicted."

"Oh," Charlie said retelling the story, "so when the sixteen-year-old is eighteen and he wants it, you'd tell him you can't have it till you get hooked?"

As Charlie described it, Lindsay was getting angry and uncomfortable, faced as he was with governing a city that had become the heroin capital of the United States. "We'd just try this in a couple of places," Lindsay responded defensively. "To test it."

"Well," said Charlie, "we got plenty of heroin in my district. We don't need any more. So I suggest you try it in Queens and Staten Island. They don't have very much there."

"Can you believe that guy?" Rangel said to me. "What a cockamamie idea."

Legalization has not worked well in European countries. The ventures of Switzerland, England, the Netherlands, and Italy into drug decriminalization have had disastrous consequences.

Switzerland's "Needle Park," touted as a way to restrict to a small area a few hundred heroin users, turned into a grotesque tourist attraction of twenty thousand heroin addicts and junkies that had to be closed down before it infected the entire city of Zurich.[36] England's foray into allowing any doctor to prescribe heroin quickly was curbed as heroin use increased.

In the Netherlands, anyone over age seventeen can drop into a marijuana "coffee shop" and pick types of marijuana just as they might choose flavors of ice cream. Adolescent pot use there jumped nearly 200 percent within a couple of years.[37] As crime and the availability of drugs rose and complaints from city residents about the decline in their quality of life multiplied, the Dutch parliament moved to trim back the number of marijuana distribution shops in Amsterdam and the amount that can be sold to an individual from twenty grams to five grams. Dutch persistence in selling pot has angered European neighbors because its anything-goes attitude toward marijuana is believed to be spreading that drug and others beyond the country's borders, notably by "drug tourism."

Italy is infrequently mentioned by advocates of legalization despite its lenient drug laws. Personal possession of small amounts of drugs has not been a crime in Italy since 1975, other than for a brief period of recriminalization between 1990 and 1993. (Even then, Italy permitted an individual to possess one dose of a drug.) Under decriminalization, possession of two to three doses of drugs such as heroin has generally been exempt from criminal sanction. Today, Italy has about two hundred thousand addicts, the highest rate of heroin addiction in Europe.[38] Of all AIDS cases in Italy, 70 percent are attributable to drug use.[39]

In contrast, Sweden offers an example of a successful restrictive drug policy. After a brief period of permitting doctors to give drugs to addicts, Sweden adopted the American policy of seeking a drug-free society in 1980. By 1988, Sweden had seen drug use drop 75 percent among young army conscripts and 66 percent among ninth-graders. Drug use rose in the 1990s because of budget cuts, unemployment, and increasing drug supplies, but it has dropped steadily since 2001 under a National Action Plan with improved funding and strict enforcement and education. "The lessons of Sweden's drug control history should be learned by others," says UN antidrug director Antonio Maria Costa.[40]

Two themes run through the attitudes of many of those who press for drug legalization. One is that there has been no progress in the war on drugs. Quite the contrary, we have in the past demonstrated the capa-bility of enormous progress. The DHHS National Household Drug Sur-vey, the nation's most extensive assessment of drug usage, reports that, from 1979 to 1993, marijuana users dropped by half, and from 1985 to 1992, cocaine users fell from 5.7 million to 1.4 million.[41] The drug-using segment of the population also is aging. In 1979, 10 percent were over age thirty-four; at the turn of the century, almost 30 percent are.[42] The number of hard-core addicts has held steady at around five to six million, a situation most experts attribute to the unavailability of treat-ment and the large number of addicts in the pipeline.[43]

More recently, drug use has not significantly decreased, and prescrip-tion drug abuse has risen sharply.[44] The reason is that the policies we have been pursuing have not been effective. It is not the criminal statutes related to drug possession, distribution, and use that are at fault. It is a broad array of policies and attitudes that I discuss in this book. There are changes in laws and policies that can sharply reduce drug use, especially initiation among teens and children, but one of them is not legalization.

The other underlying theme is the libertarian argument propounded by William Buckley, founder of the *National Review*, and *New York Times* columnist John Tierney on the right and George Soros on the left: Drug use is an issue of personal freedom and civil liberties.

This is a serious misreading of John Stuart Mill's *On Liberty*. Many libertarians cite Mill to argue that the state has no right to interfere in the private life of a citizen who uses drugs; only when an action harms someone else may the state take steps to prevent it. But Mill's concep-tion of freedom does not extend to the right of individuals to enslave themselves or to decide that they will give up their liberty. Mill wrote, "The principle of freedom cannot require that he should be free not to be free. It is not freedom to be allowed to alienate his freedom."[45]

Drug addiction is a form of enslavement. A nation devoted to indi-vidual freedom has an obligation to nourish a society and legal struc-ture that protect people, particularly children, from the slavery of drug addiction.

Even Mill's most libertarian contention—that the state may regulate only those actions that directly affect others—does not support individual drug abuse and addiction. Such conduct does affect others directly, from the battered spouse and the baby involuntarily addicted through the mother's umbilical cord to innocent bystanders injured or killed by adolescent drivers high on marijuana or cocaine. The drug addict's conduct has a direct and substantial impact on every taxpayer who foots the bill for the criminal, social service, and health care cost consequences of such actions.

Certainly a society that recognizes the state's compelling interest in banning (and stopping individuals from using) lead paint, asbestos insulation, unsafe toys, and flammable fabrics can hardly ignore its interest in banning cocaine, heroin, marijuana, methamphetamines, and hallucinogens.

Today, most kids don't use illicit drugs, but all of them are vulnerable to abuse and addiction—and all of them will be offered drugs during their teen years. It is adolescent experimentation that leads to abuse and addiction. Drugs are not dangerous because they are illegal. They are illegal because they are dangerous. Russian roulette is not a game anyone should play. Legalizing drugs not only is playing Russian roulette with children; it is also slipping a couple of extra bullets into the chamber.

CHAPTER 9

THE UNISEX LEGACY

Andrea Raines downed Ecstasy and alcohol, did methamphetamine and morphine, smoked marijuana and snorted cocaine. Throughout three years of chemical abuse, she would also make herself throw up. Now 16, Andrea said she was insecure. "I didn't like my body," she said, "I wanted to be skinnier. I wanted to be like the women you see on TV."

—MINNEAPOLIS STAR TRIBUNE, *February 10, 2006*

Dr. Alexander Wood perfected the hypodermic needle to inject morphine into the bloodstream, a method believed to free women and other patients from any unpleasant side effects and danger of addiction. Wood enthusiastically promoted his use and as a result many of his patients became morphine addicts. The first person recorded to have died from a drug overdose by hypodermic needle was Wood's wife.

—*M. Booth, in* OPIUM: A HISTORY *(1998)*

During most of the twentieth century, in health care research, treatment, and prevention, men and women were treated as one and the same, and the one was the men. Especially in the substance abuse field, it was assumed that what was good or bad for the gander was good or bad for the goose. Toward the end of the century, as researchers turned more attention to women, we learned how significant are the differences in the causes and consequences of female tobacco, alcohol, and illicit and prescription drug abuse. The nation's daughters, wives, sisters, and mothers have paid a fearful price for the failure to recognize these differences sooner and for the male-size-fits-all policies and practices that have dominated the substance abuse field.

For decades, boys smoked, drank, and used illegal drugs at much higher rates than girls. Today, thanks in good part to decades of unisex prevention strategies, that gender gap has slammed shut. Girls are at equal risk with boys to light up, binge-drink, get drunk, smoke pot, snort cocaine, and use other illegal drugs—and are even more likely to abuse addictive and dangerous prescription drugs. For years, in CASA's annual teen surveys, younger girls, ages twelve to fifteen, were shown to be at higher risk of drug use than boys their age, probably because puberty is a more difficult experience for them and because they are in closer contact with older boys. In later years, boys were at higher risk. But in 2006, for the first time in the eleven years of surveying twelve- to seventeen-year-olds, CASA found that, at every age, girls were at the same risk as or at a higher risk than boys of smoking, drinking, and drug use.[1]

That's the bad news for women's health.

The worse news is that girls and women get hooked faster and suffer harsher consequences sooner.[2]

Some six million girls and women abuse or are addicted to alcohol, fifteen million use illegal drugs and misuse prescription drugs, and more than thirty million smoke cigarettes.[3]

Girls turn to addictive substances for reasons different from those of boys. For most boys, it's something of a macho thing, sensation seeking, exhibitionist, evidenced by outrageous public acts, drunk driving, fighting. For most girls, it's inner-directed: Girls tend to use substances to control weight, alter their mood, relieve their anxiety or depression, reduce their sexual inhibitions.[4] As a result, it can be far more difficult to detect when a teenage daughter is drinking or using pills or illegal drugs.

Peer pressure is an important risk factor for all kids, but girls are generally more susceptible to the influence of their girlfriends who smoke, drink, and drug. Boys are much likelier than girls to be offered drugs by a stranger or by a parent; girls are likelier to receive offers from their female friends or boyfriends.[5] Disposable income also seems to influence girls more than boys: Among teens with fifty dollars or more of spending money per week, girls are likelier than boys to smoke, drink, get drunk, and use pot.[6]

Substances affect the sexes differently. For women, one drink has approximately the same effect as two drinks for men, and one cigarette has nearly the same carcinogenic effect as two for men.[7] Drug use and heavy drinking among girls and young women can lead to everything from brain damage and serious accidents to rape, unwanted pregnancy, and suicide. Women who smoke marijuana reduce their chance of success in fertility treatments.[8] Smoking and drinking increase the risk of breast cancer, menstrual disorders, and infertility.[9]

What's more, using the same (sometimes, even smaller) amounts of a drug, women experience more—and more severe—health problems and are likelier to become dependent. At the same level of exposure to tobacco smoke, women are up to three times likelier than men to develop lung cancer.[10] Women who use sedatives, antianxiety drugs, or hypnotics are twice as likely as men to get hooked on these drugs.[11]

For older women, the death of loved ones, financial difficulties, serious illness, or caretaking for elderly parents or grandchildren may produce stress that increases the likelihood of smoking, excessive drinking, and drug abuse. At any age, women are likelier than men to self-medicate stress and depression by smoking, drinking, and drugging.[12]

SMOKING

Parents, peers, personal concerns, and the larger social environment are key factors in determining which girls smoke and which ones don't. Parental smoking is commonly decisive: Girls appear to be more influenced than boys by their parents' smoking behavior. Daughters of smoking mothers are more likely to smoke than sons of smoking mothers.[13]

Peer influence is a factor in smoking for all teens. Those with friends who smoke are nine times likelier to smoke than their classmates whose friends don't smoke. But girls with friends who smoke are far likelier to puff away than boys with such friends.[14]

Girls smoke to be sociable, to connect with others, or to "break the ice" in social situations. A study of eleven- and thirteen-year-old girls found that girls at the top of the social pecking order—the most popular ones—are under more pressure to smoke than less popular girls. These girls see smoking as a means of enhancing their image, fitting in, or appearing mature or "cool," whereas the popular boys feel less pressure to smoke, primarily because smoking interferes with their main "cool" activity, participating in sports.[15]

Girls experience more stress, particularly from school-related pressures, than boys. They are more inclined to respond to this stress by substance use, particularly by smoking. Stress reduction is the reason girls—some as young as eight—and women most often cite for smoking.[16]

Adolescent girls are especially concerned about their weight, and many, if not most, diet at some time during middle and high school. The concern about weight and the desire for thinness are why many girls not only start to smoke but continue inhaling into adulthood. Women of all ages see nicotine as an appetite suppressant and fear the weight they might put on if they quit smoking.[17]

For whatever reasons, at the same levels of use women get hooked on nicotine faster than men and have a harder time quitting smoking.[18] In a study of twelve- and thirteen-year-old smokers, which found that 40 percent developed symptoms of tobacco dependence after just trying smoking and 53 percent after inhaling, girls displayed more symptoms of tobacco dependence than the boys. It took the girls an average of only three weeks to develop symptoms of tobacco dependence, while it took boys an average of twenty-six weeks, almost nine times longer.[19] After age sixty, fewer women than men successfully quit smoking.[20]

Smoking appears to take a greater toll on women than on men; on average, a man who smokes will lose thirteen years of life, while a woman who smokes will lose fifteen.[21] Heart disease, once considered a man's ailment, now kills more women than men.[22] Deaths related to lung cancer have been declining steadily among men since the early 1980s, but there has been a 600 percent increase in lung cancer mortality among women over the past seven decades.[23] Some 180,000 American women die from tobacco-related illnesses each year.[24]

Certain smoking consequences are unique to women. Smoking increases a woman's risk of osteoporosis; women who smoke a pack a day throughout adulthood cut their bone density up to 10 percent by the time they reach menopause. Women between the ages of forty-four and fifty-four who smoke are twice as likely to experience menopause one to two years earlier than those who have never smoked. Early menopause, coming full circle, contributes to osteoporosis.[25]

DRINKING

Men generally tend to drink more than women, but women are catching up rapidly. In the last quarter century, the gender gap in heavy drinking among high school seniors has been cut in half. From 1993 to 2001, the number of college women who were drunk in the past thirty day was up sharply. The number of women who reported drinking to get drunk more than tripled between 1977 and 1993.[26] From 1993 to 2001, the number of women who admitted being drunk three or more times in the past thirty days rose 26 percent.[27] Among younger teens, the gender gap in alcohol use and risky drinking has evaporated.[28]

Peer pressure seems more strongly associated with drinking for girls than for boys. Middle school girls who report high levels of peer pressure to drink are twice as likely to use alcohol as those who report less. This relationship between peer pressure and alcohol use is not found in boys. Girls with several close friends who smoke or drink are more than twice as likely to drink as boys with such friends.[29]

Low self-esteem is a strong predictor of alcohol abuse among girls. Girls who experience low self-esteem at age twelve are more than twice as likely to drink heavily at age fifteen as those with high self-esteem. No such powerful relationship has been identified among boys.[30]

Girls are attuned to the self-medicating potential of alcohol even before many begin to drink. As early as the sixth grade, girls are likelier than boys to believe that a "positive" effect of alcohol is its ability to allay bad moods or feelings. Girls who drink heavily are more likely than boys who do so to attribute their alcohol use to the desire to escape their problems, anger, or frustration.[31]

Depression is linked to heavy drinking in women as well as girls, and alcohol-abusing women are almost four times more likely to suffer from depression than alcohol-abusing men. (In the general population, women are approximately twice as likely to suffer from depression as men.)[32] Another strong signal of later problem drinking is sexual abuse: 69 percent of women in treatment for alcohol and/or drug abuse suffered sexual abuse as children, compared to 12 percent of men.[33] Unlike men, women who have experienced severe physical punishment as children are at an elevated risk of alcohol abuse.[34]

As is the case with smoking, women who drink heavily pay a higher price than men. These women get drunk faster, become alcoholics more quickly, and develop alcohol-related diseases, such as hypertension and brain and heart damage, more rapidly. Women who abuse alcohol are more likely than men who do so to develop cirrhosis and other liver diseases, and to develop them at lower levels of alcohol consumption.[35]

For anyone, alcohol abuse can impair learning, memory, abstract thinking, problem solving, and perceptual-motor skills (such as eye-hand coordination). But men appear to be less susceptible than women to such alcohol-induced brain impairment. Women who abuse alcohol have proportionally smaller brains in early middle age after fewer years of heavy drinking than alcohol-abusing men.[36]

Some of these gender differences are rooted in physiology. Women metabolize alcohol differently from men; their bodies contain less water and more fatty tissue compared with men of similar sizes. Because water dilutes alcohol and fat retains it, women maintain higher concentrations of alcohol in their blood. That's why one drink tends to have the same impact for a woman as two drinks for a man.[37] This physiological difference helps explain why women get intoxicated faster and experience worse hangovers even when drinking the same amount as men.

Genetics may be a more significant factor in a woman's substance abuse than in a man's. Among women, genetic factors account for up to 66 percent of the risk of alcohol dependence compared to 56 percent of the risk for men. In other words, women who end up developing alcohol-related problems tend to have a somewhat greater genetic risk of dependence than do men with such problems. [38]

DRUGGING

Teenage girls exhibit higher rates of prescription drug abuse than boys across the survey board: not only in their lifetime, but in the past year and in the past month as well.[39] They also are likelier than boys to get high on over-the-counter drugs.[40] Teenage girls are more than twice as likely as boys to be admitted to a hospital for acute drug intoxication—most often for a suicide attempt, and notably involving prescription drugs.[41]

Women have a long history of prescription drug abuse. In the late 1960s, women consumed 80 percent of the amphetamines in the United States. During that time, an estimated one to two million women were addicted to prescription drugs. By the early 1970s, women accounted for three of four Valium and Librium abuse admissions to emergency rooms and 40 percent of prescription-drug-related deaths.[42] Physicians— whether male or female—prescribe psychoactive drugs to women far more frequently than to men.[43] Women are far more likely than men to be prescribed a narcotic, antianxiety, or other potentially abusable drug.[44]

The gender gap has closed for most illegal drugs. College women use amphetamines about as much as their male classmates. Although fewer college women than men smoke pot every day, daily marijuana use has climbed more sharply among them since 1994, and that gender gap is virtually shut. The gap also has narrowed sharply for cocaine and LSD use since the mid-1990s. [45] This is particularly bad news since women become dependent on marijuana, cocaine, and heroin more quickly than men.[46]

These differences, profound in many cases, cry out for research, prevention, and treatment strategies tailored to boys and to girls, to men and to women. Our failure to craft programs for girls and women has condemned millions of them to lives scarred and ruined by smoking, drugging, and excessive drinking. Each year, scores of thousands of women die of heart disease, stroke, and cancer—and substance abuse is the number one preventable factor in each of these killing and crippling diseases.

Too many prevention and public education programs are aimed at boys. They rarely deal with the risks of depression, low self-esteem, weight-consciousness, and elimination of healthy sexual inhibitions that have such influence over a girl's alcohol or drug abuse. In treatment as well, too often the programs assume that all ages and both sexes will be helped by the same protocols. But women who have been sexually abused, or who have engaged in sexual activity while under the influence of drugs or alcohol, or who have traded sex for money in order to buy drugs or alcohol are saturated with fear and shame that make them far less likely to discuss their experiences in a group with men than in a group comprising only other women. Of women in need of treatment, 92 percent do not receive it. Stigma, embarrassment, and ignorance hide the scope of the problem and the severity of the consequences.

Central to any effort to sober up the High Society is a recognition of the different needs and risks of men and women, and of boys and girls. The tobacco and alcohol merchants have understood—and played on—these differences for decades. The failure of the public health community to take account of them has caused far too much unnecessary suffering among girls and women and among boys and men.

CHAPTER 10

FOLLOW THE TOBACCO
AND ALCOHOL MONEY

In late June, 1995, John Boehner, then an Ohio Republican representative and later House Majority Leader, walked the floor of the
House of Representatives handing out checks from Philip Morris
to individual members as they were debating legislation that the tobacco company opposed.
—WASHINGTON POST, *January 11, 2006*

Abigail Blunt, wife of House Majority Whip Roy Blunt, is a key lob-
byist for Morris.
—NEW YORK TIMES, *October 9, 2005*

Last week Maryland Attorney General Curran and 19 other state Attorneys General urged the Federal Trade Commission to take a hard
look at the role alcohol marketing plays in underage consumption.
—*Press release, Maryland Attorney General's Office,
May 16, 2006*

Lobbying by the alcohol industry helped prevent a bill to restrict
marketing of alcoholic beverages to underage drinkers from gaining
traction in Sacramento.
—SAN FRANCISCO CHRONICLE, *April 19, 2006*

If, as California Democratic power broker Jesse Unruh said in the
1960s, "Money is the mother's milk of politics," then tobacco and alcohol are two of the fattest cows.

Tobacco and alcohol money litter the corridors of power. Between
2000 and 2004, tobacco industry political action committees (PACs)
contributed more than $20 million to congressional campaigns and

another $20 million to state and local campaigns. Over that same period, alcohol industry PACs (for beer, wine, and distilled spirits) contributed more than $37 million to congressional campaigns and almost $54 million to state and local campaigns.[1] To set the stage for an accommodating presidential administration, big tobacco—led by Philip Morris, the top donor, R. J. Reynolds, and Brown and Williamson—pumped almost $17 million into the 2000 Republican campaign in support of George W. Bush.[2]

Nor is the flow of money limited to direct contributions: from 1999 to 2004, tobacco interests reported spending more than $21 million on Washington lobbyists. In 2003, the lobbying money they reported spending amounted to $127,000 for each day that Congress was in session.[3] In just one year (from July 2002 to July 2003), the top two beer manufacturers, Miller Brewing Company and Anheuser-Busch, reported spending more than $3.5 million to lobby Congress.[4] I use the term *reported spending* because lobbying reports filed with the secretary of the Senate and the clerk of the House notoriously understate the true amounts, thanks to high-priced tobacco and alcohol industry lawyers who narrowly interpret what conduct of their clients and the agents they hire constitutes lobbying.

The tobacco and alcohol merchants get their money's worth. A study of tobacco PAC contributions between 1993 and 2000 found that the amount of money received by members of Congress correlated with their protobacco voting records.[5] Another investigation revealed that congressional members who voted with the industry against proposed FDA regulation of tobacco received, on average, five times more ($27,255) in tobacco PAC money than those who voted for such regulation ($5,505).[6]

Researchers have also nailed a tight association between alcohol industry contributions to policymakers and legislative results supported by the industry. In 1999, for example, the House Appropriations Committee voted on a provision to add messages on underage drinking to a federally funded youth antidrug media campaign. The Center for Science in the Public Interest found that Representative Anne Northup, the Republican from Louisville, Kentucky, who spearheaded the successful move to strike the underage drinking provision, had received

$38,264 from alcohol-beverage industry sources. She had got nearly double the alcohol money that any other member of the Appropriations Committee had received.[7]

So substantial is the tobacco and alcohol merchants' return on their investment in members of Congress and state legislators that public health advocates have been relegated to the courts to seek relief that is legislative and regulatory in nature. This litigation strains the capacity of the judicial branch. Even more troubling, the interests of the plaintiffs' bar that sometimes represents those advocates often diverge from the public interest in protecting the health of our people.

SIX-PAC

Knowing the importance of influencing both parties, the alcohol industry spreads its cash around. In the 2004 election cycle alone, campaign contributions from the beer, wine, and liquor guys reached $11 million in individual and PAC gifts. Of that, 63 percent went to the Republicans, with the rest slipped into Democratic pockets.[8] The National Beer Wholesalers Association is the big spender of the alcohol industry, doling out $2.5 million in the 2004 election cycle. Under the association's head, David Rehr, who was a major fund-raiser for President George W. Bush, big beer's political action committee, aptly captioned "Six-Pac," catapulted into the top ten disbursing PACs and earned *Fortune Magazine*'s pick as one of the nation's ten most influential lobbying combines.[9]

The wine and liquor industries also shell out considerable cash to politicians and lobbyists on both sides of the aisle. Democrats harvest the bulk of campaign contributions from the vineyards. In the 2006 election cycle, Gallo Winery, the sixth largest congressional donor in the alcohol industry, gave 96 percent of its money to Democrats, and the Wine Institute invested almost two-thirds of its political dough in Democrats.[10] In 1999, Mike Thompson, a Democratic representative from California, led the formation of the Congressional Wine Caucus, to "engage [fellow representatives] in legislative and regulatory matters pertaining to wine issues."[11] Not surprisingly, Thompson got his biggest bucks that year from the wine industry and consistently ranked among the top five recipients of alcohol money, leading the pack in 2006.[12]

What the industry most seeks to buy with its political money is freedom from tax increases—and, in a brash display of their political muscle, in some cases even the repeal of existing taxes. In Florida, the industry successfully lobbied to reduce the state's excise tax on drinks at bars and restaurants, arguing that cheaper booze would attract more tourists and encourage more drinking, which in turn would help the state's economy and increase state revenues.[13]

The industry knows that tax increases, since they raise the price of beer and other alcohol, deter children and teens from buying these products. Such tax increases threaten the industry's financial interest in underage drinking, a source of almost a fifth of its revenues. Underage drinkers are key to the profitability of the alcohol industry not only for their current spending, but because they also seed adult excessive and alcohol-dependent drinkers who are the source of at least another 20 percent of industry sales. Of the $129 billion spent on alcohol in 2001, $23 billion was attributable to underage drinking and $26 billion to pathological adult drinking, which accounted for almost 40 percent of alcohol sales that year. Some estimates place the value as high as 50 percent of alcohol sales.[14] The industry's tenacious efforts to kill tax increases that would reduce underage drinking make a mockery of their protestations that they do not encourage underage consumption of beer and alcohol.

There is nothing either new or partisan about the beer industry's interest in underage drinkers. In 1978, when I was Secretary of Health, Education, and Welfare (HEW), I remember riding in a car with House Speaker Jim Wright, heading for a Democratic Party fund-raiser for Florida congressman Claude Pepper. I mentioned that I was thinking about proposing a sharp increase in the tax on beer in order to discourage underage drinking. "There's been no increase in any alcohol taxes since 1951," I pointed out. Wright's response was instant and insistent: "You can't do that. Joe Six-Packs are our people!" Other Democratic congressmen in the limo chimed in. "Your bill would be dead on arrival," they chorused, "The beer guys will kill it." I never sent the bill forward, even though I tried to argue with them that a hike in the tax on beer and alcohol would be a Triple Crown winner: a win for the budget, a win for the children by reducing underage drinking, and a win in reducing health care costs by curbing adult alcoholism and alcohol abuse.

Thanks to the industry's successful effort to keep taxes down, over the past fifty years the real cost of alcoholic beverages has plunged. Not since 1991 has Congress increased federal taxes on alcohol. Over the ensuing fifteen years, the average real price of beer dropped 9 percent, and the modest 1991 tax hike lost more than a third of its value to inflation.[15] Restoring the federal excise tax on beer to its real value of fifty years ago would require an increase of almost 300 percent.[16] In 2005 the alcohol industry had the chutzpah to seek repeal of the 1991 tax increase. They failed; that was just too much for legislators to gulp down.[17]

All fifty states, Washington, D.C., and Puerto Rico place excise taxes on beer, wine, and hard liquor, but rates vary widely, and few have raised taxes in order to discourage underage drinking. Where political money flows like beer from an open tap, state taxes stay low. Missouri, headquarters of Anheuser-Busch, has a ridiculously low alcohol tax of 6 cents a gallon. In 2002, Anheuser-Busch contributed $235,000 to Missouri state legislators. Vermont, meanwhile, sets its excise tax at 26.5 cents a gallon.[18] The same pattern holds true for wine. Excise taxes vary from $2.50 per gallon in Alaska and $1.75 in Iowa, states with no wine industry, down to 20 cents in California and 19 cents in New York, two of the top wine-producing states.[19] In most states, taxes on beer, wine, and liquor have not increased significantly in decades.

Industry campaign contributions crush public opinion, since most politicians follow the money like alley cats after the scent of fish in the garbage. In a 2001 survey, 54 percent of respondents thought that alcohol taxes should be increased; an even higher proportion thought the revenue from such taxes should be dedicated to preventing and treating alcoholism and alcohol abuse.[20] In another poll, 71 percent supported increasing the national beer tax and committing the revenues to substance abuse prevention.[21] Beer bucks speak louder to legislators, drowning out the concern of the two-thirds of Americans who consider it inappropriate for politicians to accept money from the beer industry and then vote on legislation to reduce the taxes on beer.

In 2006, the American Medical Association (AMA) called for increases in federal and state taxes on beer, wine, and liquor, noting that "tax increases lead to lower alcohol consumption rates among adults and youth, fewer binge drinking episodes, and lower traffic fatality rates." The AMA "reaffirm[ed] the concept that alcohol is an addictive drug and its abuse is one of the nation's leading drug problems" and urged that funds from increased taxes be used to prevent underage and abusive drinking, treat alcohol addicts, and support public health programs for vulnerable populations.[22]

In the face of the AMA's concern about vulnerable populations, alcohol merchants target blacks, who suffer disproportionately from higher rates of alcohol-related death, disease, and injury, and the rapidly growing Latino community. In San Francisco, 31 percent of billboards in neighborhoods of Latinos advertise alcohol, as do 23 percent in those of African-Americans, compared to only 12 to 13 percent in those of whites and Asian-Americans.[23] There are also more liquor licenses granted in black and Latino city neighborhoods than in white ones, thanks to the power of the alcohol industry, even though researchers have found that the presence of liquor stores and bars tends to increase violence.[24]

By law there can be no cigarette ads on broadcast television.[25] For the alcohol industry, however, any such restrictions are a matter of self-determination. The broadcast networks adhere to an industry practice that prohibits hard liquor commercials on network television.[26] With the arrival of cable television, alcohol executives have hawked their wares there and have poured big dollars into local stations that accept their advertising. From 2001 to 2005, underage youth exposure to alcohol advertising on television jumped 41 percent, thanks largely to increases in liquor commercials on cable TV.[27]

In 2002 NBC indicated it was going to accept hard liquor advertising. The congressional clamor was so great that the network backed off, fearing federal legislation that would impose on all alcohol advertising the same sort of prohibition imposed on tobacco advertising.[28] The network—and the broadcast and beer industries—were especially concerned that in acting on such legislation Congress might also decide to ban beer advertising. Public health advocates had been pushing for such a ban. If the Congress moved to ban hard liquor commercials on television, the beer and broadcast executives knew that the liquor industry would join with the public health advocates to press for a prohibition of beer commercials as well.

The networks have long accepted beer advertising and claim that they would not be able to afford to run professional and college athletic events without the funds from such commercials—an argument that echoes their claims a generation ago when they tried to hang onto cigarette advertising. These athletic events provide the beer merchants an opportunity get their message across to underage teens, who make up a significant part of the audience. NBC was not about to risk that ad revenue, and the beer merchants were not about to risk their access to the youth market.

The importance that the alcohol industry places on advertising to underage drinkers can be seen from the enormous investment they make in advertising on radio shows where the audience is disproportionately composed of twelve- to twenty-year-olds. Such youths comprise 15 percent of the population, and the Institute of Medicine has recommended that the alcohol industry refrain from advertising on broadcasts where the audience of twelve- to twenty-year-olds exceeds that percentage. In fact, in radio markets, 71 percent of total underage exposure to radio alcohol advertising occurred on programs with disproportionately large youth audiences, with 32 percent of such exposure on programs where more than 30 percent (twice the population proportion) of the audience is underage. In the Dallas radio market, 90 percent of alcohol advertising is on radio shows that exceed the 15 percent threshold; in Washington, D.C., Atlanta, and Seattle, more than 80 percent; in Los Angeles and Chicago, more than 75 percent.[29] The beer and liquor merchants have set 30 percent as an industry standard (under pressure, down from 50 percent in 2003 to the lower percentage standard that the wine industry had established for itself), a threshold they widely disregard in the top markets.[30]

INHALE THE MONEY

The tobacco industry has long been as skittish as an old lady crossing a thoroughfare in Manhattan about the impact of taxation on sales. In

1981, the *Journal of Law and Economics* published a study demonstrating that a 10 percent rise in the price of cigarettes leads to a 12 percent decline in consumption among twelve- to seventeen-year-olds.[31] A 1982 R. J. Reynolds tobacco company document agreed that if prices were raised 10 percent, the number of kids who smoked could drop almost 12 percent.[32]

Here's how Philip Morris put the matter in 1995: "[Past] increases in the [federal and state] excise and other similar taxes . . . have had an adverse impact on sales of cigarettes. Any future increases . . . could result in volume declines for the cigarette industry."[33] A decade earlier they had declared, "Of all the concerns, there is one—taxation—that alarms us the most. While marketing restrictions and public and passive smoking [restrictions] do depress volume, in our experience taxation depresses it much more severely. Our concern for taxation is, therefore, central to our thinking."[34]

Philip Morris puts its money where its mouth is. The company invested more than $10 million in the election of George W. Bush in 2000 in order to make certain that this president's no-new-taxes commitment covered excise taxes on cigarettes.[35] In Virginia, the tobacco giant invested almost $1 million in politicians (along with expensive gifts, meals, and trips on the company's private jet worth lots more) in the early 2000s as the state legislature was considering a cigarette tax hike. As a result, in 2004 Virginia's first cigarette tax increase in half a century kept the commonwealth's rate lower than that of forty-one other states. Further, to atone to Philip Morris for the tax increase, the Virginia legislature at the same time approved a special ten-year tax break for the company. [36]

Prevalence rates among smokers tend to reflect rates of state cigarette taxes. The highest prevalence rates for smoking are in West Virginia (27 percent) and Tennessee (26 percent), which have among the lowest taxes in the nation on cigarettes. States with the smallest smoking prevalence rates, such as Utah (11 percent), and California (15 percent), tax cigarettes at a much higher rate.[37] No wonder the tobacco companies spend so much money in campaigns to buy seats in state legislatures and rooms in governors' mansions.

The tobacco industry has not enjoyed the extraordinary success of the beer and alcohol industry in holding back tax increases. For the most part, cigarette taxes have climbed over the past two decades, and these increases have often been designed to reduce smoking, particularly among children and teens. They reflect the fact that most Americans believe that cigarette taxes should be raised substantially in order to help state and local governments pay for the costs of treating smoking-related diseases.[38] Even in the tobacco-growing states like Kentucky and Maryland, citizens have supported higher cigarette taxes.[39]

At the federal level, cigarette taxes have risen from $16.80 to $40.95 per thousand cigarettes between 1990 and 2002.[40] In New York City, where Mayor Michael Bloomberg has used tax increases to push the price of a pack of cigarettes to more than seven dollars, smoking decreased by 11 percent between 2002 and 2003. More significantly, in the wake of the Bloomberg tax increase, the number of high school smokers dropped 36 percent.[41] Bloomberg wants another tax increase to take the price of a pack of cigarettes over eight dollars because, as he put it, "It will save lives by keeping children from starting and helping adults quit." But he has been blocked by a New York state legislature beholden to tobacco interests. Even the most modest tax increases have an impact. In Kentucky, Governor Ernie Fletcher, a physician, pushed through the state legislature an increase in the cigarette tax from three to thirty cents a pack. Though the tax is low and smoking prevalence rates in the state are still high, since the tax took effect cigarette consumption in Kentucky has been falling by 2 percent annually.[42]

Tobacco company damage control is to seek ways to offset tax-caused price increases. In 2002, more than 63 percent of cigarette marketing budgets, some $8 billion dollars, went to price discounts for cigarette wholesalers and retailers. The companies spent another billion dollars in free cigarette promotions, giving away samples, offering coupons for free smokes, and buy-one-get-one-free campaigns.[43] Price discounts and freebies are aimed at the most price-sensitive customers: kids and the poor. Children and teens, of course, are the industry's key to maintaining a stream of future customers. The industry sees the poor similarly to the way P. T. Barnum saw circus customers—as suckers at the other end of a smoking-drug delivery system. Distributing free cigarettes is so important to the industry that in 2006 R. J. Reynolds sued to invalidate a Seattle city ordinance that bans the practice.

In the 1990s, the nicotine merchants created "little cigars," by 2005 a $400-million-a-year industry, to avoid the excise tax on cigarettes. In 2006, forty states, led by Iowa attorney general Tim Miller, asked the U.S. Treasury Department to bar tobacco companies from pushing these products as "little cigars" in order to avoid higher cigarette excise taxes that deter teen smoking, noting that "little cigars" appeal to young smokers because they are cheaper than cigarettes. The American Heart and Lung Associations point out that "these 'little cigars' are blatantly aimed at our children, . . . are cheaper and more affordable to kids, . . . and are often sold individually rather than in packs because their classification exempts them from state laws setting minimum pack sizes for cigarettes."[44]

For a sense of how critical low prices are to an industry in search of replacement smokers, one has only to examine the industry's shameless smuggling scheme to kill a Canadian tax increase and the charges of the European Commission that one company supported a black market to sidestep taxes in the European Union.

In the early 1990s, Canada raised taxes on cigarettes sold there by the equivalent of $2.26 American ($3.50 Canadian) a carton. The tobacco industry claimed that the tax hike precipitated a sharp increase in smuggling and related violence, as criminals arranged to ship Canadian cigarettes to the United States and smuggled them back into Canada free of taxes.[45] To make their case, tobacco companies surreptitiously fostered this cross-border smuggling. In an exchange of letters with the managing director of British American Tobacco, the chairman of Imperial Tobacco discussed ways in which they could manipulate prices so that "an increasing volume of our domestic sales in Canada will be exported [to the United States] then smuggled back for sale here [in Canada]."[46] The two companies kept prices down in the states close to Canada in order to encourage Canadian criminals to purchase cigarettes in the United States and then smuggle them to Canada for illegal sale at prices less than the higher-taxed Canadian cigarettes. The companies used this scam to persuade the Canadian parliament to repeal the higher cigarette tax.[47]

Convinced that a similarly sordid scheme was designed to avoid the impact of high European cigarette taxes, the European Commission accused R. J. Reynolds of selling black-market cigarettes to drug barons and organized crime, to resell them at lower prices free of European Union (EU) taxes. In a civil lawsuit filed in New York, the Commission claimed that as a result EU nations had lost "hundreds of millions of euros" during the 1990s. The Commission also charged that Reynolds conspired with the criminal underworld in central and eastern Europe, accepting "dirty money" with full knowledge that many of the cigarettes it sold would be smuggled into western European Union nations. The commission alleged that Reynolds made it "part of their operating business plan to sell cigarettes to and through criminal organizations and to accept criminal proceeds in payment for cigarettes by secret and surreptitious means."[48] The European Union's New York suit was dismissed for lack of jurisdiction, so its charges have never been aired on the merits.[49]

Right behind higher taxes on big tobacco's hit list are laws to create smoke-free environments. The industry pulls out all the stops to fight bans on smoking in enclosed spaces, buildings, restaurants, and taxi cabs and tries to kill laws like those in California and Washington that ban smoking at beaches and in public parks. By making it difficult to smoke and branding the practice as socially unacceptable, such restrictions have a significant impact in reducing smoking, particularly among office workers and middle-class and affluent segments of the population. The industry creates phony restaurant associations and enlists minority restaurant owners and bars with under-the-table payments to fight such laws for fear of losing business.

In 1978, when I declared the Health, Education, and Welfare Department's headquarters the nation's first smoke-free building, I noted that, in enclosed spaces, "You can eat alone, you can drink alone, but you cannot smoke alone." The Tobacco Institute, then the industry's lobbying muscle in Washington, unsuccessfully tried to get Congress to overturn my decision in order to, as they put it, "protect smokers' rights."

Here again, New York City (along with Beverly Hills) set the bar high. In 1986, Mayor Ed Koch asked me to head a mayoral committee on smoking and health. Our committee recommended that restaurants, closed sports arenas, and convention halls reserve at least half their seats for nonsmokers, and that smoking be banned outright in retail stores, hearing rooms, taxis, restrooms, and theaters. When I reported to Koch,

I said I realized that passing such an ordinance was hopeless; the tobacco interests would spend millions to kill the bill in the City Council.

"Nonsense," Koch said. "You propose the toughest law that makes sense. I'll get it passed."

I expressed skepticism about his nonchalance. "But they'll take the tobacco money," I responded.

"This is New York," Koch agreed. "Of course they'll take the tobacco money. Then they'll vote for your bill."

City Council members did take the money. Then, led by Peter Vallone, who at the time chaired the council's health committee, they voted unanimously for the bill.

With the evidence mounting that there is no loss of business, and employers fearing lawsuits by workers subjected to involuntary secondhand smoke, states and communities are putting in place broad prohibitions against smoking in public spaces, offices, factories, restaurants, and bars. A reflection of favorable public attitudes and the commercial value of such restrictions is that the Westin Hotel chain has gone completely smoke-free in the United States.[50] Faced with the fact that secondhand smoke kills approximately seventy thousand Americans a year and cripples many thousands more, the tobacco industry settled a case in Florida brought by flight attendants who collected $300 million because of diseases and deaths suffered when smoking was permitted on poorly ventilated jet planes. They and their attorneys, Stanley and Susan Rosenblatt, have used the money to establish the Flight Attendants Medical Research Institute to support research into secondhand smoke.[51]

The tobacco industry is very much a "Do as I say, not as I do" business. When Andrew Tisch, then head of the Lorillard subsidiary of Loews Inc., tried to get Senator Frank Lautenberg to back off his amendment to require that all airline flights be smoke-free, the senator asked, "Does your father, Larry, smoke?"

"No," replied Andrew.

"Does your Uncle Bob smoke?"

"No."

"Do you smoke?"

Andrew again replied in the negative.

"OK," Lautenberg said, "I'll drop my amendment when you come back and tell me that your father, your uncle, and you are smoking a pack a day!"

Lautenberg's amendment promptly became the law of the land.

Also high on big tobacco's hit list are any effective public education programs directed at discouraging children and teens from smoking and encouraging adult smokers to quit. When I was at HEW and started the national antismoking campaign in 1978, I learned firsthand how terrified the nicotine pushers are of public education campaigns. They battled furiously to kill my request to Congress for just $12 million to mount such a campaign.

In 2006, in the *American Journal for Public Health* Forum on Youth Smoking, physicians Pamela Ling and Stan Glantz reviewed thousands of tobacco company documents and found that the industry had dissected the transition from the first cigarette as a teen to becoming a pack-a-day smoker at twenty-five as a series of stages, and that it had developed marketing strategies to encourage initial experimentation by teens and then increases in smoking during school, military service, new jobs, leisure, and social activities.[52]

Florida mounted a multiyear effort to address smoking among children through a public education campaign designed by teens and aimed at the teen population. The fundamental concept was that the tobacco hawkers are telling lies to manipulate kids into smoking their stuff: Don't let these adults trick you and get you hooked; rebel against them by not smoking. As Florida governor Lawton Chiles sought $18 million from the state legislature to fund this program, he called me for material on the dangers of smoking for kids. When he won the battle, I called to congratulate him. "Joe," he said, "I damn near had to sink the state with public works to get the votes to pass this legislation!" This potent program, continued by Governor Jeb Bush, brought a 38 percent reduction in teen smoking over two years—from 18.4 percent in 2000 to 11.4 percent in 2002—and a sharp reduction in marijuana smoking.[53] But cigarette companies never die; they don't even fade away. In 2005, Jeb Bush had to sink the state again with public favors for legislators to hang on to just $1 million for this program.

But the Florida advertising strategy became the conceptual basis for the American Legacy Foundation's truth® campaign. That effort, driven by foundation president Cheryl Healton, is much edgier, but it's built on the same basic principle—Don't let the bastards manipulate you!—and has proven even more effective. In its first two years, the truth® campaign has been credited with keeping at least three hundred thousand children and teens from starting smoking. That initial impact promises to save $1 billion in health care costs each year.[54] The campaign sparked all former Secretaries of Health, U.S. Surgeons General, and heads of the Centers for Disease Control and Prevention, Republican and Democrat, to form a Citizens Commission to Protect the truth® (which I chair) and counter tobacco merchants who are trying to kill the program.

For years, the big political dollars of the tobacco industry have paralyzed the U.S. Congress and most state legislatures. As a result, public health advocates have been forced to seek from courts what legislators beholden to big tobacco refuse to provide. In 1994, state attorneys general filed lawsuits to force big tobacco to reimburse their states for the health care costs of treating people with ailments related to tobacco use and to curb tobacco advertising and promotion aimed at children and teens.

Senator John McCain and others interested in the antismoking effort understood the weaknesses of a judicial solution or settlement. In the spring of 1998, McCain introduced and held hearings in the Commerce Committee he chaired on a bill that would have written into law a tough, government-enforceable version of the relief the state attorneys general were seeking.

House Speaker Newt Gingrich initially sounded like the brass section of a band of public health advocates clamoring for the McCain bill rather than a court settlement. Then Philip Morris—the eight-hundred-pound gorilla of the nicotine pushers—and other tobacco companies threatened to turn off their Republican Party money spigots. In a maneuver that must have warmed Machiavelli in his chilly grave, the tobacco merchants reminded Speaker Gingrich and Senate Majority Leader Trent Lott that three of every four of their political dollars go to the Republicans. The House Speaker shifted his attack from tobacco executives to the McCain bill and public health advocates. Lott promptly sandbagged McCain's legislative effort, leaving the tobacco industry free to negotiate a far more favorable deal with the states and their plaintiffs' lawyers.

On November 23, 1998, the attorneys general of forty-six states and the big tobacco companies (Brown and Williamson Tobacco Corporation, Lorillard Tobacco Company, Philip Morris Incorporated, R. J. Reynolds Tobacco Company, Commonwealth Tobacco, and Liggett and Myers) signed the Master Settlement Agreement (MSA). The companies agreed to pay $246 billion to the states, desist from marketing targeted at youth, end all outdoor advertising, severely restrict other traditional marketing practices, endow a national research foundation, and fund a public education campaign.[55]

The MSA highlights the pitfalls and limitations of a court's playing legislature and the difference between the interests of plaintiffs' lawyers, politicians, and public health advocates. So determined were the plaintiffs' lawyers to get their fees and so anxious were the states to ease budget crunches that the agreement did not even require that the money received from the tobacco companies be used for tobacco control and prevention and the treatment of tobacco-related diseases!

Well aware that competing pressures on governors and state legislatures would quickly divert the funds from antismoking efforts, the tobacco companies happily agreed to give the states maximum flexibility to spend the settlement payments. Most settlement money received by the states has been used for budget shortfalls. Only 20 percent has been devoted to health-related programs—in many states not even tobacco-related health efforts.[56] Michigan has sold off a significant part of its future share of the settlement in exchange for a much smaller lump sum payment, than it would otherwise have rerceived under the MSA, to be used for economic development.[57] Other states, including California, New Jersey, and Wisconsin, has made such sales, as has Nassau county in New York.[58]

Under the MSA, the tobacco companies agreed to fund the public education campaign for five years, but thereafter only if they continued to control 99.05 of the cigarette market. No public health advocate would have agreed to such a preposterous provision, and indeed, the companies fell below that market share before the ink was dry on the settlement they signed. The tobacco merchants have since refused to continue funding the public education effort and have taken to the courts in attempts to stop Cheryl Healton's effective truth® media campaign.

The MSA has had only marginal success in curbing marketing to kids. Tobacco company marketing doubled after the settlement to more than $15 billion a year, or $42 million a day in 2005.[59] A study of advertising patterns in thirty-eight national magazines, published in the *New England Journal of Medicine*, determined that the amount spent to advertise in youth-oriented publications the three brands most popular with teens and other young people—Camel, Marlboro, and Newport—has soared since the settlement.[60] In response, five states—Arizona, California, New York, Ohio, and Washington—filed suit against R. J. Reynolds in 2001 to enforce the restrictions against marketing to youth contained in the settlement agreement. The California court found the company in violation of the MSA and compelled it to pay sanctions.[61] The willingness of big tobacco to take risks and to pay sanctions is compelling evidence of how important children and teens are to their future profits.

BUTTS AND BOOZE: POLITICAL PARTNERS

There are revealing similarities between the tactics of the tobacco and alcohol merchants. Both are threatened by independent public health campaigns, especially edgy ones aimed at discouraging children and teens from smoking and drinking. Both prefer to conduct any such efforts on their own terms, because they know how to send subliminal messages of legitimacy and approval of smoking and excessive drinking. The Philip Morris campaign urging parents to talk to their kids carries the implicit message that smoking is just swell for adults. The alcohol industry's designated-driver campaign carries the implicit message that everyone else can drink up a storm; its "drink responsibly" campaign subliminally signals to its underage purchasers that the key message is "responsible" as far as their drinking is concerned. (Indeed, while the number of Americans who call themselves drinkers has held at about 50 percent since 1979. In 2005 43 percent reported bingeing at least monthly versus 29 percent in 1996, and almost three-fourths reported drinking in the last week versus about half in 1966.[62])

Both the tobacco pushers and the alcohol merchants make their products attractive to children and teens and seek high visibility in media and at events with large audiences of kids. Both have tried to sugar-coat their products to make them attractive to young teens: tobacco companies with chocolate, raspberry, and other flavored cigarettes; alcohol with sweetened and fruit-flavored alcopops, zippers, and other products. Both oppose tough, highly visible warning labels on their packaging and full revelation of their ingredients.

Both battle tenaciously to hold down tax increases well below covering the costs their products impose on society. In 2005, the total tax take from federal, state, and local taxes on tobacco was $20 billion; the health care costs due to smoking totaled $97 billion. The revenue from federal, state, and local taxes on alcohol was about $18 billion; the health care cost of alcohol abuse exceeded $100 billion.[63]

The overall direct costs of smoking and alcohol abuse—including, health care, crime, lost productivity, disability, and social welfare for those like abused children and those who lose parents—adds many more billions of dollars annually.

Both tobacco and alcohol company executives are largely responsible for government policies that put virtually all public resources into shoveling up the ravages of smoking and excessive drinking—treating the killing and crippling diseases and accidents and policing and prosecuting the crime—and that starve research on prevention efforts and public health education campaigns. The alcohol and tobacco merchants supported my requests as Secretary of HEW for funds to treat and research lung cancer and cardiovascular and respiratory diseases, and they battled to kill my requests for funds to research and promote persuasive public health education.

More than any other culprits, with their enormous investments in campaign contributions and lobbying, the tobacco and alcohol merchants are responsible for the upside-down-cake public policy that puts ninety-six cents of every dollar of the more than 100 billion spent on tobacco, alcohol, and drug abuse into health care, criminal justice, and social services, while only four cents goes to prevention and treatment. Their control of so many federal and state legislators and public officials through their hefty campaign contributions makes the most convincing case for campaign finance reform. Getting the tobacco and alcohol money out of American politics—even significantly reducing its influence—would save millions of lives, eliminate untold crippling diseases, and reduce violent crime and accidents.

CHAPTER 11

SOBERING UP
THE HIGH SOCIETY

In the late 1970s and early 1980s, the public health community, parents, and politicians saw the degrading and life-destroying experiences of addicts and young Americans like basketball phenomenon Len Bias as a wake-up call to reject the drug culture of the 1970s.

The result was astonishing.

From 1979 to 1992, illegal drug use by Americans twelve and over plummeted from 25.4 million people to 12.0 million, the lowest point since the early 1960s.[1] Among twelve- to seventeen-year-olds, illegal drug use dropped from 3.3 million to 1.1 million.[2]

Tragically, in the 1990s we lost that momentum. By 2005, overall drug use had climbed to 20 million Americans, almost double the 1992 low, and despite some decline since 2002, teen drug use stood at 2.6 million.[3] The proportion of twelve- to seventeen-year-olds offered marijuana has gone from 37 percent in 1996 to 39 percent in 2006.[4] Over roughly the same period, from 1992 to 2003, while the population increased 14 percent, adult abuse of prescription drugs rose 81 percent, and teen abuse shot up 212 percent.[5] By 2003, 15.1 million Americans were abusing prescription drugs, including 2.3 million teens.[6] The number of alcoholics and alcohol abusers continued to hover around 16 to 20 million, not much different from when I was Secretary of Health, Education, and Welfare in the late 1970s.[7] Only in smoking have we experienced declines from the 1992 levels among both adults and teens,[8] although even this substance use has been leveling off since 2005.

For all the billions of dollars spent and all the huffing and puffing over the years since 1992, the nation has not been able to blow down much of the house of drug and alcohol abuse and addiction. Whatever we have been doing for the past decade and a half—however noble and well-intentioned the government programs, prevention and treatment techniques, parental and societal conduct and cajoling—our policies and actions have not delivered significant reductions in drug and alcohol abuse and addiction. Indeed, with the explosion of prescription drug abuse, for caring parents the situation has gotten worse. Mothers and fathers are likely to be concerned whatever the drug their sons or daughters get into—whether illegal drugs like marijuana and cocaine or addictive prescription drugs like opioids or central nervous stimulants or depressants—and since the lows of 1992, the odds of their children's using some such substance have gone up.

Political leadership is essential. The importance of this leadership can be seen from the actions and inactions of the two presidents who have dominated the post-Reagan years.

Bill Clinton was the first president to take on the tobacco industry, and his stern and consistent antismoking words and actions were a key element in the decline of teen smoking and in invigorating widespread grassroots campaigns—from states suing the tobacco merchants and localities increasing taxes and mandating smoke-free space to public health advocates mounting education and "quit" campaigns. During the Clinton years, the number of teen smokers dropped by 30 percent.[9]

But Clinton paid little attention to illegal drug use. Indeed, his often quoted statement that "I smoked marijuana, but I didn't inhale" sent an unintended but influential message to kids that at least some pot smoking might be OK so long as you don't inhale. Teen marijuana use doubled during his presidency.[10]

Our other dominant national leader during this period, George W. Bush, is a recovering alcoholic and drug user. He has repudiated his substance abuse. But as president, he has shied away from the issue. He has done nothing to curb the actions of the tobacco and alcohol merchants to make their products attractive to children and teens when a public presidential scolding would likely have significantly restrained them. W's ideological commitment to no new taxes cuts no slack for increases in tobacco and alcohol excise levies that would make it too expensive for many children to buy cigarettes and alcohol. And he has been missing in action on illegal and prescription drug abuse.

Conservatives and liberals need to shed the ideological myopia in their view of substance abuse.

Many conservatives see drug and alcohol abuse and addiction not as a disease, but as self-indulgence or a moral weakness. Nor do most conservatives consider spending on treatment and prevention investments that will pay dividends in fewer government social programs over the long run. They oppose allocating additional public funds for treatment programs for prisoners, mothers on welfare, and parents caught up in child welfare systems. By refusing to support efforts to attack the root of the substance abuse epidemic, these conservatives are, in effect, increasing taxes on their constituents by burdening them with the cost of illness, crime, social welfare, homelessness, and broken families related to smoking, drugging, and excessive drinking. Indeed, they seem not to understand that their commitment to preserve marriage and the family would be strengthened by an effective assault on the substance abuse and addiction that lurk in the dark corners of so many marital split-ups and so much domestic violence. It is remarkable to see conservatives and libertarians diss as "nannyism" expenditures for government public health initiatives to discourage smoking and alcohol and drug abuse when they are investments that, if successful, will pay off in less government because of the reduced need for health care, criminal justice, and social programs that are a consequence of such abuse.

Liberals like libertarian George Soros are no better. Adopting their view that marijuana (and for some, all drugs) should be legalized would in our free, capitalistic society create an opportunity for a titanic new industry on a par with today's tobacco and alcohol behemoths. The marijuana (and other drug) manufacturers would certainly follow in the successful footsteps of the nicotine pushers and alcohol merchants—killing tax efforts to curb use, marketing cleverly to seduce teens, claiming First Amendment protection for their "commercial free speech," and selling candy-flavored pot and brownies to make their stuff more palatable to youngsters. Increased use would soon spawn lots more of the same social problems, such as illness, crime, child neglect and abuse, domestic violence, and welfare dependency, that we experience from substance abuse today. Progressive Democrats would call for more government programs and restrictions (which libertarians abhor) to combat these problems.

Then there is the reasonable center that most politicians claim as their political turf and that has dominated substance abuse policy. This moderate middle has isolated substance abuse and addiction as a separate matter, done little to remove its stigma, and ignored its implication in virtually every domestic problem the nation faces. The moderate middle has sought to act incrementally, taking measured steps that avoid offending settled constituencies at home and friendly nations abroad. But moderate approaches are not appropriate for an epidemic that touches every family and circle of friends and is implicated in most all our domestic problems. It's time to abandon the cautious, step-by-step approach and take some giant leaps. To paraphrase British prime minister David Lloyd George, we cannot conquer the chasm of substance abuse and addiction by gingerly taking one step at a time.

Can we take the leap?

We can—if our people understand that substance abuse and addiction is a chronic disease that infects our nation's intractable social problems and appreciate that, unless we deal with this epidemic, we will never grapple fully with those problems.

SMASHING THE STIGMA

My harshest judgment of the medical profession and the public health community is their failure to educate our society that substance abuse and addiction is a disease, not a moral failing or easily abandoned act of self-indulgence. That the medicine men and women are capable of such education can be seen from the monumental and effective efforts they have mounted to educate the nation (and the world) about AIDS. In the course of that undertaking, they have revolutionized thinking about condom use, discussed intimate details of sexual activities, and inspired understanding of heterosexual and homosexual conduct with a public candor unimaginable just a few years ago.

True, individuals who inhale their first joint, swallow their first drink, snort their first line of cocaine, or pop their first pill are certainly responsible and can be held accountable for their conduct. If they had never experimented in the first place, they wouldn't have gotten hooked or become abusers. But most people who make that first choice do so at an age when they are not capable of appreciating the consequences of their choice.

How are they any different from the teen who lights up the first cigarette or overeats or diets for the first time? When that teen becomes a regular smoker, we don't say that he should not expect some medical help to quit or surgery for his lung cancer. When the young girl who embarks on her first diet to become as thin as the model she admired in *Vanity Fair* turns into an anorexic or a bulimic, we don't say that she is not entitled to treatment. When a patient who has been warned by his physician to stay away from fatty food because of high cholesterol has a heart attack or stroke because he breaks his diet, should he be denied care because of his lack of willpower?

Addiction is a chronic disease more like diabetes and high blood pressure than like a broken arm or influenza. It cannot be fixed or cured in a single round of therapy, with a surgical procedure or one regimen of pharmaceuticals. Perpetual care is as critical to treating the alcoholic or drug addict as taking insulin or hypertension pills is to the care of the diabetic or the victim of high blood pressure. When the diabetic eats too much candy or the hypertensive patient goes off his pills because they are inhibiting his sexual prowess, we don't condemn him. But let a cocaine or heroin addict slip, and the condemnation bell peals. The medical and public health professionals have done an abysmal job in educating the American people about the medical reality of drug and alcohol abuse and addiction. Their failure to instruct the nation about addiction as they have about AIDS permits the High Society to treat those afflicted with this disease as the biblical lepers of modern-day America, and to relegate this disease to the dark corner of the health care closet the way Lord Rochester hid his demented wife in *Jane Eyre*.

If a man's wife has cancer, or a woman's husband has a serious heart ailment, the family freely talks about the condition and watches over the afflicted family member. If a child has multiple sclerosis or epilepsy, parents freely talk about it, and family members are attentive and compassionate. But if a spouse is a drunk, or a child is hooked on cocaine, marijuana, or heroin, it becomes the family secret. Spouses and parents are guilty and ashamed; it is this guilt and embarrassment that the medicine men and women of our nation must lead the way to stamping out.

Alcoholics Anonymous—perhaps the most effective (and cost-effective) regimen yet devised—has helped weld this iron curtain of secrecy. Based on sincere beliefs that anonymity is an essential ingredient of the successful Twelve Step program, AA participants and chapters resist any efforts to have their members go public. Many AA members tell me that secrecy is essential for individuals to enter the program. Anonymity is understandable with respect to any individual who does not wish to be identified. My own belief is that this commitment to anonymity is also necessitated by the way society has treated this disease of body, mind, and spirit. The reluctance of employers to hire recovering alcoholics or drug addicts and the difficulty anyone who admits alcoholism or drug addiction has in obtaining health insurance encourage AA members to support secrecy as a sacred tenet of recovery. It is time for AA and its members to encourage those who are willing to come forward, like faces and voices of recovery, to speak about their experience. More openness from those in recovery from alcohol and drug addiction will help many others confront their problem and help our society understand that this is a disease that millions are in recovery from.

When I started the National Center on Addiction and Substance Abuse (CASA) at Columbia University in 1992, former first lady Betty Ford said, "If you do nothing else, if you can just peel the stigma off this disease, you will have accomplished great things." After fifteen years of intense work in this field, I have come to appreciate the significance of her statement.

Stigma denies substance abuse and addiction its proper place as a chronic disease. It permits the medical profession, and the health insurers, to refuse to accept relapses as understandable human frailty, part and parcel of the chronic nature of the illness, the way relapses are accepted in other chronic ailments like hypertension, asthma, and diabetes.

To appreciate the insidious impact of stigma, consider how society treats individuals who become diabetic as a result of obesity from overeating. They are viewed as victims of a dreadful disease, meriting health insurance coverage and medical treatment. The fact that they have not been able to control their food intake is not condemned as evidence of moral deficiency or self-indulgence. Compare the alcoholics or drug addicts who cannot control their drinking or drugging: They are often viewed as morally weak and self-indulgent; their condition is not universally accepted as a disease.

Nowhere does stigma do more damage than to our young. Only 6.2 percent of college students who are alcohol-dependent seek help. CASA's survey of college students found that while 88 percent feel that school services to deal with substance abuse problems are accessible, 37 percent said that fear of social stigma—being embarrassed or scared that someone will find out—keeps students from seeking help.[11]

PROFESSIONALIZING PROVIDERS

A most disturbing characteristic of many of those who treat substance abuse and addiction is their pit bull penchant for attacking treatment providers who use techniques different from theirs. The therapeutic communities that use no drugs criticize the residential treatment centers that use drugs (sometimes for extended periods) to ease the withdrawal symptoms of their patients. The high-end treatment centers look down on the public programs that rely on methadone as either a permanent or (long-term) temporary method of caring for heroin addicts. The methadone mavens disdain those who insist on treating heroin without any drug therapy for abandoning a valuable tool that would increase their success rate. Many nonresidential programs look on residential programs as unnecessarily expensive rip-offs. Providers who use single-sex programs look askance at those who employ coed programs. Many in Alcoholics Anonymous put down any program other than their Twelve Steps to recovery, especially those programs that use pharmaceuticals. Those who believe that spirituality or religion is a key component of recovery reject those who promote nonspiritual programs—and vice versa. Counselors who treat alcoholics and regard a patient's return to moderate drinking as possible (even desirable) are scorned as irresponsible by the rest of the field, which holds that complete abstinence is the only solution. Rare is the drug and alcohol treatment provider who recognizes that all of the above are dedicated to helping those who have become addicted to drugs and alcohol.

In no other field of health care do I find such attitudes. There are many ways to treat the same cancers: radiation, chemotherapy, surgery, pills, diet. Physicians using one method do not criticize those using another. Similarly, there are scores of different procedures for treating serious cardiovascular diseases: open-heart surgery, stents, diet, exercise, heart pumps, angioplasty, artificial hearts. Here again, cardiologists preferring one method do not look down on those who consider another more effective. It is essential for practicioners of different substance abuse treatment modalities to develop a similar measure of mutual respect.

This canine snarling among the drug and alcohol treatment communities stems from the field's lack of professional standards, institutions, and courtesies, which are part and parcel of the medical profession. Physicians are subjected to rigorous academic and clinical training during four years of medical school and another four years (at least) of residency training in teaching hospitals. Throughout their careers they must comply with demanding standards of state medical boards and professional societies, including continuing education. If substance abuse is to be accorded its proper status as a disease, then those who treat it should be subject to the same high standards of education, training, and continuing education as physicians and nurses. It is essential to develop professional institutions throughout the treatment community comparable to those that the world of medicine adopted after the 1910 Flexner report exposed rampant quackery and an urgent need for education, licensing, and state boards to establish and police professional standards for physicians. Subjecting all substance abuse treatment providers to the same demanding standards of education, training, and practice would provide the basis for mutual respect and an end to the sniping that marks the treatment community today. Such standards would also reinforce the need for holistic approaches in treatment—confronting the physical, mental, emotional, and spiritual needs of the patient and attending to the patient's surrounding circumstances of family, friends, and task in life.

Another important benefit can flow from such professionalization. Sobering up the High Society requires a host of federal, state, and local government actions—such as making major increases in research funds; conditioning federal aid to prisons on providing treatment to inmates who need it; conditioning such aid to schools on getting the drugs out and effective education programs in; according substance abuse treatment equal reimbursement status with mental and physical health care under Medicare, Medicaid, and private health insurance; and supporting courts and prosecutors with professional resources to deal with drug- and alcohol-abusing offenders. Essential to convincing governments and legislators to enact such measures is an organization that assembles the combined energies of the entire substance abuse field in an American Substance Abuse and Addiction Association, comparable to the American Heart or Lung or Mental Health Associations. Such an organization requires a substantial measure of collaboration and understanding of common interests among various substance abuse treatment and advocacy constituencies that can spring from professionalizing the field.

CURBING AVAILABILITY AND ATTRACTIVENESS

The overriding obligation of our public officials is to support the efforts of parents and others who most influence the young to raise drug-free children.

Fulfilling that obligation begins with curbing the wide availability and calculated attractiveness of the legal drugs, nicotine and alcohol, to children and teens. Self-regulation of marketing practices has been a notable failure. So has the enforcement of laws prohibiting the sale of cigarettes and alcohol to minors. Our public officials can no longer stand by while tobacco and alcohol merchants market their drugs in ways that are attractive to children and teens, nor can they look the other way while stores, bars, and restaurants sell these legal drugs to underage consumers. Cigarette and alcohol manufacturers should be held accountable for the actions of the stores, bars, and restaurants that repeatedly sell their products to underage consumers.

Tobacco and alcohol merchants are not entitled to a First Amendment right to commercial speech in order to fend off reasonable government restrictions on their marketing practices. Since millions of our children are at risk, the government has the power to prohibit any marketing on television (cable or broadcast), to require the labeling of these products with vividly displayed warnings, and to mandate labels and package inserts identifying all ingredients. Justice Oliver Wendell Holmes, Jr., in a famous opinion, wrote, "The most stringent protection of free speech would not protect a man falsely shouting fire in a theater and causing a panic."[12] In view of the killing and crippling consequences of using tobacco as intended and of underage alcohol use, those who seek to make these products tempting to children are shouting fire in a theater crowded with children and teens. The tobacco and alcohol peddlers are not entitled to legal protection to market their products to this audience, package them in ways that will be attractive to it, or saturate with their images events and publications that large numbers of children and teens view. All alcohol and beer advertising should be banned from television. The Congress could follow the lead of the European Parliament and ban all product placement of alcohol and tobacco products on television and in films.

The Food and Drug Administration has the power to curb the availability of prescription drugs for abuse. It can require as conditions of its approval that pharmaceutical companies formulate dangerous and addictive drugs in ways that make abuse difficult and develop detailed plans to tighten control of the drugs at the first signs of abuse.

We also need effective international arrangements to curb alcohol abuse, especially by children. The treaty concerning tobacco products provides a precedent. In 2004, the Bush administration signed the World Health Organization's Framework Convention on Tobacco Control, the first international treaty on health. More than 140 nations have ratified the treaty, unfortunately not including the United States because the administration refuses to submit it to the U.S. Senate for ratification. Nations ratifying the treaty commit themselves to limit tobacco advertising, promotion; and event sponsorship; to increase cigarette taxes in order to discourage underage smoking and help pay the cost of treating individuals with tobacco-related diseases; to enlarge warning labels on cigarette packages; to end smoking in public places; and to crack down on tobacco smuggling and make it more difficult for tobacco companies to influence legislation on smoking.

The World Health Organization should establish a similar framework for an international agreement on alcohol. Under such a treaty, nations should commit themselves to discourage sales of alcohol products to minors; to impose severe penalties on those who do so; to restrict alcohol advertising in and around places like schools where minors congregate and in publications where teens and children are a significant part of the readership; to prohibit sponsorship of broadcasts and athletic and entertainment events by beer, wine, and alcohol companies where teens and children comprise a significant part of the audience; and to require the labeling of alcohol products with the dangers of underage drinking (as some nations now do with respect to pregnant women), with their ingredients and caloric content, and with the adverse consequences of excessive drinking.

There's no need for states, localities, and the federal government to await international agreement. They can take action to make the sale of tobacco products and alcohol to underage children and teens a serious offense. The power to tax can be employed to increase the price of cigarettes and beer and thus discourage teen use. The power to license is another important tool. Retailers, bars, and restaurants that sell tobacco products or alcohol to underage customers (or others they have reason to know are purchasing items such as cigarettes and beer for underage customers) should be subject to heavy fines and to the suspension, and revocation of licenses to do business. Young purchasers should be required to provide the same sort of photo identification that airlines require, and the penalties for making, selling, or using a phony ID should be increased. The smoking age can be raised to twenty-one.

We must mount a far more effective effort to block the entry of illegal drugs into the United States and to eliminate their production within the country. This undertaking demands the kind of attention we have committed to keeping chemical, biological, and nuclear weapons out of our nation. Marijuana, cocaine, heroin, Ecstasy, and other illegal drugs have demonstrated a far deadlier capability for mass destruction.

For decades the State Department and the foreign policy establishment have put the matter of drug control in the back of the international bus. Their concerns have been the Cold War, nuclear proliferation, commercial protections for our industries, and terrorism. During the mid-1960s, when I was serving as a presidential aide in the White House, we detected early symptoms of the spread of heroin addiction. I repeatedly asked Secretary of State Dean Rusk to press Turkey, then the chief source of heroin smuggled into the United States, to destroy its poppy fields and illegal drug operations. Rusk invariably responded, "We need Turkey as an ally to help contain the Soviet Union. We must be extremely measured in how we approach the Turkish government about poppy growth and heroin production."

That attitude—permitting other foreign policy concerns to trump our interest in curbing illegal drug production and exports to the United States—endures to this day. Indeed, thanks in good measure to the Bush administration tactics with respect to the Taliban and terrorism, the opium trade has mushroomed in Afghanistan. The relatively inexpensive heroin exported from that nation poses a far more clear and present danger to our children and our people than the threat of terrorism from the Taliban. In addition, in June 2006, Secretary of Defense Donald Rumsfeld announced plans to move Black Hawk helicopters from their drug interdiction mission in the Bahamas to operations in Iraq and Afghanistan. This decision was made despite warnings by several House members, including two Republican committee chairmen, and Bahamian officials that such a move would gut the area's antidrug effort.[13]

International agreements are required to commit the entire world community to reducing the availability (and curbing the use) of illegal drugs like heroin, cocaine, and Ecstasy. The United States should put this issue at the top of its foreign policy agenda, along with trade, nuclear proliferation, and terrorism. The world needs to strengthen United Nations drug treaties, to enlist all nations to eliminate drug production within their borders, to increase penalties for drug dealers and smugglers, to impose severe penalties on those who sell to teens and children, to tighten banking laws and increase penalties to make it difficult and costly to launder drug money, and to establish formal military and policing arrangements to curb drug production and distribution.[14] We should be as aggressive in seeking sanctions to pressure Afghanistan and Colombia to eliminate their drug production and exports as we are in trying to get North Korea and Iran to close down their nuclear weapon development and prevent them from exporting nuclear materials.

THE FAITH COMMUNITY

The faith community has a powerful opportunity to counter substance abuse and addiction and help provide support to parents trying to bring up their children in a drug-free environment. Priests, ministers, rabbis, and imams should understand the importance of religious involvement in keeping teens away from drugs and the stress and strain on parents trying to do so in today's self-indulgent society. Even for children, appreciating that they are creatures of God, imbued with free will and an inherent dignity, can be crucial to whether they risk degrading themselves through substance abuse and addiction. Teens who attend religious services regularly are less likely to use drugs, alcohol, and tobacco than those who do not.[15]

The clergy are woefully prepared to deal with substance abuse and addiction in their congregations. When surveyed, more than 90 percent of parish priests, rabbis, and ministers indicate that drug abuse, particularly involving alcohol, is a significant problem among their congregations, more often than not involved in family-shattering experiences like spousal violence, child abuse, adultery, and divorce.[16] Yet, barely more than 10 percent of seminarians and rabbinical students complete any course work in how to spot substance abuse and addiction and what to do when it's been identified.[17]

Therein lies a serious problem, considering Americans often feel most comfortable turning to their clergy for help with a substance abuse problem in their family. Priests, ministers, and rabbis are readily accessible, discreet, and available to help at low or no cost, and they enjoy preexisting relationships with their congregants. All clergy should be required to receive substance abuse training in their seminaries. Then they will be prepared to help prevent substance abuse through sermons, youth and adult study groups, religious counseling, working with local treatment facilities and physicians, and developing support systems for substance abusers and their families affiliated with their place of worship.

PACKAGING PREVENTION

Prevention should be laser-beamed on children and teens.

What does it take to dissuade kids from experimenting with drugs? Experimentation is the essential first step on the road toward abuse and addiction, and no one experiments thinking she or he is going to get hooked. What are the situations and circumstances that influence the risk a child will try, abuse, or get hooked on tobacco, alcohol, illegal drugs, or pharmaceuticals?

CASA's in-depth teen surveys and other research have gone a long way toward identifying the social and psychological factors that influence the risk that a teen will smoke, drink, or use drugs. The next step is to act on such research. Public health programs should be crafted with those factors in mind and should also make parents aware of the signals of substance abuse risk. Physicians and nurses should know what questions to ask to determine the level of risk for their adolescent patients.

The failure to act on what we know is inexcusable, particularly with respect to the difference between boys and girls. Unisex programs have proved pretty much a failure, whether in treatment, in the pediatrician's office, or in the television, magazine, and newspaper antidrug ads of the federal government. Public education programs directed at children and teens, though conceived to have unisex appeal, tend to be aimed at situations and characteristics that influence boys. Few focus on depression, anxiety, and stress—three characteristics that more commonly increase the risk that girls will smoke, drink, and use drugs. Even fewer (if any) confront the fact that girls who binge-drink do so because they want to be one of the boys—even though one drink has the impact on them that takes two for boys—or that girls drink to reduce their sexual inhibitions.

Nor are all teens the same. Efforts to discourage teens from smoking, drinking, and using drugs should take account of cultural and ethnic differences: What will move a suburban white teen may be quite different from what will move an inner-city Hispanic or African-American teen. What will discourage an urban teen from smoking pot or trying meth may not turn off a rural teenager. Different prevention strokes are appropriate for folks at different ages. Kids at the various stages of their life—from ten to twenty—use or don't use for quite different reasons, and during the teen years, attitudes can change every few months.

As with treatment, a holistic approach is key. It is more than a matter of simply telling kids not to smoke, drink, or use drugs. It is a matter of recognizing the conditions that increase a teen's risk—and reducing their incidence. Public education and prevention programs must be persistent and relevant to the generation they seek to persuade. Each new generation needs to hear the message in terms that it can understand.

Systemwide approaches can produce extraordinary results. In New York City, Mayor Michael Bloomberg and his health commissioner, Dr. Thomas Frieden, used all the tools at their disposal to attack the tobacco problem. They sharply raised taxes to increase the cost of a pack of cigarettes to more than seven dollars. That reduced teen smoking initiation and also priced cigarettes out of the hands of many poor people. They passed laws prohibiting smoking in virtually all enclosed spaces: restaurants, office buildings, museums, and all other public spaces. That helped reduce smoking among the more affluent, who found it increasingly difficult to find any enclosed place to light up in. When the public health battle shifted to the enforcement arena, the New York Police Department created the Cigarette Interdiction Group to stop cigarette smuggling aimed at avoiding the city's high taxes,[18] and New York City Health Department inspectors made sure violators of public smoke-free space laws were fined. The city also mounted a program to help people quit, with television ads offering free medications such as patches to help smokers break their habit. As a result, New York City experienced dramatic reductions in smoking, especially among high school students, and smoking-related deaths fell by more than eight hundred a year from 2000 to 2005.[19]

A MOM-AND-POP OPERATION

When all is said and done, preventing teen substance abuse is a Mom-and-Pop operation. Parents cannot outsource their responsibility to law enforcement, public health agencies, or schools and colleges. The fundamental obligation of those broader institutions is significant, but secondary. And while there is much room for improvement in curbing the availability of legal and illegal drugs to the nation's children and teens and targeting public health campaigns, the reality is that such substances—and many commonplace prescription and over-the-counter drugs, as well as household products like aerosol cans and other inhalants—will always be within reach of kids seeking a high. That puts a premium on vesting children with the will and skills to say no, and parents are uniquely positioned to do this.

Parent power is the most potent, the least appreciated, and the most underutilized resource we have in the struggle to raise children free of drug and alcohol abuse and addiction. When mothers and fathers appreciate their potential to influence their teens—and use it firmly and sensitively—we will have taken a giant leap to turn back this scourge that has destroyed so many children and brought grief to so many families and friends. The front line for America's drug problem is not in legislative hearing rooms or courtrooms run by politicians and judges. It is in living rooms and dining rooms, and across kitchen tables, in the hands of parents and families.

Parents who are engaged in their children's lives have the best chance of having children who do not engage in drug and alcohol use. This means everything from having frequent family dinners, helping with homework, and attending athletic and other events in which their children participate to setting firm but reasonable standards of conduct, including curfews, and making clear that smoking, drinking, and drug use are unacceptable. There are no silver bullets, but involved parents who send a clear message of disapproval of substance use dramatically reduce the odds that their teen will get involved in tobacco, alcohol, or drugs.[20]

The most basic parental involvement—eating dinner as a family—has an enormous impact in reducing a child's risk of drug use. CASA studies and surveys consistently demonstrate that the more often teens have dinner with their parents, the less likely they are to smoke, drink, or use drugs. Time together over dinner offers parents a chance to speak to their children—and to listen to them. Hearing and seeing their children regularly enables parents to spot subtle characteristics, such as high stress, low self-esteem, and persistent boredom, that signal potential trouble.

It is important for parents to understand that binge drinking or smoking pot is not some benign rite of adolescent passage, but a dangerous and unacceptable practice. The parental medium—actions, words, body language—is the most persuasive message that kids hear. The message for smoking and illegal drug use is simple: No. Never. The message for alcohol use is more complex: No for children and teens, moderation for adults. Excessive drinking is the taboo for all. The parents who reinforce this message repeatedly and are engaged in the lives of their children are the parents likeliest to raise drug-free kids.

Parents should realize that they are not pals. They have a critical standard- and boundary-setting responsibility that inevitably will prompt some teen resistance. That is to be expected. Indeed, parents who always get along with their teens are probably doing something wrong.

Parent power is key to getting drugs out of American middle and high schools. When parents shout, "We're mad as hell and we're not going to take it anymore!" school administrators and teachers will take steps to get drugs out of America's middle and high schools. The willingness of parents to tackle this problem is a signal example of parents' engagement that will inspire their own children to stay drug-free.

I am calling for a dramatic shift in our nation's attitude toward drug and alcohol abuse and addiction—acceptance of such abuse and addiction as a chronic disease and recognition of its impact on the most intractable domestic problems we confront. With such acceptance and recognition, we will appreciate the benefits of a revolution in our criminal justice, health care, and social service systems. We can seize the opportunity that prosecutors, courts, and prisons offer to reclaim hundreds of thousands of addicts. We can see the importance of the kind of major investment in substance abuse research that we have made in cancer, cardiovascular disease, and AIDS. We can reclaim families caught up in the child welfare systems.

With such a shift in attitude, we can recast all aspects of substance abuse in America: research and practice, demand and supply, prevention and treatment. The revolution can improve the quality of life of our people and, by example, of others across the world. I'm calling for the same kind of defining change in attitude that we—and with our leadership, much of the world—have experienced with smoking and AIDS.

Focus on our children is central to curbing drug and alcohol abuse in the future. Parents are primary, but there's plenty that schools, churches, local, state, and federal government, and the entertainment industry should do. The sooner their attitude toward substance abuse and addiction changes and they accept their share of responsibility to protect our children from drug and alcohol abuse, the sooner we will see an America where parents don't have to go to bed each night in fear that their teenage daughter or son will end up an alcohol or drug abuser or addict, or a victim of reckless driving or sexual assault by some drunken friend.

In his monumental study of history, the brilliant British historian Arnold Toynbee found that the great civilizations were destroyed not by an external enemy, but from within. "Civilizations," he said, "die from suicide, not by murder." Of all the internal dangers our nation faces, none poses a greater threat to our children and families and none is complicit in more domestic ills than substance abuse and addiction.

This is our enemy within.

The judgment of history will be harsh if we fail to defeat that enemy—and deservedly so, when the stakes are our children and there is so much we can do to help them.

ACKNOWLEDGMENTS

Life and this country have been very good to me. God blessed me with extraordinary parents who nourished me with love and sacrificed to educate me. The Jesuits at Brooklyn Prep and Holy Cross and the professors at Harvard Law School not only opened and honed my mind, they gave me a sense of the transcendent importance of social justice. My law practice, with clients like the *Washington Post* during the Watergate years, and my government service in Robert McNamara's Defense Department and Lyndon Johnson's White House, and as President Jimmy Carter's Secretary of Health, Education, and Welfare, were exhilarating and abundant in satisfaction. I have been fortunate to work with talented men and women who have given me extraordinary opportunities, recognized my successes and tolerated my mistakes, helped me get up when I fell, and instilled values that focused my energies.

When I returned to private law practice in Washington and New York after my years at HEW, I missed the satisfaction of trying to make the world, or some part of it, a little better. I did not believe that I was putting to best use the talents God had given me, my unique experience, and my good fortune. I was itching to take on another task in life but had no idea where I could make a difference. I got a spark of encouragement at a dinner with Lady Bird Johnson at the LBJ Library in 1991. As we got up from the table, she put her hands on my arms and looked at me. "Joe, you were so young when you worked for Lyndon. How old are you now?"

"I'm sixty, Mrs. Johnson," I answered.

"Well. Let me give you some advice," she said. "Between now and seventy-five you work very hard and play very hard. Because after that it gets a little difficult."

I began to reflect on my experience in search of clues for the best way to commit my energies.

Much of my navy service in the Office of the Judge Advocate General had been spent defending, on appeal, sailors and marines convicted at courts-martial for offenses related to illegal drugs (usually marijuana) and alcohol, either possession or drunkenness, or for assaults and rapes committed while the defendant was high on such substances.

While LBJ's chief domestic aide, I helped push through Congress the Drug Rehabilitation Act of 1966, authorizing the first federal funds to treat addicts. In preparing the president's message on crime, we recommended (a first for any national leader) that, in the absence of disorderly conduct or some other offense, states treat drunkenness—then the nation's number one crime—as a disease requiring detoxification and treatment.

In the 1960s, I helped consolidate law enforcement responsibilities related to the nation's burgeoning drug problem in the Justice Department in an independent Bureau of Narcotics and Dangerous Drugs (now the Drug Enforcement Administration).

After I left the White House in 1969, I served as a member of the Special Committee on Crime Prevention and Control in the District of Columbia. We tried to focus public attention on the district's epidemic of heroin addiction and the related rise in crime.

As Secretary of Health, Education, and Welfare, when I mounted the nation's antismoking campaign in 1978 people interested in fighting alcoholism and alcohol abuse asked me to take up their cause. I was visited by Mercedes McCambridge, the movie actress who had won an Oscar for her portrayal of the tough political hatchet in *All The King's Men*, the 1949 film classic inspired by Louisiana governor Huey P. Long. "You talk about tobacco all the time," she said, "but you never talk about alcoholism. That's an even worse problem. I know. I've been through it. I struggle with it every day." We went to work preparing a program on alcoholism that I announced in May 1979.

In the early 1980s, at Governor Hugh Carey's request I studied substance abuse in the state of New York. On Chrysler's board of directors, I confronted the difficulty in reducing smoking and alcohol, marijuana, and cocaine abuse and their impact on productivity and health care costs. In 1982 and 1983, as special counsel to the House Ethics Committee, I found widespread pill popping, illegal drug use, and alcohol abuse among teen pages and Capitol Hill employees.

In the mid-1980s, as counsel for Johnson & Johnson, I got to know Jim Burke, chairman and CEO of the pharmaceutical company. Burke planned to chair the Partnership for a Drug-Free America. "You could really do something about this and you ought to," he said. "There's no good public policy research out there. You could make a helluva contribution." Burke confronted me with articles I had written attacking the war on drugs as too narrowly focused on criminal punishment, interdiction, and illegal drugs and calling for more research, prevention, and treatment. "Don't just write about this," he challenged. "Do something!"

I began discussing the problem of substance abuse with people around the nation: doctors, businesspeople, lawyers, film and television artists and producers, editors and reporters, government officials, frontline experts in voluntary agencies, and recovering alcoholics and drug addicts. I saw the problem as addiction—regardless of whether the substance was alcohol, nicotine, or illegal or prescription drugs. To me, substance abuse was among the most pernicious threats to our society, and our political leaders were not facing up to it. I struggled with what role, if any, I might be able to play. Buoyed by the support of family and friends, I decided to put together a new organization, a think/action tank that would assemble people with all the professional skills needed to research and combat the abuse of all substances.

In March 1991, I took Dr. Steven Schroeder, newly installed president of the Robert Wood Johnson Foundation, through my basic idea to examine the problem in every sector of society, not simply criminal justice and health, but business, sports, schools, cities, and social welfare. We would bring to bear all the skills needed to combat substance abuse—not simply medicine and law enforcement, but anthropology, communications, economics, epidemiology, law, psychology, public health, religion, statistics, and social services. He agreed to provide the seed money for this enterprise.

Thus was born the National Center on Addiction and Substance Abuse at Columbia University. The name lent itself to the acronym CASA, the Italian and Spanish word for house. In my mind, it symbolized our bringing under one roof all the skills needed to attack all substance abuse in all corners of society.

I worked hard to recruit a committed board of directors. Jim Burke agreed to serve. In search of someone from a company that was a national icon interested in youngsters, I asked Don Keough, then president of Coca-Cola, to join the board and commit Coca-Cola to being a founding supporter. I had seen Keough's marketing genius in action and knew that, if he committed, he would deliver. He committed in one phone conversation.

Seeking a representative of the labor movement, I asked Lane Kirkland, president of the AFL-CIO, to suggest someone who would have the respect of the labor movement and express their view vigorously.

"What about Doug Fraser?" Kirkland asked. "He's retired from the United Auto Workers, but he arbitrates disputes among our unions and he sure as hell is respected." I called Fraser that very day. He immediately agreed to serve.

My next call was to LaSalle Leffall, who chaired the department of Surgery at Howard University's medical school and hospital. He had been president of the American Cancer Society when I was HEW Secretary, and I knew that he considered smoking the most deadly threat to the health of blacks. He signed up.

I called Frank Wells, president of Disney and a colleague from his days as a practicing attorney in New York. When Wells invited me to his home to talk the project over, I flew to Los Angeles and met with him at 6:30 one morning. He came downstairs, freshly showered after his morning jog. The meeting lasted almost three hours. As we talked, Frank worked over my draft mission statement, insisting that we make it "simple, like a Disney movie, so everyone can understand what you're about."

By the end of the meeting, we had crafted CASA's missions. Then Frank said, "I'm onboard. This is an enormous problem for the nation, and God knows, there's plenty of it in the entertainment industry."

I considered it important to have a Hispanic on the board, but I wanted no mere token. I called friends in Texas, California, New York, and Washington. I discovered Manuel Pacheco, then president of the University of Arizona. Pacheco had been president of the University of

Houston–Downtown and among the first academic leaders to ask business leaders what they wanted their college graduates to learn. I called Pacheco and introduced myself, and we spoke at length. He agreed to join the board.

I asked my friend John Rosenwald, then vice chair of Bear Sterns and one of the nation's wisest and most generous philanthropists, to come aboard as our investment adviser. He did and, on the spot, became our first contributor.

As president of Columbia University, Mike Sovern joined the board and established the precedent that the president of the university would always serve as a member.

My call to Barbara Jordan brought back a flood of memories. I had gotten to know her during my years on the White House staff. Lyndon Johnson was peacock-proud of his discovery of Barbara, the first black elected to the Texas senate. When we were setting up a presidential task force on income maintenance, I sent a list of names in to LBJ, including Northwest Industries chairman Ben Heineman as chair and, as members, the financier Andre Mayer, Bob McNamara, and several top-flight economists. Johnson approved the list and wrote, "Add Barbara Jordan." Never having heard of her, I checked with White House aide Marvin Watson, who told me, "She's a Negro Texas state senator, a friend of the president's." I assumed that, as a local Texas politician, she would be over her head. Since she was a friend of LBJ's, I waited for an appropriate moment, over dinner alone one evening, to raise the issue with him. "You know, Mr. President, this income maintenance group is high-powered and the subject is complex as hell. You suggested I add Barbara Jordan. If you want to do something for her, I can find another task force to put her on."

LBJ exploded. "Let me tell you something. She didn't go to Harvard and she never worked on Wall Street, but she's got more brains and common sense in her pinky fingernail than all those other members put together. She's going to be the first Negro governor or United States senator from the state of Texas. Put her on your Goddamn task force."

I did, and she dominated its deliberations. Barbara Jordan later became the first black woman elected to Congress from the South. Now, years later, she was teaching at the LBJ School of Public Affairs in

Austin. I knew she was interested in the impact of alcohol on African-Americans; she had written the introduction to a pamphlet on the subject.

Barbara was reluctant to join the CASA board because of her declining health. She never spoke about it, but she was suffering from multiple sclerosis, which confined her to a wheelchair, and leukemia. I asked her to serve for a couple of years to get us off the ground. She agreed and was such a powerful board member that John Rosenwald once remarked, "Barbara Jordan is the most interesting and compelling board member I've ever served with."

When the health trade press reported that I was launching CASA, Betty Ford sent me a wonderful letter of support: "Your early awareness of the dangers of smoking helped change the habits of an entire nation. Your warnings about a serious health hazard saved thousands of lives. I was delighted that you are including alcohol and prescription drugs in your studies."

I called to thank her. "This nation has needed an organization like this for so long," she said. "I'm so glad you're doing this. If there's anything I can do to help, let me know."

I jumped at the opening. "You can come on the board as a founding member. We have no recovering individual on the board, and you'd add enormous prestige."

There was a pause of five or ten seconds, which seemed like five or ten minutes to me. Then Betty said, "If I can work out my schedule to do the meetings, I will."

"We'll work out the schedule," I said.

"OK, Joe," she said.

In 1992 I abandoned the practice of law completely and devoted myself totally to building CASA into a national asset.

As was the case when I went to HEW, I had no sense of making a sacrifice in leaving a lucrative law practice. I was riding a great wave, convinced that I was putting whatever talent, celebrity, energy, and contacts I had to right use.

Today CASA is recognized as the gold standard in this field with the brightest professionals on substance abuse ever assembled in one organization. Since 1992, a number of distinguished and committed Americans have served on the CASA board: Lee Bollinger, Ursula Burns, Columba Bush, Ken Chenault, Jamie Lee Curtis, Jamie Dimon, Peter Dolan, Mary Fisher, Vic Ganzi, Leo Kelmenson, David Kessler, Monk Malloy, Joe Plumeri, Nancy Reagan, Shari Redstone, Linda Johnson Rice, Mike Roth, George Rupp, Mickey Schulhof, Lou Sullivan, John Sweeney, and Michael Wiener.

For fifteen years we have been probing the problem of substance abuse in our nation. This book is a distillation of what I have learned about our High Society.

Several people read all or parts of this manuscript: Peggy Collins, John Demers, Lauren Duran, Susan Foster, Herb Kleber, Jon Morgenstern, and Elizabeth Planet. Many CASA staffers helped with research, fact checking, and administrative mechanics: Rachel Adams, Kirsten Byerts, Jane Carlson, Jennie Hauser, Barbara Kurzweil, Jennie Leszkiewicz, David Man, Liz Peters, Amy Schlosberg, and Roger Vaughan. Elizabeth Planet worked on Chapter 5.

Nicole Grunfeld was my research assistant throughout work on this book. She is a young attorney with a penetrating eye for the fault lines in any analysis and meticulous standards of accuracy and excellence. This is a better book because of her care, dedication, and insistence on "getting it right."

Join Together, which posts on its Web site everyday just about everything of significance in the world of substance abuse, has been an invaluable resource thanks to the thoughtful creativity of its founding director, David Rosenbloom.

My assistant, Jane Nealy, once again provided invaluable service as drafts made their way through the word-processing system and to and from the editors. JoAnn McCauley kept my schedule going. Rush Russell and Sue Brown kept the CASA research and administrative trains running on time while I worked on this manuscript.

As he has done with three of my earlier books, Peter Osnos offered perceptive insights that greatly enriched this manuscript. He is a remarkable editor and publisher, and I'm greatly indebted to him. I had the benefit of Clive Priddle, Robert Kimzey, and Margaret Ritchie as editors, along with Morgen Van Vorst, Melissa Raymond, and Shana Murph. Nina D'Amario designed the cover. Led by its new publisher, Susan Weinberg, the entire team at Public Affairs Books is better than first-class.

I owe special thanks to my wife, Hilary, who lived through the many weekends, early mornings, and late evenings I spent in the spectacular study she has created for me in Westport, Connecticut. She is the love of my life and has been for more than a quarter century, during which she has showered me with love, sage advice, and her spectacular sense of humor.

Finally, I appreciate the support and understanding of my children, Mark, Joe III, Claudia, Brooke, and Frick, and my grandchildren, Joe IV (Jack), Pete, Brian, Russell, Evan, Olivia, and Nicky, who saw less of me during the writing. Grandpa is back!

With eternal gratitude to all who helped, as always what's on these pages is my responsibility alone.

JAC, Jr.
March 2007

DISEASES/CONDITIONS ATTRIBUTABLE TO SUBSTANCE ABUSE*

Disease Category	Substance	Population Attributable Risks**
Abortion	Smoking	15%
AIDS—Adults	IV Drug Use	32%
AIDS—<13 yrs	IV Drug Use	55%
Anal Cancer	Smoking	46%
Angina Pectoris	Smoking	16%
Asthma	Smoking and Passive Smoke	27%
Bladder Cancer—Males	Smoking	53%
Bladder Cancer—Females	Smoking	43%
Brain Tumor	Smoking	20%
Brain Tumor	Smoking	27%
Breast Cancer	Alcohol	13%
Burns	Alcohol and Drugs	25%
Cardiomyopathy	Alcohol	40%
Cataracts—Female	Smoking	6%
Cervical Cancer	Smoking	21%
Cheek and Gum Cancer	Smokeless tobacco	87%
Cirrhosis	Alcohol	74%
Colorectal Cancer	Alcohol	17%

continues

*The National Center on Addiction and Substance Abuse at Columbia University. *The Cost of Substance Abuse to America's Health Care System: Medicaid Hospital Costs*. July 1993.
**Population Attributable Risk (PAR) is an epidemiologic term meaning the percentage of a given illness that could be prevented if the use of the substance were eliminated. In other words, the PAR for cigarettes and lung cancer is 87%, indicating that 87% of lung cancers could have been prevented if there were no cigarette smoking.

Disease Category	Substance	Population Attributable Risks
Congenital Defects	Smoking	21%
Congenital Syphilis	Cocaine	9%
COPD—Male	Smoking	84%
COPD—Female	Smoking	79%
Coronary Artery Disease	Smoking	74%
Coronary Heart Disease	Smoking	52%
Crohn's Disease	Smoking	59%
Dementia	Alcohol and Drugs	11%
Diabetes—Female	Smoking	8%
Duodenal Ulcers	Alcohol	5%
Duodenal Ulcers	Smoking	52%
Ectopic Pregnancy	Smoking	74%
Endocarditis	IV Drugs	75%
Epilepsy	Alcohol	30%
Esophageal Cancer	Alcohol and Smoking	80%
Head and Neck Cancer	Alcohol and Smoking	50%
Hepatitis A	IV Drugs	6%
Hepatitis B	IV Drugs	12%
Hepatitis C	IV Drugs	36%
Hypertension	Alcohol	11%
Influenza	Smoking	45%
Kidney Cancer	Smoking	33%
Laryngeal Cancer—Male	Alcohol and Smoking	80%
Laryngeal Cancer—Female	Alcohol and Smoking	94%
Leukemia	Smoking	30%
Liver Cancer	Alcohol	29%
Low Back Pain	Smoking	10%
Low Birth Weight	Smoking	42%
Lower Respiratory Illness (Acute Bronchitis & Pneumonia)	Passive Smoke	24%
Lung Cancer—Male	Smoking	88%
Lung Cancer—Female	Smoking	74%
Myocardial Infarction—Female	Smoking	76%
Myocardial Infarction—Male	Smoking	33%
Oral Cavity Cancer	Alcohol and Smokeless Tobacco	85%
Other Respir. Diseases—Male	Smoking	37%

Disease Category	Substance	Population Attributable Risks
Other Respir. Diseases—Female	Smoking	35%
Pancreatic Cancer—Male	Smoking	41%
Pancreatic Cancer—Female	Smoking	19%
Pancreatitis, Chronic	Alcohol	72%
Pancreatitis, Acute	Alcohol	47%
Pelvic Inflammatory Disease	Smoking	33%
Peptic Ulcers—Female	Smoking	29%
Perinatal Death	Smoking	17%
Periodontitis	Smoking	40%
Peripheral Vascular Disease (PVD)	Smoking	75%
Pharyngeal Cancer	Alcohol and Smoking	80%
Pneumonia—Female	Smoking	35%
Pneumonia—Male	Smoking	36%
Pregnancy—Bleeding	Smoking	19%
Pregnancy—Premature Rupture	Smoking	32%
Pregnancy—Spontan. Abortion	Smoking and Cocaine	41%
Pregnancy—Abrupt Placentae	Smoking	42%
Pregnancy—Placenta Previa	Smoking	43%
Preterm Delivery	Smoking	25%
Renal Cancer—Male	Smoking	39%
Renal Cancer—Female	Smoking	32%
Renal Pelvis Cancer	Smoking	60%
Rheumatoid Arthritis	Smoking	17%
Seizures	Alcohol	41%
Stomach Cancer—Male	Smoking	39%
Stomach Cancer—Female	Smoking	33%
Stomach Ulcers	Alcohol	13%
Stomach Ulcers—Male	Smoking	34%
Stroke	Smoking and Cocaine	65%
Trauma	Alcohol and Drugs	40%
Tubal Pregnancy	Smoking	36%
Ureter Cancer	Smoking	71%

SOURCE NOTES

Many of the data in this volume come from a variety of sources that attempt to measure the extent of illegal drug use, as well as the extent of underage smoking and drinking.

Survey data based on the use of illegal drugs, and of the teen use of legal substances like alcohol and cigarettes, are usually self-reported. As a result, researchers believe that they understate the extent of such use. The most extensive survey, the National Survey on Drug Use and Health (formerly the National Household Survey on Drug Abuse), is conducted by the Substance Abuse and Mental Health Services Administration of the U.S. Department of Health and Human Services (SAMHSA). It was conducted from 1971 to 1988 every three years; since 1990 it has been conducted annually. Across this period, SAMHSA has made many changes in its sampling and methodology to improve the survey; the most recent change was in 2002. While direct comparisons of rates between these years of methodological change must be done with caution, I have used that survey to establish broad trends of significance because it offers the most extensive survey data available. The other government surveys, Monitoring the Future Survey conducted by the National Institute on Drug Abuse since 1975 largely to measure behaviors of high school students, and the Youth Risk Behavior Survey conducted by the Centers for Disease Control and Prevention since 1990 to measure health risk behavior, reflect essentially the same broad trends. These two surveys also make changes periodically to enhance their validity. The three surveys offer the best available data to measure trends in drug, alcohol, tobacco, and prescription drug use.

The Drug Abuse Warning Network (DAWN) is a national surveillance system that has been monitoring drug-related emergency room visits since 1972 and is conducted by SAMHSA. In 2003, the number of sites surveyed was increased. Again, it offers the best available data to assess changes in such emergency room admissions over the years.

The text and source notes use the following abbreviations:

AMA   American Medical Association
BJS   Bureau of Justice Statistics
CAMY   Center on Alcohol Marketing and Youth
CASA   National Center on Addiction and Substance Abuse at
             Columbia University
CDC   Centers for Disease Control and Prevention
DASIS   Drug and Alcohol Services Information System
DAWN   Drug Abuse Warning Network
DHHS   U.S. Department of Health and Human Services
NIAAA   National Institute on Alcohol Abuse and Alcoholism
NHSDA   National Household Survey on Drug Abuse
NIDA   National Institute on Drug Abuse
NIH   National Institutes of Health
NSDUH   National Survey of Drug Use and Health
OAS   Office of Applied Studies, SAMHSA
SAMHSA   Substance Abuse and Mental Health Services
             Administration
TEDS   Treatment Episode Data Set
YRBS   Youth Risk Behavior Surveillance System

PROLOGUE

1. Paul Gahlinger, *Illegal drugs: A complete guide to their history, chemistry, use and abuse* (New York: Plume, 2004), viii.

2. OAS, SAMHSA, *Results from the 2004 National Survey of Drug Use and Health: National findings*, DHHS Pub. No. SMA 02–3758 (Rockville, MD: DHHS, 2005).

CHAPTER ONE

1. There are 2.5 million children and 1.5 million adults who take prescribed stimulants for attention deficit–hyperactivity disorder (ADHD)—S. E. Nissen, "ADHD drugs and cardiovascular risk," *New England Journal of Medicine* 354 (2006, 14): 1445–1448. Eight million people use antidepressants—G. Anand, *Approval is near on a new drug for depression*, June 12, 2002, retrieved November 27, 2007, http://global.factiva.com. There are more than fifteen million people

abusing prescription opioids, depressants, and stimulants—CASA, *Under the counter: The diversion and abuse of controlled prescription drugs in the U.S.* (New York: Author, 2005). Sixty-one million people currently smoke cigarettes—OAS, SAMHSA, *Results from the 2005 National Survey of Drug Use and Health: National findings*, DHHS Pub. No. SMA 06-4194 (Rockville, MD: DHHS, 2006). 180 thousand people depend on or abuse inhalants—National Inhalant Prevention Coalition, *Guidelines for medical examiners, coroners and pathologists: Determining inhalant deaths*, citing OAS, *Results from the 2001 National Household Survey on Drug Abuse: Volume 1: Summary of national findings*, retrieved November 21, 2006, http://www.inhalants.org/final_medical.htm. Sixteen to twenty million Americans abuse alcohol or are addicted to it—NIAAA, *Alcoholism: Getting the facts*, 2004, retrieved November 17, 2006, http://pubs.niaaa.nih.gov/publications/GettheFacts_HTML/facts.htm. Over one million children use steroids—CDC, "Youth risk behavior surveillance—United States, 2003," *MMWR Surveillance Summeries* 53 (2004, SS-2). Twenty-five million Americans use marijuana—OAS, SAMHSA, *Results from the 2005 National Survey*. There are 6 million Americans who use cocaine, 1.3 million who use methamphetamine, and 1 million who regularly use Ecstasy and hallucinogens—Ibid. Half a million Americans are heroin users—J. F. Epstein, J. C. Gfroerer, and OAS, *Emerging trends in drug abuse: Heroin abuse in the United States*, March 2, 2006, retrieved November 30, 2006, http://www.oas.samhsa.gov/NHSDA/Treatan/treana11.htm). These numbers are very likely low because almost all of them are based on self-reporting, and researchers have found that individuals tend to underestimate self-reporting of smoking, drinking, and illegal and nonmedical prescription drug use.

2. OAS, SAMHSA, *Results from the 2004 National Survey of Drug Use and Health: National findings*, DHHS Pub. No. SMA 05-4602 (Rockville, MD: DHHS, 2005).

3. CASA Report, *Under the Counter: The Diversion and Abuse of Controlled Prescription Drugs in the U.S.* (New York: 2005), 12.

4. MSNBC, "Antipsychotic drug use among kids soars," May 3, 2006, retrieved November 28, 2006, http://www.msnbc.com.

5. OAS, SAMHSA, *Results from the 2004 National Survey*; CASA, *National survey of American attitudes on substance abuse IX: Teen dating practices and sexual activity* (New York: 2004); CASA, *National survey of American attitudes on substance abuse X: Teens and parents* (New York: 2005); CASA, *National survey of American attitudes on substance abuse XI: Teens and parents* (New York: 2006).

6. OAS, SAMHSA, *National Household Survey on Drug Abuse: Main findings 1992*, DHHS Publication No. SMA 94-3012 (Rockville, MD: DHHS, Public Health Service, 1995); OAS, SAMHSA, *Results from the 2004 National Survey of Drug Use and Health*: OAS, SAMHSA, *Results from the 2005 National*

http://web1.whs.osd.mil/mmid/casualty/GWSUM.pdf; Operation Enduring Freedom (2001–present, as of April 9, 2005), http://web1.whs.osd.mil/mmid/casualty/OEFDEATHS.pdf; Operation Iraqi Freedom (2003–present, as of April 8, 2005), http://web1.whs.osd.mil/mmid/casualty/oif-deaths-total.pdf; U.S. Department of Transportation, *Traffic safety facts 2003: Figure 1: Fatal crashes 1975–2003*, January 2005, retrieved May 6, 2005, http://www-nrd.nhtsa.dot.gov; OAS, *Results from the 2005 National Survey*.

32. Vietnam Conflict (1964–1973), casualty summary as of June 15, 2004, http://web1.whs.osd.mil/mmid/CASUALTY/vietnam.pdf.

33. CDC, *Cigarette smoking-related mortality*, 2005, retrieved June 27, 2005, http://www.cdc.gov/TOBACCO/research_data/health_consequences/mortali.htm; Iraq and Afghanistan, http://icasualties.org/oif.

34. CASA, *Rethinking rites of passage: Substance abuse on America's Campuses* (New York: 1994), 15.

35. CASA, *Wasting the best and the brightest: Substance abuse at America's colleges and universities* (New York: 2007).

36. Survey conducted by CASA under confidentiality agreement.

37. J. D. Grant, J. F. Scherrer, M. T. Lynskey, M. J. Lyons, S. A. Eisen, and M. T. Tsuang, "Adolescent alcohol use is a risk factor for adult alcohol and drug dependence: Evidence from a twin design," *Psychological Medicine* 36 (2006): 109–118; A. Golub and B. D. Johnson, "Variation in youthful risks of progression from alcohol and tobacco to marijuana and to hard drugs across generations," *American Journal of Public Health* 91 (2001): 225–232.

38. OAS, SAMHSA, *Results from the 2004 National Survey*.

39. CAMY, *Overexposed: Youth a target of alcohol advertising in magazines* (Washington, DC: Author, 2002); F. Craig, C. Garfield, P. Chung, and P. Rathouz, "Alcohol advertising in magazines and adolescent readership," *Journal of the American Medical Association* 289 (2003): 2424–2429; CAMY, *Television: Alcohol's vast adland: Executive summary*, 2005, retrieved August 5, 2005, http://camp.org/research.

CHAPTER TWO

1. CDC, *Annual smoking-attributable mortality, years of potential life lost, and economic costs: United States 1995–1999*, retrieved August 17, 2005, http://www.cdc.gov/mmwr/preview/mmwrhtml.

2. P. M. Gahlinger, *Illegal drugs: A complete guide to their history, chemistry, use and abuse* (New York: Plume, 2004).

3. CASA teen surveys.

4. C. McCarthy, *Kicking the habit by reclaiming the sacred*, 2005, retrieved August 17, 2005, http://www.4women.gov/pyph/articles/kicking_habit.html.

5. R. Kluger, *Ashes to ashes* (New York: Knopf, 1996), 9.

6. Schneider Institute for Health Policy and Robert Wood Johnson Foundation, *Substance abuse: The nation's number one health problem* (Princeton, NJ: Robert Wood Johnson Foundation, 2001), 11.

7. J. T. Scharf, *History of Maryland: From the earliest periods to the present day* (Hatboro, PA: Tradition Press, 1967); R. R. Vernellia, *Course outline: Tobacco, health and the law*, 1999, retrieved June 22, 2005, http://academic.udayton.edu/health/syllabi/tobacco.

8. G. Borio, *Tobacco timeline: The eighteenth century: Snuff holds sway*, 2005, retrieved June 9, 2005, http://www.tobacco.org/resources/history.

9. Kluger, 14.

10. Ibid.

11. Ibid., 12–14.

12. R. R. Vernellia, *Course outline*.

13. Ibid., 18.

14. T. M. Matthewson, "Smoke signals: Cigarettes, advertising and the American way of life" at the Valentine Museum, Richmond, Virginia. *Technology and Culture*, 1992:33(3), 560–563.

15. Kluger, 18–19.

16. S. Chapman, "Great expectorations! The decline of public spitting: Lessons for passive smoking?" *British Medical Journal* 311 (1995): 1685–1686; "No spitting in Washington," *New York Times*, May 3, 1903.

17. Kluger, 18–19.

18. Ibid., 63.

19. Ibid., 61.

20. G. Thain and C. Sutton, *Advertising regulation in tobacco prevention and control*, 1998, retrieved June 24, 2005, http://www.tobaccolaw.org/documents.

21. A. M. Brandt, "Recruiting women smokers: The engineering of consent," *Journal of the American Medical Women's Association* 51(1996, 1–2): 63–66.

22. Goode, 197.

23. Museum of Broadcast Communications, *Columbia Broadcasting System*, 2006, retrieved November 14, 2006, http://museum.tv/archives/etv/C/htmlC/columbiabroa.

24. TC Online. (1998). *Tobacco use and the United States military: A long-standing problem (Editorial)*. Retrieved February 8, 2007, http://tc.bmj.com/cgi/content/full/7/3/219.

25. J. Alicoate, *The 1951 Film Daily year book of motion pictures* (New York: Film Daily, 1951). The precise number is 4.394 billion.

26. M. N. Gardner and A. M. Brandt, "The doctor's choice is America's choice: The physician in U.S. cigarette advertisements, 1930–1953," *American Journal of Public Health* 96 (2006,2): 222–232.

27. Tobacco Documents Online, *Pollay advertisements*, 2006, retrieved December 27, 2006, http://tobaccodocuments.org/pollay_ads/Came01.05.html?pattern=113%2C597#images.

28. E. L. Wynder and E. A. Graham, "Tobacco smoking as a possible etiologic factor in bronchiogenic carcinoma: A study of six hundred and eighty-four proven cases," *Journal of the American Medical Association*, 143 (1950, 4): 329–336.

29. CDC, *Achievements in public health, 1900–1999; Tobacco use—United States 1900–1999*, 1999, retrieved August 17, 2005, http://www.cdc.gov/mmwr/preview/mmwrhtml.

30. Schneider Institute, 11.

31. R. H. Carmona, "Prepared remarks: Launch of report of the Surgeon General; The health consequences of smoking," May 27, 2004, retrieved June 22, 2005, http://www.surgeongeneral.gov/news/speeches; Schneider Institute, 11.

32. U.S. Department of Health, Education, and Welfare, Public Health Service, *Smoking and health: Report of the Advisory Committee to the Surgeon General of the Public Health Service* (Washington, DC: Department of Health, Education, and Welfare, 1964).

33. Schneider Institute, 11.

34. *Time*, "The beneficent monster," June 12, 1978, retrieved January 11, 2007, http://www.time.com/time/; A. Fairchild and J. Colgrove, "Out of the ashes: The life, death, and rebirth of the cigarette in the united States," *American Journal of Public Health* 94 (2004, 2): 192–204.

35. U.S. Public Health Service, *Smoking and health: A report of the Surgeon General* (Washington, DC: U.S. Public Health Service, Office of Smoking and Health, 1979).

36. DHHS and Office of Smoking and Health, *The health consequences of smoking: Nicotine addiction: A report of the Surgeon General* (Rockville, MD: DHHS, Public Health Service, 1988).

37. Schneider Institute, 11; American Heart Association, *Tobacco industry's targeting of youth, minorities and women*, 2005, retrieved June 27, 2005, http://www.americanheart.org.

38. S. J. Anderson, S. A. Glantz, and P. M. Ling "Emotions for sale: Cigarette advertising and women's psychological needs," *Tobacco Control* 14 (2005): 127–135.

39. S. Craig and T. Moellinger, "'So rich, mild and fresh': A critical look at TV cigarette commercials: 1948–1971," *Journal of Communication Inquiry* 25 (2001, 1): 55–71.

40. American Heart Association, Tobacco industry's targeting.

41. National Association of African Americans for Positive Imagery, *1990 uptown coalition*, 1990, retrieved June 23, 2005, http://www.naaapi.org/campaigns/1990.asp.

42. American Heart Association, Tobacco industry's targeting.

43. Ibid.

44. J. P. Pierce, W. S. Choi, E. A. Gilpin, A. J. Farkas, and C. C. Berry, "Tobacco industry promotion of cigarettes and adolescent smoking," *Journal of the American Medical Association* 279 (1998, 7): 511–515.

45. U.S. Federal Trade Commission, *In the matter of R. J. Reynolds Company, a corporation, Docket No. 9285: Complaint*, 1997, retrieved November 14, 2006, http://www.ftc.gov/os/1997/05/d9285cmp.htm.

46. P. M. Fischer, M. P. Schwartz, J. W. Richards, A. O. Goldstein, and T. H. Rojas, "Brand logo recognition by children aged 3 to 6 years: Mickey Mouse and Old Joe the Camel," *Journal of the American Medical Association* 266 (1991, 22): 3145–3148.

47. CDC and Tobacco Information and Prevention Source, *Chronology of significant developments related to smoking and health*, February 15, 2006, retrieved November 14, 2006, http://www.cdc.gov/tobacco/overview/chron96.htm.

48. Ibid.

49. OAS, SAMHSA, *Results from the 2004 National Survey of Drug Use and Health: National findings*, DHHS Pub. No. SMA 02-3758 (Rockville, MD: DHHS, 2005).

50. Campaign for Tobacco-Free Kids, *Smoking and kids: Fact sheet*, August 9, 2005, retrieved November 16, 2006, http://tobaccofreekids.org.

51. R. Beyer, *The greatest stories never told: 100 tales from history to astonish, bewilder and stupefy* (New York: HarperCollins, 2003).

52. Fraunces Tavern, *The birth of a landmark*, 2005, retrieved August 22, 2005, http://www.frauncestavern.com.

53. Ibid.

54. E. Burns, *The spirits of America: A social history of alcohol* (Philadelphia: Temple University Press, 2004), 14.

55. A. Barr, *Drink: A social history of America* (New York: Carroll & Graf, 1999), 256.

56. G. Edwards, *Alcohol: The world's favorite drug* (New York: St. Martin's Press, 2000), 74; NIAAA and Division of Epidemiology and Prevention Research, *U.S. apparent per capita ethanol consumption for the United States: 1850–2002*, 2005, retrieved June 29, 2005, http://www.niaaa.nih.gov/databases.

57. Edwards, 75.

58. Barr, 149.

59. Edwards, 76–77.

60. Ibid., 79.

61. Burns, 82–86, 115.

62. Ibid., 148–151.

63. Barr, 329.

64. M. E. Lender and J. M. Martin, *Drinking in America* (New York: Free Press, 1987), 108; Barr, 147.

65. Barr, 335.

66. Houghton Mifflin College Division, *Reader's companion to U.S. women's history: Prohibition and temperance*, 2005, retrieved July 29, 2005, http://college.hmco.com/history.

67. Lender and Martin, 196–197.

68. Odessa Pictures, *A round for the house: The history of drinking in America*, 2004, retrieved January 31, 2005, http://www.odessapictures.com.

69. Houghton Mifflin College Division, *Reader's companion to American history: Volstead Act*, 2005, retrieved July 26, 2005, http://college.hmco.com/history.

70. Lender and Martin, 173; Edwards, 105, 110; AMA, *Chronology of AMA history: 1941 to 1960*, 2005, retrieved August 25, 2005, http://www.ama-assn.org/ama/pub/category/1926.html.

71. Lender and Martin, 170.

72. AMA, *Chronology*; AMA, *Minimum legal drinking age: Brief history of the minimum legal drinking age*, 2005, retrieved August 25, 2005, http://www.ama-assn.org/ama/pub/category; Twenty-sixth Amendment to the U.S. Constitution, 2005, retrieved August 29, 2005, http://www.nps.gov/malu/documents/amend26.htm; see also M. A. Males, *The scapegoat generation: America's war on adolescents* (Monroe, ME: Common Courage Press, 1996), 194.

73. J. A. Califano, *The 1982 report on drug abuse and alcoholism* (New York: Warner Books, 1982), 156.

74. Ibid., 155–156.

75. Barr, 261.

76. National Highway Traffic Safety Administration, *Fact sheet: Minimum drinking age laws*, 2006, retrieved December 4, 2006, http://www.nhtsa.dot.gov/people/injury/alcohol/Community%20Guides%20HTML/PDFs/Public_App7.pdf.

77. CASA, *The commercial value of underage and pathological drinking to the alcohol industry* (New York: 2006); S. E. Foster, R. D. Vaughan, W. H. Foster, and J. A. Califano, "Alcohol consumption and expenditures for underage drinking and adult excessive drinking," *Journal of the American Medical Association* 289 (8): 989–995; OAS, SAMHSA, *Results from the 2001 national household survey on drug abuse: Volume 1: summary of national findings*, NHSDA Series H-17, DHHS Publication No. SMA 02-3758 (Rockville, MD: DHHS, SAMHSA, OAS, 2002).

78. National Council on Alcoholism and Drug Dependence, *Facts and information: Alcoholism and drug dependence are America's number one health problem*, June 2002, retrieved December 7, 2006, http://www.ncadd.org/facts/numberoneprob.html; CASA, *Teen Tipplers: America's underage drinking epidemic* (New York: Author, 2003); National Council on Alcoholism and Drug Dependence, *Facts and information: Alcoholism and alcohol-related problems*, 2006, retrieved December 7, 2006, http://www.ncadd.org/facts/problems.html.

79. U.S. Information Agency electronic journal, *Drug use: A concern for over a century: Illicit drugs in the United States*, 1997, retrieved November 15, 2006, http://usinfo.state.gov/journals.

80. E. M. Brecher and Editors of *Consumer Reports*, *Chapter 2: The Consumers Union Report on licit and illicit drugs: Opiates for pain relief, for tranquilizers,*

and for pleasure, 1972, retrieved November 20, 2006, http://www.druglibrary
.org/schaffer/library/studies/cu/cu2.html; S. R. Kandall, "Women and addiction
in the United States—1850–1920, in C. L. Wetherington and A. B. Roman
(Eds.), *Drug addiction research and the health of women*, 33–52 (Rockville, MD:
DHHS, NIH, NIDA, 1998).

81. Merriam-Webster, *The American Heritage Dictionary of the English Language*, 2006, retreived August 10, 2005, http://dictionary.reference.com/
search?q=morphism.

82. R. Askwith, *How aspirin turned hero*, 1998, retrieved August 10, 2005,
http://opiods.com/heroin/heroininhistory.html.

83. CASA, *Women under the influence* (Baltimore: Johns Hopkins University Press, 2006), 74.

84. Gahlinger, 39; University of Buffalo, Addiction Research Unit, *Before
prohibition: Images from the prohibition era when many psychotropic substances
were legally available in America and Europe*, 2005, retrieved August 29, 2005,
http://wings.buffalo.edu/aru/preprohibition.htm.

85. J. Jonnes, *Hep-cats, narcs, and pipe dreams: A history of America's romance
with illegal drugs* (New York: Scribner, 1996), 20.

86. Freud, S. (2007). *Freudian slips: Cocaine 1884: From "Über Coca,"* Centralblatt für die ges. Therapie, 2, pp. 289–314, 1884 V. The Effect of coca on the
healthy human body. Retrieved February 9, 2007, http://www.heretical.com/
freudian/coca1884.html.

87. Gahlinger, 39.

88. D. Clark, *Substance use and misuse: Some historical perspectives*, 2003, retrieved November 5, 2004, http://www.dcresearch.net; M. R. Aldrich, "Historical notes on women addicts," *Journal of Psychoactive Drugs* 26 (2006, 1):
61–64; M. Sandmaier, *The invisible alcoholics: Women and alcohol* (Bradenton,
FL: Human Services Institute TAB Books, 1992); Kandall.

89. Jonnes, 21–25; C. Whitebread, *The history of the non-medical use of drugs
in the United States*, 1995, retrieved August 29, 2005, http://druglibrary.org/
schaffer/History/whiteb1.htm.

90. Gahlinger, 27, 58.

91. Brecher, et al.

92. U.S. Government Office of Technology Assessment, *Appendix A: Drug
control policy in the United States: Historical perspectives*, 2006, retrieved November 15, 2006, http://www.drugtext.org/library/reports/ota/appa.htm.

93. Congressional Research Service of the Library of Congress, *Drug use: A
U.S. concern for over a century*, 1997, retrieved August 11, 2005, http://
usinfo.state.gov/journals/itgic; Gahlinger, 36.

94. Gahlinger, 48.

95. R. G. Kaiser, "CIA says it has new details of its drug tests on humans,"
Washington Post, July 16, 1977, A3; J. Wolf, "Problem reopened in death
of man in CIA drug test," *Chicago Sun-Times*, June 3, 1994, 31; G. Tasker,

"Inquiry into CIA researcher's '53 death inconclusive," *Baltimore Sun*, November 29, 1994, 1B.

96. B. Kennedy, *The tranquilizing of America: How mood-altering prescription drugs changed the cultural landscape*, 1999, retrieved August 16, 2006, http://www.cnn.com/SPECIALS/1999/century/episodes/06/currents/.

97. F. Engstrom, "Psychotropic drugs: Modern medicine's alternative to purgatives, straightjackets, and asylums," *Postgraduate Medicine* 101 (1997, 3): 198–200; J. M. Metzl and J. Angel, "Assessing the impact of SSRI antidepressants on popular notion of women's depressive illness," *Social Science and Medicine* 58 (2004, 3): 577–584.

98. Brecher et al.

99. J. O. Cole, L. A. Bolling, and B. J. Peake, "Stimulant drugs—Medical needs, alternative indications and related problems," in J. R. Cooper, D. J. Czechowicz, S. P. Molinari, and R. C. Petersen (Eds.), *Impact of prescription drug diversion control systems on medical practice and patient care: NIDA research monograph 131* (Rockville, MD: DHHS, Public Health Service, NIH, NIDA, 1993), 89–108.

100. Ibid.

101. CASA, Women under the influence, 79.

102. Ibid.

103. Gahlinger, 53; University of Virginia Library, *The psychedelic '60s*, 2004, retrieved August 17, 2005, http://www.lib.virginia.edu/small/exhibits/sixties/.

104. OAS, *Substance use among women in the United States*, DHHS Pub. No. SMA 97-3162 (Rockville, MD: DHHS, SAMHSA, 1997); Gahlinger, 37.

105. Gahlinger, 64.

106. S. Peele, "Running scared: We're too frightened to deal with the real issues in adolescent substance abuse," *Health Education Review* 2 (1987): 423–432; L. D. Harrison, M. Backenheimer, and J. A. Inciardi, *The nature and extent of marijuana use in the United States*, October 3, 2006, retrieved December 8, 2006, http://www.cedro-uva.org/lib/harrison.cannabis.03.html; DHHS and NIH, *National Institute on Drug Abuse research report series 7: Marijuana abuse* (Washington, DC: 2005); E. M. Brecher and Editors of *Consumer Reports*, *Chapter 52: The Consumers Union Report on licit and illicit drugs: LSD today: The search for a rational perspective*, 1972, retrieved November 20, 2006, http://www.druglibrary.org/schaffer/library/studies/cu/cu52.html; S. R. Kandall, *Women and addiction in the United States: 1920 to the present*, 2006, retrieved December 8, 2006, http://www.nida.nih.gov/PDF/DARHW/053-080_Kandall2.pdf.

107. Join Together, "Alaska supreme court upholds marijuana use at home," September 20, 2004, retrieved November 20, 2006, http://www.jointogether.org.

108. Kennedy.

109. Johnston, L. D., Bachman, J. G., & O'Malley, P. M. (1980). *Highlights from student drug use in America, 1975-1980*. (DHHS Publication No. [ADM] 81-1066). Rockville, MD: National Institute on Drug Abuse.

110. Gahlinger, 242.

111. Ibid., 245.

112. S. Jenkins, "'A dream within a dream': Celtics pick Bias," *Washington Post*, June 18, 1986, D1, D5; B. Brubaker, "Bias: Much pressure, little relief," *Washington Post*, June 22, 1986, B1, B15.

113. N. Reagan, "The need for intolerance," *Washington Post*, July 7, 1986, A1.

114. Schneider Institute, 8.

115. CASA, *Under the counter: The diversion and abuse of controlled prescription drugs in the U.S.* (New York: 2005), 16.

116. Ibid., 21.

117. Ibid., 3.

118. International Narcotics Control Board, *Narcotic drugs: Estimated world requirements for 2004: Statistics for 2002* (New York: United Nations, 2004).

CHAPTER 3

1. Lyndon Johnson, *Special message to the Congress on crime in America*, February 6, 1967, retrieved November 30, 2006, http://www.presidency.ucsb.edu/ws/index.php?pid=28394.

2. In passing, on page 268 of J. A. Califano, *The 1982 report on drug abuse and alcoholism* (New York: Warner Books, 1982).

3. Drug Abuse Warning Network, *The DAWN report: Highlights from DAWN: New York City, 2002* (Rockville, MD: U.S. Department of Health and Human Services, 2006).

4. OAS, SAMHSA, *Drug abuse warning network, 2004: National estimates of drug-related emergency department visits: DAWN series D–28*, 2006, retrieved November 18, 2006, http://DAWNinfo.samhsa.gov. OAS, SAMHSA, Results from the 2005 National Survey.

5. D. M. Ewalt, *Special report: America's drunkest cities*, August 22, 2006, retrieved November 24, 2006, http://www.forbes.com/2006/08/22.

6. Center for Substance Abuse Research, "Methamphetamine treatment admissions rates higher than those of cocaine and/or heroin in western states," *Cesar/Fax* 14 (2005, 12): 1.

7. Ibid.

8. P. Belluck, "Methadone, once the way out, suddenly grows as a killer drug," *New York Times*, February 9, 2003, retrieved November 24, 2006, http://query.nytimes.com/gst.

9. CASA, *Under the counter: The diversion and abuse of controlled prescription drugs in the U.S.* (New York: 2005), 32.

10. OAS, SAMHSA, *NSDUH report: Substance use among older adults: 2002 and 2003 update*, April 22, 2005, retrieved November 16, 2006, http://www.oas.samhsa.gov/2k5/olderadults/olderadults.htm.

11. D. B. Kandel, K. Yamaguchi, K. Chen, "Stages of progression in drug involvement from adolescence to adulthood: Further evidence for the gateway theory," *Journal of Studies on Alcohol* 53 (1992, 5): 447–457.

12. OAS, SAMHSA, Results from the 2001 National Survey.

13. CASA and American Legacy Foundation, *Report on teen cigarette smoking and marijuana use* (New York: 2003), 3.

14. Ibid., 4.

15. CASA, *Cigarettes, alcohol, marijuana*. See also articles by D. B. Kandel cited in the CASA report.

16. CASA, *Cigarettes, alcohol, marijuana*, 42, 3, 9.

17. Ibid., 21.

18. CASA, *Teen tipplers*, 19.

19. CASA, *Cigarettes, alcohol, marijuana*, 22.

20. Ibid., 33.

21. Ibid.

22. CASA, *Non-medical marijuana: Rite of passage or Russian roulette?* (New York: 1999), 22–23; CASA, *Substance Abuse and the American Adolescent: A Report by the Commission on Substance Abuse Among American Adolescents.* (New York: 1997), 13.

23. CASA, *Cigarettes, alcohol, marijuana*, 17.

24. DHHS, *Smoking and health: Report of the Advisory Committee to the Surgeon General of the Public Health Service.* (Washington, DC: Author, 1964); *Time*, The government report, January 17, 1964, retrieved November 30, 2006, http://www.time.com/time/magazine.

25. CASA, *Non-medical marijuana II: Rite of passage or Russian roulette? A CASA white paper* (New York: 2004), 3.

26. I. J. Selikoff, E. C. Hammond, and H. Seidman, "Mortality experience of insulation workers in the United States and Canada, 1943–1976," *Annals of the New York Academy of Science* 330 (1979): 91–116.

27. N. Swan, *NIDA notes: Brain scans open window to view cocaine's effects on the brain*, July 1998, retrieved December 13, 2006, http://www.nida.nih.gov/NIDA_NNotes/NNVol13N2/Brain.html.

28. G. Di Chiara, "The role of dopamine in drug abuse viewed from the perspective of its role in motivation," *Drug and Alcohol Dependence* 38 (1995): 95–137.

29. C. L. Walters, J. N. Cleck, Y. Kuo, and J. A. Blendy, "µ-Opioid Receptor and CREB activation are required for nicotine reward," *Neuron* 46 (2005, 6): 933–943.

30. *Medical News Today*, "Strength of cocaine cravings linked to brain response," March 17, 2006, retrieved December 13, 2006, http://www.medical newstoday.com; D. I. Lubman, M. Yücel, and C. Pantelis, "Addiction, a condition of compulsive behaviour? Neuroimaging and neuropsychological evidence of inhibitory dysregulation," *Addiction* 99 (2004): 1491–1502.

31. R. Mathias, *Pathological obesity and drug addiction share common brain characteristics*, October 2001, retrieved December 4, 2006, http://www.nida.nih.gov/NIDA_Notes/NNVol16N4/pathological.html.

32. CASA, *Under the counter*, 3.

33. Ibid., 4.

34. OAS, *The DAWN report: Highlights from DAWN: Los Angeles, 2002* (Rockville, MD: DHHS, 2004); Drug Abuse Warning Network, *The DAWN report: Amphetamine and methamphetamine emergency department visits, 1995–2002* (Rockville, MD: DHHS, 2004).

35. *The DAWN report: Amphetamine and methamphetamine emergency department visits, 1995–2002* (Rockville, MD: DHHS, 2004).

36. DHHS and SAMHSA, *Fact sheet: Alcohol use in adolescents is associated with psychological distress and depression*, August 2002, retrieved November 30, 2006, http://alcoholfreechildren.org; G. Chang, L. Sherritt, and J. R. Knight, "Adolescent cigarette smoking and mental health symptoms," *Journal of Adolescent Health* 26 (2005): 517–522.

CHAPTER 4

1. CASA, *1995 CASA National Survey of American Attitudes on Substance Abuse I* (New York: 1995); CASA, *1996 CASA National Survey of American Attitudes on Substance Abuse II: Teens and Their Parents* (New York: 1996); CASA, *1997 CASA National Survey of American Attitudes on Substance Abuse III: Teens, Their Parents, Teachers and Principals* (New York: 1997); CASA, *1998 CASA National Survey of American Attitudes on Substance Abuse IV: Teens, Teachers and Principals* (New York: 1998); CASA, *1999 CASA National Survey of American Attitudes on Substance Abuse V: Teens and Their Parents* (New York: 1999); CASA, *2001 CASA National Survey of American Attitudes on Substance Abuse VI: Teens* (New York: 2001); CASA, *2002 CASA National Survey of American Attitudes on Substance Abuse VII: Teens, Parents and Siblings* (New York: 2002); CASA, *2003 CASA National Survey of American Attitudes on Substance Abuse VIII: Teens and Parents* (New York: 2003); CASA, *2004 CASA National Survey of American Attitudes on Substance Abuse IX: Teen Dating Practices and Sexual Activity* (New York: 2004); CASA, *National Survey of American Attitudes on Substance Abuse X: Teens and Parents* (New York: 2005); CASA, *National Survey of American Attitudes on Substance Abuse XI: Teens and Parents* (New York: 2006).

2. N. D. Volkow, *Exploring the why's of adolescent drug abuse*, September 2004, retrieved November 21, 2006, http://www.nida.nih.gov/NIDA_notes.

3. OAS, SAMHSA, *Results from the 2003 National Survey of Drug Use and Health: National findings*, DHHS Pub. No. SMA 02–3758 (Rockville, MD: DHHS, 2004); U.S. Public Health Service and Office of the Surgeon General,

Youth and tobacco: Tobacco use among young people: A report of the Surgeon General (Washington, DC: U.S. Public Health Service, Office of Smoking and Health, 1995).

4. CASA, *Teen tipplers: America's underage drinking epidemic* (New York: 2003), 4.

5. OAS, SAMHSA, *Age of first use among admissions for drugs: 1993 and 2003*, 2006, Retrieved December 5, 2006, http://www.oas.samhsa.gov.

6. In 1992, the rate of past month's use among youth was 5.3 percent. OAS, SAMHSA, *National Household Survey on Drug Abuse: Main findings 1992*, DHHS Pub. No. SMA 94-3012 (Rockville, MD: DHHS, Public Health Service, 1995). Applied to the census, the number was 1.1 million. U.S. Census Bureau. (2007). *U.S. population estimates by age, sex, race, and Hispanic origin: 1980 to 1999.* Retrieved February 1, 2007, http://www.census.gov/popest/archives/1990s/nat-detail-layout.txt. In 2005, the rate of current drug use among youth was 9.9 percent. OAS, SAMHSA, *Results from the 2005 National Survey of Drug Use and Health: National findings*, DHHS Pub. No. SMA 06-4194 (Rockville, MD: DHHS, 2006). Applied to the Census, that number is approximately 2.6 million youth. U.S. Census Bureau, & Bureau of Labor Statistics. (2006). *Current Population Survey (CPS): December 2005.* Retrieved February 1, 2007, http://www.census.gov/cps/.

7. CASA, *Under the counter: The diversion and abuse of controlled prescription drugs in the U.S.* (New York: 2005), 4.

8. CASA, *Women under the influence*, 81–82.

9. OAS, SAMHSA, *Results from the 2005 National Survey.*

10. DHHS and NIAAA, *Make a difference: Talk to your child about alcohol*, 2006, retrieved December 7, 2006, http://pubs.niaaa.nih.gov/publications/MakeADiff_html.

11. CASA, *Wasting the best and the brightest: Substance abuse at America's colleges and universities* (New York: 2007).

12. CAMY, *Drinking and risky sexual behavior* (Washington, DC: 2003); Henry J. Kaiser Foundation, *Substance use and risky sexual behavior: Attitudes and practices among adolescents and young adults*, February 2002, retrieved December 12, 2006, http://www.kff.org; L. Remez, "Adolescent drug users more likely to become pregnant, elect abortion," *Family Planning Perspectives* 24 (1992, 6): 281–282.

13. R. J. Bonnie, M. E. O'Connell, and Committee on Developing a Strategy to Reduce and Prevent Underage Drinking (Eds.), *Reducing underage drinking: A collective responsibility* (Washington, DC: Board on Children, Youth and Families, Division of Behavioral and Social Sciences and Education, Research Council and Institute of Medicine, 2004).

14. J. Tressler, "Teen driver pleads guilty in death," *Sun News*, November 14, 2006, retrieved November 20, 2006, http://www.myrtlebeachonline.com.

15. D. Kavanaugh, "Girls gets 2 years in fatal shooting," *Albuquerque Journal*, July 6, 2005, retrieved November 30, 2006, http://www.abqjournal.com/north/369367north_news07-06-05.htm.

16. *Star Tribune*, "Wrongful-death suit over fraternity drinking is settled," November 18, 2006. retrieved November 20, 2006, http://www.startribune.com/462/story/821618.html.

17. CASA, *National Survey X, CASA National Survey XI*.

18. CASA, *"You've got drugs!": Prescription drug pushers on the internet: A CASA white paper* (New York: 2004), 4, 6.

19. E. W. Boyer, M. Shannon, and P. L. Hibberd, (2006). "The internet and psychoactive substance use among innovative drug users," *Pediatrics* 115 (2006): 302–305.

20. CASA, *National Survey XI*.

21. CASA, *National Survey X*.

22. CASA, *National Survey XI*.

23. CASA, *National Survey V*.

24. CASA, *1999 CASA National Survey*.

25. "Who's who say what's hot," retrieved March 2, 2006, www.groupmag.com.

26. CASA, *National Survey X; CASA, National Survey XI*.

27. R. Sherer "FDA Panel: No Black Box Warning for ADHD Drugs," *Psychiatric Times*, Vol XXIII, No. 6 (May 2006).

28. D. Costello, "Their drugs of choice; teens turn to Vicodin, Ritalin and other easily obtained prescription pills," *Los Angeles Times*, February 7, 2005, F1.

29. J. Sterba, "ADD drug Adderall finds black market on school campuses," *Arizona Daily Star*, November 17, 2004, A1.

30. SAMHSA, *Prevention alert: Trouble in the medicine chest: RX drug abuse growing*, March 7, 2003, retrieved November 30, 2006, http://ncadi.samhsa.gov/govpubs.

31. Costello.

32. CASA. *National Survey XI*.

33. CASA, *1997 CASA National Survey*.

34. R. Russell, personal communication, March 15, 2006.

35. K. V. Finn and H. J. Willert, "Alcohol and drugs in schools: Teachers' reactions to the problem," *Phi Delta Kappan* 88 (2006, 1): 37–40.

36. Ibid.

37. K. Schnackel, "Do something now about drug-infected schools: Editorial," *Post Standard/Herald-Journal*, April 7, 2006, A17.

38. S. T. Ennett, N. S. Tobler, C. L. Ringwalt, and R. L. Flewelling, "How effective is drug abuse resistance education? A meta-analysis of Project DARE outcome evaluations," *American Journal of Public Health* 84 (1994, 9): 1394–1401; D. R. Lynam, R. Milich, R. Zimmermann, S. P. Novak, T. K. Logan, C. Martin, C. Leukefeld, and R. Clayton, "Project DARE: No effects at

10-year follow-up," *Journal of Consulting and Clinical Psychology* 67 (1999, 4): 590–593.

39. M. Jameson, "Anti-drug overdose? Many school prevention programs don't help, scientists say, and may even do harm," *Los Angeles Times*, May 15, 2006, retrieved November 28, 2006, http://www.latimes.com/features/health; S. L. West and K. K. O'Neal, "Project D.A.R.E. outcome effectiveness revisited," *American Journal of Public Health* 94 (2004, 6): 1027–1029.

40. K. Zernike, "Antidrug program says it will adopt a new strategy," *New York Times*, 2001, retrieved November 17, 2006, http://www.nytimes.com/2001/02/15/national/15DARE.html.

41. E. M. Shepard, *The economic costs of D.A.R.E.* (Syracuse, NY: Le Moyne College Institute of Industrial Relations, 2001).

42. National Center for Education Statistics, *Violence and discipline problems in U.S. public schools: 1996–97*, 1998, retrieved August 10, 2000, http://nces.ed.gov.

43. Student Drug Testing Coalition, *Student drug testing information*, 2006, retrieved December 11, 2006, http://www.studentdrugtesting.org/.

44. Jameson.

45. A. Mann, *Relationships matter: Impact of parental, peer factors on teen, young adult substance abuse*, 2003, retrieved November 21, 2006, http://www.nida.nih.gov/NIDA_Notes/NNVol18N2/Relationships.html.

46. S. Inskeep, *Accepting the reality of drug addiction*, NPR interview, June 6, 2006, retrieved June 12, 2006, http://www.lexis-nexis.com.

47. CASA, *National Survey X*.

48. Ibid.

49. Ibid.

50. J. Connic, *Study finds Westport girls more likely to abuse substances*, May 19, 2006, retrieved November 15, 2006, http://www.westportnow.com.

51. CASA, *Teen tipplers*, 5.

52. CASA, *National Survey XI*.

53. CASA, *National Survey X*.

54. Ibid.

55. A. Beam, "Midlands teens say alcohol easily obtained: They say drinking common at parties, even when parents are present," *The State*, Columbia, SC, August 24, 2006, A6.

56. F. Santos, "Keeping tabs on teenage drinking: New measures seek to hold adults accountable for what happens at home," *New York Times*, July 2, 2006, retrieved November 29, 2006, http://select.nytimes.com/search.

57. B. Hughes, "Couple gets plea deal in teen drinking party," *Journal News* (Westchester County, NY), November 3, 2006, retrieved November 17, 2006, http://www.thejournalnews.com.

58. J. Nesbitt, "Underage drinking starts close to home," *Charlotte Observer*, August 9, 2005, retrieved November 17, 2006, http://www.charlotte.com.

59. S. K. Wickham, "Drinking-party mom speaks up," *Union Leader* (Manchester, NM), March 19, 2006, retrieved March 30, 2006, http://web.lexis-nexis.com.

60. *Newsday*, "Adults on the hook: New Long Beach law is a step in the right direction on underage drinking," August 23, 2006, retrieved August 23, 2006, http://www.newsday.com/news/opinion.

61. L. Brody and J. Petrick, "Parents get probation in teen party case," the *Bergen County Record*, August 11, 2006, retrieved August 17, 2006, http://web.lexis-nexis.com.

62. J. Chenevey, "Women warned about wild spring breaks," December 19, 2006, retrieved December 19, 2006, http://www.cbsnews.com/; AMA, *Sex and intoxication among women more common on spring break according to AMA poll*, March 8, 2006, retrieved December 19, 2006, http://www.ama-assn.org/ama/pub/category/16083.html.

63. Associated Press, "In Aruba, suspect's dad, 2nd man ordered freed," *Philadelphia Daily News*, June 27, 2005, 9; R. Subramanian, "Eschew alcohol to set example for teens," *El Paso Times*, June 23, 2006, 5B; K. St. John and H. K. Lee, "Berkeley: student death tied to drinking: Police say friends' contest to consume alcohol proved fatal," *San Francisco Chronicle*, March 30, 2004, B1; "Timely warning: Spring break alarm on 'gone wild' behavior applies to both sexes," *The News Journal*, March 13, 2006, 4A.

64. CASA, *Rethinking rites of passage: Substance abuse on America's campuses* (New York: 1994), 17.

65. A. M. White, C. L. Kraus, and H. S. Schwartzwelder, "Many college freshman drink at levels far beyond the binge threshold," *Alcoholism Clinical and Experimental Research* 30 (22006, 6): 1006–1010.

66. Associated Press, "Yale to limit drinking, tailgating for Harvard game," October 27, 2005, retrieved November 20, 2006, http://sports.espn.go.com/ncf/news/story?id=2205570.

67. Ibid.

68. R. Rivera, "Reining in academy drinking: Shore patrol tries to curb midshipmen's off-campus alcohol excesses," *Washington Post*, April 25, 2006, retrieved April 25, 2006, http://www.washingtonpost.com.

69. *MSNBC.com*, "College's staff tries to curb "penny pints" binges," April 24, 2006, retrieved April 24, 2006, http://www.msnbc.com/id/12454355.

70. H. Wechsler, J. E. Lee, M. Kuo, M. Seibring, T. F. Nelson, and H. Lee, "Trends in college binge drinking during a period of increased prevention efforts," *Journal of American College Health* 50 (2002, 5): 203–217.

71. CASA, *Women under the influence* (Baltimore: Johns Hopkins University Press, 2006); E. Emery, G. P. Ritter-Richardson, A. L. Strozier, and R. J. McDermott, "Using focus group interviews to identify salient issues concerning college students' alcohol abuse," *Journal of American College Health* 41 (1993, 5): 195–198.

72. CASA, *Wasting the best and the brightest*.

73. "Arrests for alcohol rise on campuses," *Chronicle of Higher Education* 53 (2006, 10): 40.

74. CASA, *Wasting the best and the brightest.*

75. J. Garreau, "A dose of genius: "Smart pills" are on the rise: But is taking them wise?" *Washington Post,* June 11, 2006, retrieved June 12, 2006, http://www.washingtonpost.com.

76. Spin.com, *Everybody's talking about . . . "brain steroid" for scholars on the rise,* June 14, 2006, retrieved November 20, 2006, http://www.spin.com/features.

77. Garreau.

78. R. Davis and A. DeBarros, "Alcohol and fire a deadly mix; Fatalities especially high in off-campus housing," *USA Today,* August 30, 2006, retrieved August 31, 2006, http://www.usatoday.com.

79. *Denver Channel,* "Chapter's charter revoked after alcohol violations," September 9, 2006, retrieved November 20, 2006, http://www.thedenver channel.com/print; *South End Newspaper,* "Hazing to close sorority at University of Michigan," April 7, 2005, retrieved November 20, 2006, http://www.southend.wayne.edu/modules/news; *San Francisco Gate,* "Fla. fraternity shut after hazing claims," November 9, 2006, retrieved November 20, 2006, http://sfgate.com/cgi-bin/article.cgi?.

80. T. Lewin, "Does it work? Substance-free dorms: Clean living on campus," Education Life Supplement, *New York Times,* November 6, 2005, 4A; State University of New York College at Brockport, *Counseling center: Substance abuse counseling,* November 20, 2006, retrieved November 20, 2006, http://www.brockport.edu/cc/substance.html; Cornell College, *Counseling center: Substance use and abuse issues,* November 20, 2006, retrieved November 20, 2006, http://cornellcollege.edu/counseling/suba.shtml.

81. D. P. Nixon, "Georgetown mandates alcohol education," *The Hoya,* September 18, 2006, retrieved September 20, 2006, http://web.lexis-nexis.com; M. Abramson, "New college students' first course is on alcohol," *Contra Costa Times,* September 26, 2006, retrieved September 27, 2006, http://www.contra coststimes.com.

82. A. Jones, "UGA today opens center to fight alcohol," *The Atlanta Journal-Constitution,* October 6, 2006, retrieved October 6, 2006, http://w3.nexis.com/new/delivery.

83. *CNN.com,* "'Recovery dorms' offer student support: Dedicated housing helps ease temptations,"* January 18, 2005, retrieved November 21, 2006, http://www.uh.edu/ednews/2005/cnn.

84. J. Cummins, "University of Oklahoma to ban alcohol: Recent death leads to "dry" campus," *MSNBC.com,* December 14, 2004, retrieved November 20, 2006, http://www.msnbc.msn.com/id/6712195; M. Belt, "Officers crack down on underage drinking," *Lawrence Journal-World,* May 28, 2004, retrieved November 20, 2006, http://www2.ljworld.com/news/2004.

85. R. Traister, "The rise and fall of Kate Moss," *Ottawa Citizen*, October 16, 2005, C6.

86. A. O. Goldstein, R. A. Sobel, and G. R. Newman, "Tobacco and alcohol use in G-Rated children's animated films," *Journal of the American Medical Association* 281 (1999, 12): 1131–1136.

87. CASA, *Teen tipplers*, 5.

88. MSNBC.com, "Turner to ax smoking scenes from cartoons," August 21, 2006, retrieved August 21, 2006, http://www.msnbc.com/id/14452732.

89. American Legacy Foundation, *Exposure to pro-tobacco advertising and marketing by America's youth continues despite sweeping restrictions implemented five years ago*, December 11, 2003, retrieved November 21, 2006, http://www .americanlegacy.org/402.html.

90. American Legacy Foundation, *Youth exposure to smoking in movies* (Washington, DC: Author, 2004).

91. J. D. Sargent, M. L. Beach, A. M. Adachi-Mejia, J. J. Gibson, L. T. Titus-Ernstoff, C. P. Carusi, et al., "Exposure to movie smoking: Its relation to smoking initiation among US adolescents," *Pediatrics* 116 (2005, 5): 1183–1191.

92. CASA. *National Survey X*.

93. T. Howard, "More prime time shows go for a drink," *USA Today*, October 9, 2006, 1B.

94. M. C. Bonneville, K. Kozar, C. Hussey, and K. Patrick, *Factors influencing children as they consider role models*, 2006, retrieved November 30, 2006, http://www.ccfi.educ.ubc.ca/publications/insights/v10n01/articles/gender .html; T. L. Ziemer, "Study says kids emulate athletes: What kids learn from famous athletes on and off the field," *ABC News*, October 13, 2000, retrieved November 20, 2006, http://abcnews.go.com/Sports; Henry J. Kaiser Foundation, *A national survey of kids (and their parents) about famous athletes as role models: Summary of findings*, 2000, retrieved December 20, 2006, http:// www.kff.org/.

95. L. D. Johnston, P. M. O'Malley, J. G. Bachman, and J. E. Schulenberg, *Monitoring the Future national results on adolescent drug use: Overview of key findings, 2005*, NIH Publication No. 06-5882 (Bethesda, MD: NIDA, 2006); CDC, *Trends in the prevalence of marijuana, cocaine, and other illegal drugs*, 2005, retrieved December 27, 2006, http://www.cdc.gov/healthyyouth/yrbs/pdf/ trends/2005_YRBS_Drug-Use.pdf.

96. CASA, *Under the counter*, 4.

97. Ibid, 6.

98. Ibid, 4.

99. H. Araton, "Bonds will beat out Aaron, but he'll never beat the rap," *New York Times*, May 30, 2006, D1.

100. M. Fainaru-Wada and L. Williams, *Game of shadows* (New York: Gotham Books, 2006).

101. *Modern Brewery Age*, "Anheuser-Busch Inc. acquires four Sea World theme parks," October 9, 1989, retrieved November 17, 2006, http://www.find articles.com/p/articles.

102. S. Wieberg, "Colorado treads carefully in relationship with Coors," *USA Today*, November 16, 2005, retrieved May 1, 2006, http://www.usatoday.com.

103. S. L. Myers, "Mayor fights ad at Shea on tobacco," *New York Times*, February 4, 1994, B3.

104. *Marin Institute*, "Watchdogs stop Coors' co-promotion with "Scary Movie 4": Beer maker exposed for marketing to youth in PG–13 movies," May 1, 2006, retrieved May 3, 2006, http://www.nexis.com/research/pnews.

105. J. B. Arndofer, "The death of beer," *Advertising Age* 76 (2005, 18): 1–2.

106. NIAAA, *National Advisory Council on Alcohol Abuse and Alcoholism Summary of meeting: February 2–3, 2005*, February 2005, retrieved December 5, 2006, http://www.niaaa.nih.gov/.

107. R. L. Collins, T. Schell, P. L. Ellickson, and D. McCaffrey, "Predictors of beer advertising awareness among eighth graders," *Addiction* 98 (2003, 9): 1297–1306; S. E. Martin, L. B. Snyder, M. Hamilton, F. Fleming-Milici, M. D. Slater, A. Stacy, et al., "Alcohol advertising and youth," *Alcoholism Clinical and Experimental Research* 26 (2002, 6): 900–906.

108. J. W. Grube and L. Wallack, "Television beer advertising and drinking knowledge, beliefs, and intentions among schoolchildren," *American Journal of Public Health* 84 (1994, 2): 254–259.

109. R. Beachamp, *The bull terrier*, November 17, 2006, retrieved November 17, 2006, http://www.petpublishing.com/dogken/breeds/bullterr.shtml.

110. K. Raugust, *Animation World* "Bud-weis-er: Computer-generated frogs and lizards give Bud a boost," 1998, retrieved December 5, 2006, http://www.awn.com/mag/issue3.7/3.7pages/3.7raugustbud.html.

111. Ibid.

112. CAMY, *Television: Alcohol's vast adland*.

113. CAMY, *Radio Daze: Alcohol Ads Tune in Underage Youth* (Washington, DC: 2003); CAMY, *Youth overexposed: Alcohol advertising in magazines 2001–2003: Executive summary* (Washington, DC: 2005).

114. CAMY, *Youth overexposed*.

115. H. Richardson, *Raising more voices than mugs: Changing the college environment through media advocacy* (Washington, DC: U.S. Department of Education, DHHS, 1994).

116. *Business Wire*, "TNS media intelligence profiles the advertising side of March madness: The biggest spenders increasing ad rates and dunking on the competition," March 10, 2006, retrieved November 17, 2006, http://www .businesswire.com.

117. J. F. Mosher, "Flavored alcoholic beverages: An international marketing campaign that targets youth," *Journal of Public Health Policy* 26 (2005, 3): 326–342.

118. P. Franson, "Fast-growing malternatives threaten grape expectations," *Winebusiness.com*, November 1, 2002, retrieved November 17, 2006, http://www.winebusiness.com/referencelibrary/webarticle.cfm?dataId=10744.

119. Center for Science in the Public Interest, *What teens and adults are saying about "Alcopops": Major findings* (Washington, DC: 2001).

120. AMA, *Girlie drinks . . . women's diseases: Teenage drinking survey results*, 2006, retrieved December 22, 2006, http://www.alcoholpolicymd.com/.

121. Island Breeze by Bacardi, *Great taste! 1/2 the calories of traditional spirit! 1/2 the calories of wine!* 2006, retrieved November 17, 2006, http://www.island breeze.com/home_html.aspx.

122. Bacardi U.S.A., Inc., "Kim Cattrall to be the face of Island Breeze by Bacardi," press release, April 13, 2005, retrieved November 17, 2006, http://www.prnewswire.com.

123. Cocktails by Jenn, "It's in the bag with the cocktails by Jenn "Handbags are a girl's best friend" contest," press release, September 25, 2005, retrieved November 17, 2006, http://www.prnewswire.com/cgi-bin/stories.pl?.

124. J. Butschli, "Glass bottle launch: A-B company's beverage 'a-peels' to women," *Packaging World Magazine*, September 2006, retrieved November 17, 2006, http://www.packworld.com/print.php?id=21975.

125. D. Leinwand, "Parents warned about 24-proof gelatin," *USA Today*, July 3, 2002, retrieved November 20, 2006, http://www.usatoday.com/news/nation.

126. M. Fass, *Panel rejects bid to upset ban on alcoholic "Freaky Ice,"* January 13, 2006, retrieved November 20, 2006, http://www.law.com/jsp/law.

127. CAMY, *Exposure of African-American youth to alcohol advertising: Executive summary* (Washington, DC: 2006).

128. M. Jordan, "Cerveza, Si o No? The beer industry's embrace of Hispanic market prompts a backlash from activists," *Wall Street Journal*, March 29, 2006, B1.

129. Ibid.

130. Johnson, L. D., P. M. O'Malley, J. G. Bachman, and J. E. Schulenberg, 2005. *Monitoring the Future National Survey Results on Drug Use, 1975–2004: Volume I, Secondary School Students*. Bethesda, MD. National Institute on Drug Abuse, 599, table D-63.

131. S. E. Foster, R. D. Vaughan, W. H. Foster, and J. A. Califano, "Estimate of the commercial value of underage drinking and adult abusive and dependent drinking to the alcohol industry," *Archives of Pediatrics and Adolescent Medicine* 160 (2006, 5): 473–478.

132. *Youth Risk Behavior Study (YRBS), 2005* [Data File]. Atlanta, GA: U.S. Department of Health and Human Services, Centers for Disease Control and Prevention, National Center for Chronic Disease Prevention and Health Promotion.

133. CASA, *Teen tipplers*, 3.

134. OAS, SAMHSA, *Results from the 2004 National Survey.*

135. J. Miller, T. Naimi, R. Brewer, and S. Jones, "Binge drinking and associated health risk behaviors among high school students," *Pediatrics, Official Journal of the American Academy of Pediatrics* 119 (2007, 1): 76–85.

136. CASA, *Wasting the Best and the Brightest.*

137. R. W. Hingson, T. Heeren, and M. R. Winter, "Age at drinking onset and alcohol dependence: Age of onset, duration, and severity," *Archives of Pediatrics and Adolescent Medicine* 160 (2006, 7): 739–746.

138. K. Butler, "The grim neurology of teenage drinking," *New York Times,* July 4, 2006, retrieved December 14, 2006, http://select.nytimes.com.

139. Campaign for Tobacco Free Kids, *Research center: You need to know the truth,* 2006, retrieved November 21, 2006, http://www.tobaccofreekids.org/research/.

140. Washington Post, "Memos highlight importance of "'younger adult smokers,'" January 15, 1998, retrieved November 21, 2006, http://www.washington post.com.

141. R. Wellman, D. Sugarman, and J. Winikoff, "The extent to which tobacco marketing and tobacco use in films contribute to children's use of tobacco: A meta-analysis," *Archives of Pediatrics and Adolescent Medicine* (December 2006).

142. *Court TV Online,* "FTC dismisses Joe Camel advertising suit," January 27, 2006, retrieved November 20, 2006, http://www.courttv.com/archive/legaldocs/tobacco/ftc_012799.html.

143. Biography Resource Center Online, *Louis Vincent Gerstner, Jr.,* 2006, retrieved November 21, 2006, http://www.galenet.com.

144. Office of New York State Attorney General Eliot Spitzer, *Attorneys general and R. J. Reynolds reach historic settlement to end the sale of flavored cigarettes: Press release,* October 11, 2006, retrieved October 11, 2006, http://oag.state.ny.us/press/2006/oct/oct11a_06.html.

145. *CNN Interactive,* "Secret memos show cigarette-maker targeted teens," January 15, 1998, retrieved November 20, 2006, http://www.cnn.com/HEALTH/9801/15/tobacco.kid.settlement; L. Szabo, "Flavored cigarettes, colorful wrappers ignite fire," *USA Today,* January 5, 2005, retrieved November 27, 2006, http://usatoday.printthis.clickability.com.

146. American Lung Association, *Tobacco policy trend alert: From Joe Camel to Kauai Kolada: The marketing of candy-flavored cigarettes,* 2005, retrieved December 22, 2006, http://www.lungusa.org; Szabo.

147. Office of New York State Attorney General Eliot Spitzer.

148. Join Together, "Study says more teens smoking cigars," December 5, 2005, retrieved November 20, 2006, http://www.jointogether.org/news/research/summaries/2005; C. D. Delnevo, J. Foulds, and M. Hrywna, "Trading tobacco: Are youths choosing cigars over cigarettes?" *American Journal of Public Health* 95 (2005, 12): 2123.

149. OAS, SAMHSA, *Results from the 2004 National Survey.*

150. D. Brown, "Nicotine up sharply in many cigarettes," *Washington Post*, August 31, 2006, A1; Massachusetts Tobacco Control Program, Massachusetts Department of Public Health, *Change in nicotine yields 1998–2004*, 2006, retrieved December 22, 2006, http://www.mass.gov/dph/mtcp/reports/nicotine _yields_1998_2004_report.pdf.

151. *Washington Post*, "Big tobacco, lawless as ever: Profiting by manipulating addictions that kill," September 5, 2006, retrieved September 5, 2006, http://www.washingtonpost.com.

152. In 2004 and 2005, 9.3 percent of eighth-graders were current smokers—L. Johnston, P. O'Malley, J. Bachman, and J. Schulenberg, "Decline in teen smoking appears to be nearing its end," *University of Michigan News Service*, December 20, 2005; L. D. Johnston, P. M. O'Malley, J. G. Bachman, and J. E. Schulenberg, *Monitoring the future: National results on adolescent drug use: Overview of key findings*, 2004, 2005, retrieved December 22, 2006, http://www.monitoringthe future.org/pubs/monographs/overview2004.pdf; L. D. Johnston, P. M. O'Malley, J. G. Bachman, and J. E. Schulenberg, *Monitoring the future: National results on adolescent drug use: Overview of key findings*, 2005, 2006, retrieved December 22, 2006, http://www.monitoringthefuture.org/pubs/monographs/overview2005.pdf.

153. *CASA analysis of the National Household Survey on Drug Abuse (NHSDA)*, *1979, 1982, 1985, 1988, 1990–2001* [Data file], and the *National Survey on Drug Use and Health (NSDUH)*, *2002, 2003, 2004, 2005* [Data file]. Rockville, MD: U.S. Department of Health and Human Services, Substance Abuse and Mental Health Services Administration. See Source Note A.

154. Ibid.

155. Ibid.

CHAPTER 5

1. J. M. McGinnis and W. H. Foege, "Mortality and morbidity attributable to use of addictive substances in the United States," *Proceedings of the Association of American Physicians* 111 (1999, 2): 109–111; CDC, *National vital statistics report: Deaths: Preliminary data for 2000*, October 9, 2001, retrieved November 8, 2006, http://www.cdc.gov/nchs/data/nvsr/nvsr49/nvsr49_12.pdf.

2. Schneider Institute for Health Policy and Robert Wood Johnson Foundation, *Substance abuse: The nation's number one health problem* (Princeton, NJ: Robert Wood Johnson Foundation, 2001), 6; CDC, *Tobacco information and prevention source*, 2006, retrieved November 8, 2006, http://www.cdc.gov/ tobacco/issue.htm.

3. CDC, *Deaths: Final data for 2003 tables for E-Stat*, August 30, 2006, retrieved November 8, 2006, http://www.cdc.gov/nchs/data/hestat/finaldeaths03 _tables.pdf.

4. Schneider Institute, 6.

5. Ibid.

6. J. M. McGinnis and W. H. Foege, "Actual causes of death in the United States," *Journal of the American Medical Association* 270 (1993, 18): 2207–2212.

7. Ibid.

8. Ibid.

9. McGinnis and Foege, "Mortality and Morbidity."

10. Ibid.

11. K. M. Flegal, B. I. Graubard, D. F. Williamson, and H. G. Mitchell, "Excess deaths associated with underweight, overweight, and obesity," *Journal of the American Medical Association* 293 (2005, 15): 1861–1867.

12. Schneider Institute, 6.

13. A. Jacobs, "Battling H.I.V. where sex meets crystal meth," *New York Times*, February 21, 2006, retrieved October 23, 2006, http://www.nytimes.com.

14. J. M. Walsh, R. Flegel, R., R. Atkins, L. A. Cangianelli, C. Cooper, C. Welsh, et al., "Drug and alcohol use among drivers admitted to a level-1 trauma center," *Accident Analysis and Prevention* 37 (2005): 894–901.

15. Ibid.

16. Ibid.

17. L. J. Bilncoe, A. G. Seay, E. Zaloshnja, T. R. Miller, E. O. Romano, S. Luchter, et al., *The economic impact of motor vehicle crashes 2000* (Washington, DC: U.S. Department of Transportation, National Highway Traffic Safety Administration, 2002).

18. OAS, *NSDUH report: Pregnancy and substance use* (Rockville, MD: DHHS, SAMHSA, 2004).

19. CDC. *Fetal alcohol spectrum disorders: Frequently asked questions*, 2006, retrieved November 7, 2006, http://www.cdc.gov.

20. J. Lee, L. A. Croen, K. H. Backstrand, C. K. Yoshida, L. H. Henning, C. Lindan, et al., "Maternal and infant characteristics associated with perinatal arterial stroke in the infant," *Journal of the American Medical Association* 293 (2005, 6): 723–729; A. Greenough and Z. Kassim, "Effects of substance abuse during pregnancy," *Journal of the Royal Society for the Promotion of Health* 125 (2005, 5): 212–213.

21. American Lung Association, *Women and smoking fact sheet*, March 2006, retrieved October 24, 2006, http://www.lungusa.org/site.

22. M. D. Cornelius and N. L. Day, "The effects of tobacco use during and after pregnancy on exposed children: Relevance of findings for alcohol research," *Alcohol Research and Health* 24 (2000, 4): 242–249.

23. DHHS, *The health consequences of involuntary exposure to tobacco smoke: A report of the Surgeon General* (Washington, DC: DHHS, CDC, National Center for Chronic Disease Prevention and Health Promotion, Office of Smoking and Health, 2006); Greenough and Kassim.

24. DHHS, *The health consequences*.

25. Ibid.

26. A. Quindlen, "Public and private: Please don't inhale," *New York Times*, February 3, 1993, retrieved January 20, 2006, http://www.nytimes.com.

27. DHHS, *The health consequences*.

28. CDC, *Annual smoking-attributable mortality, years of potential life lost, and economic costs: United States 1995–1999*, 2002, retrieved August 17, 2005, http://www.cdc.gov/mmwr/preview/mmwrhtml.

29. M. Kerr, "Mortality rate would plunge without passive smoking," Reuters, May 10, 2006, retrieved November 7, 2006, http://global.factiva.com.

30. Narcotic Addict Rehabilitation Act of 1966, Pub. L. No. 89-793, § (1966).

31. T. L. Mark, R. M. Coffey, D. R. McKusick, H. Harwood, E. King, E. Bouchery, et al., *National estimates of expenditures for mental health services and substance abuse treatment, 1991–2001* (Rockville, MD: SAMHSA, 2005).

32. Ibid. (Applying 7 percent annual rate of increase in health care costs.)

33. Ibid. (Applying 7 percent annual rate of increase in health care costs.)

34. OAS, *National and state estimates of the drug abuse treatment gap: 2000 National Household Survey on Drug Abuse* (Rockville, MD: SAMHSA, 2002). See also DHHS, *Closing the drug abuse treatment gap: A report to the president of the United States, September 2001* (Washington, DC: 2001).

35. CASA, *Behind bars: Substance abuse and America's prison population* (New York: 1998).

36. CASA, *No safe haven: Children of substance abusing parents* (New York: 1999), 36–37.

37. CASA, *CASAWORKS for families: A promising approach to welfare reform and substance-abusing women* (New York: 2001), 3.

38. SAMHSA, *Strategies for developing treatment programs for people with co-occurring substance abuse and mental disorders* (Rockville, MD: Author, 2003); NIDA, *Treatment of drug-dependent individuals with comorbid mental disorders: NIDA research monograph 172* (Rockville, MD: DHHS, NIH, 1997).

39. NIDA, *Treatment for drug-exposed women and children: Advances in research methodology: NIDA research monograph 165* (Rockville, MD: DHHS, NIH, 1996); NIDA, *Medications development for the treatment of pregnant addicts and their infants: NIDA research monograph 149* (Rockville, MD: DHHS, Public Health Service, NIH, 1995).

40. A. Margolin, H. D. Kleber, S. K. Avants, J. Konefal, F. Gawin, E. Stark, et al., "Acupuncture for the treatment of cocaine addiction: A randomized controlled trial," *Journal of the American Medical Association* 287 (2002, 1): 55–63.

41. OAS, *The DASIS report: Characteristics of repeat admissions to substance abuse treatment* (Rockville, MD: SAMHSA, 2002); NIDA, *Relapse and recovery in drug abuse* (Rockville, MD: DHHS, Public Health Service, 1986).

42. S. L. Ettner, D. Huang, E. Evans, D. R. Ash, M. Hardy, M. Jourabchi, et al., "Benefit-cost in the California Treatment Outcome Project: Does substance abuse treatment 'pay for itself'?" *Health Services Research* 41 (2006, 1): 192–213.

43. C. P. Rydell and S. S. Everingham, *Controlling cocaine: Supply versus demand programs* (Santa Monica, CA: RAND, 1994); D. R. Gerstein, R. A. Johnson, H. Harwood, D. Fountain, N. Suter, and K. Malloy, *Evaluating recovery services: The California Drug and Alcohol Treatment Assessment (CALDATA): Executive summary* (Sacramento: State of California, Department of Alcohol and Drug Programs, 1994).

44. L. J. Walter, L. Ackerson, and S. Allen, "Medicaid chemical dependency patients in a commercial health plan: Do high medical costs come down over time?" *Journal of Behavioral Health Services and Research* 32 (2005, 3): 253–263.

45. Join Together, *State leadership needs to improve addiction treatment, prevention*, February 24, 2006, retrieved November 8, 2006, http://www.jointogether.org/news.

46. CASA, *Missed opportunity: National survey of primary care physicians and patients on substance abuse* (New York: 2000), 5.

47. Ibid, 9–11.

48. American Lung Association *Secondhand smoke fact sheet*, August 2006, retrieved November 8, 2006, http://www.lungusa.org/site.

49. P. Ehrlich, J. K. Brown, and R. Drongowski, "Characterization of the drug-positive adolescent trauma population: Should we, do we, and does it make a difference if we test?" *Journal of Pediatric Surgery* 41 (2006, 5): 927–930.

50. G. D'Onofrio and L. C. Degutis, "Preventive care in the emergency department: Screening and brief intervention for alcohol problems in the emergency department: A systematic review," *Academic Emergency Medicine* 9 (2002, 6): 627–638; L. M. Gentilello, P. Duggan, D. Drummond, A. Tonnesen, E. E. Degner, R. P. Fischer, and R. L. Reed 2nd, "Major injury as a unique opportunity to initiate treatment in the alcoholic," *American Journal of Surgery* 156 (1998, 6): 558–561; L. M. Gentilello, F. P. Rivara, D. M. Donovan, G. J. Jurkovich, E. Daranciang, C. W. Dunn, A. Villaveces, M. Copass, and R. R. Ries, "Alcohol interventions in a trauma center as a means of reducing the risk of injury recurrence," *Annals of Surgery* 230 (1999, 4): 473.

51. L. Barclay, "Denial of care due to alcohol use: A newsmaker interview with Larry M. Gentilello, MD," *Medscape Medical News*, October 27, 2005.

52. F. P. Rivara et al., "Screening trauma patients for alcohol problems: Are insurance companies barriers?" *Journal of Trauma, Injury, Infection and Critical Care* 48 (2000, 115).

53. H. Moses, E. R. Dorsey, D. H. Matheson, and S. O. Thier, "Financial anatomy of biomedical research," *Journal of the American Association* 294 (2005, 11): 1333–1342.

54. NIH, Office of the Budget, *What's new? Budget request—FY 2007*, 2006, retrieved November 8, 2006, http://officeofbudget.od.nih.gov.NIH chart.

55. Ibid.

56. G. Chang, L. Sherritt, and J. R. Knight, "Adolescent cigarette smoking and mental health symptoms," *Journal of Adolescent Health* 36 (2005): 517–522.

57. Centers for Medicare and Medicaid Services, *National health expenditure data*, June 7, 2006, retrieved November 7, 2006, http://www.cms.hhs.gov/NationalHealthExpendData/.

58. Ibid.

59. J. A. Califano, *Radical surgery: What's next for America's health care* (New York: Times Books, 1994).

60. Schneider Institute. Applying 7 percent annual rate of increase in health care expenditures.

61. J. A. Califano, "A national attack on addiction is long overdue," *New York Times*, September 23, 1986, retrieved October 23, 2006, http://www.nytimes.com.

62. CASA, *The cost of substance abuse to America's health care system: Report 1: Medicaid hospital costs* (New York: 1993). CASA's 1993 paper estimated that total hospital costs (including psychiatric facility costs) represented 28 percent of total Medicaid spending in 1994. Assuming the 28 percent remained the same from 1994 to 2003, when we apply that percentage to the combined federal and state payments under the Medicaid program in 2004 ($291 billion; see Centers for Medicare and Medicaid Services, June 7, 2006), we get $81 billion. If 20 percent of this total is still attributable to substance abuse (as CASA estimated it was in 1993), then at least $16 billion of Medicaid's inpatient hospital costs are attributable to substance abuse.

63. Ibid.

64. Walter et al.

65. CASA, *The cost of substance abuse*.

66. In 2004, total Medicare spending was up to $309 billion (see Centers for Medicare and Medicaid Services. *National Health Expenditure Data*, http://www.cms.hhs.gov/NationalHealthExpendData/), with 40 percent of that amount ($124 billion; see Medicare Payment Advisory Commission, *Healthcare spending and the Medicare program*, June 2004 and 2005, www.medpac.gov) attributable to inpatient hospital costs. I applied the 25 percent figure from the 1994 CASA paper to the $124 billion in Medicare spending on inpatient hospital costs in 2003 and came up with $31 billion of Medicare spending on inpatient hospital care attributable to substance abuse.

67. CASA, *The cost of substance abuse to America's health care system: Report 2: Medicare hospital costs* (New York: 1994).

68. Office of National Drug Control Policy *National drug control strategy February 2005: Appendix A: National drug control budget: Summary*, February 2005, retrieved November 12, 2006, http://www.whitehousedrugpolicy.gov.

69. National Association of Counties, *The meth epidemic in America: Two new surveys of U.S. counties: The effect of meth abuse on hospital emergency rooms, the challenges of treating meth abuse* (Washington, DC: National Association of Counties, 2006).

70. Ibid.

71. American Heart Association and American Stroke Association, *Heart disease and stroke statistics—2006 update*, 2007, retrieved January 29, 2007, http://www.americanheart.org/downloadable/heart/1139325127381Statupdate2006.pdf.; M. Glynn and P. Rhodes, *Estimated HIV prevalence in the United States at the end of 2003*, 2005, retrieved January 29, 2007, http://www.american heart.org/downloadable/heart/1139325127381Statupdate2000.pdf; RAND, and Agency for Health Care Policy and Research, *HIV cost and services utilization study: Policy brief: A portrait of the HIV+ population in America*, 2007, retrieved January 29, 2007, http://www.rand.org/pubs/research_briefs/RB4523/index1.html; American Cancer Society. *Cancer facts & figures 2005*, 2005, retrieved January 29, 2007, http://www.cancer.org/downloads/STT/CAFF2005 f4PWSecured.pdf; National Institutes of Health, National Heart, Lung, and Blood Institute, *Fact book fiscal year 2003*, retrieved January 29, 2007, http://www.nhlbi.nih.gov/about/03factbk.pdf.

72. C. Bartucchi, R. N. Alsever, C. Nevin-Woods, W. M. Thomas, R. O. Estacio, B. B. Bartelson, et al., "Reduction in the incidence of acute myocardial infarction associated with a citywide smoking ordinance," *Circulation* 114 (2006): 1490–1496.

73. Schneider Institute, 19.

CHAPTER 6

1. The National Center on Addiction and Substance Abuse (CASA) at Columbia University. (2004). *CASA analysis of Survey of Inmates in Local Jails, 2002*. Washington, DC: U.S. Department of Justice, Office of Justice Programs, Bureau of Justice Statistics.

2. CASA, *Behind bars: Substance abuse and America's prison population* (New York: 1998), 4–5.

3. P. M. Harrison and A. J. Beck, "Prison and jail inmates at midyear 2005," *Bureau of Justice Statistics Bulletin*, May 2006.

4. International Centre for Prison Studies, *Prison brief for United States of America*, April 8, 2005, retrieved July 7, 2005, http://www.kcl.ac.uk/depsta/rel/icps/worldbrief/north_america_records.

5. U.S. Census Bureau, *Population estimates 2004: Table 1: Annual estimates of the population for incorporated places over 100,000*, June 30, 2005, retrieved December 4, 2006, http://www.census.gov/popest/cities/tables/SUB-EST2004.

6. Sterling, E. E., & Stewart, J. (June 24, 2006). *Undo this legacy of Len Bias's death*. Retrieved November 27, http://www.washingtonpost.com.; Harrison and Beck, Prison and jail inmates at midyear 2005.

7. P. M. Harrison and A. J. Beck, *Bureau of Justice Statistics Bulletin: Prisoners in 2005*, NCJ 215092 (Washington, DC: U.S. Department of Justice, Office of Justice Programs, 2006).

8. CASA, *Behind bars: Substance abuse and America's prison population* (New York: 1998), 2, 7.

9. National Institute of Corrections, *Caught in the net: The impact of drug policies on women and families: Executive summary*, 2004, retrieved December 4, 2006, http://www.fairlaws4families.org; Harrison and Beck, NCJ 215092; G. Hill and P. Harrison, *Female prisoners under state or federal jurisdiction*, Bureau of Justice Statistics, National Prisoner Statistics Data Series NPS-1 (Washington, DC: Bureau of Justice Statistics, 2005); G. Hill and P. Harrison, *Male prisoners under state or federal jurisdiction*, Bureau of Justice Statistics, National Prisoner Statistics Data Series NPS-1 (Washington, DC: Bureau of Justice Statistics, 2005).

10. P. M. Harrison and A. J. Beck, *Prison and jail inmates at midyear 2004*, NCJ 208801 (Washington, DC: U.S. Department of Justice, Office of Justice Programs, Bureau of Justice, 2005); Harrison and Beck, NCJ 215092; Hill and Harrison, *Female prisoners*, NPS–1; Hill and Harrison, *Male prisoners*, NPS–1; National Institute of Corrections, *Caught in the net*.

11. J. A. Califano, "A new prescription: Investing in substance-abuse treatment would take a big bite out of crime," *Washington Monthly*, October 1998, retrieved December 20, 2006, http://www.washingtonmonthly.com/features/1998/9810.califano.prescription.html.

12. CASA, *Behind bars*, 104.

13. CASA, *Criminal neglect: Substance abuse, juvenile justice and the children left behind* (New York: 2004), 4, 27.

14. M. Brush, "Company focus: 3 prison stocks poised to break out," *MSN Money*, January 15, 2005, retrieved November 26, 2006, http://moneycentral.msn.com/content/P105034.asp?Printer.

15. Institute on Money in State Politics, *Policy Lock-down: Prison interests court political players: Executive summary*, April 2006, retrieved December 4, 2006, http://www.followthemoney.org.

16. A. Cheung, *Prison privatization and the use of incarceration* (Washington, DC: Sentencing Project, 2004).

17. Ibid.

18. T. L. Besser and M. M. Hanson, *The development of last resort: The impact of new state prisons on small town economies* (Ames: Department of Sociology, Iowa State University, 2003).

19. B. Lambert, "High overtime in Nassau jail upsets pact on pay raises," *New York Times*, August 6, 2005, retrieved August 8, 2005, http://www.nytimes.com/2005/08/06/nyregion.

20. Z. R. Dowdy, "Crime and punishment: How the U.S. prison system makes minority communities pay," *New Crisis Magazine* (July-August 2002): 32–37.

21. Besser and Hanson, 6–7.

22. S. E. McGregor, "Senseless census," *Amsterdam News*, October 20, 2005, retrieved December 1, 2006, http://www.prisonpolicy.org/news/amsterdamnews10202005.html.

23. Harrison and Beck, NCJ 208801; Federal Bureau of Investigation, *Crime in the United States: Table 1*, September 2006, retrieved December 22, 2006, http://www.fbi.gov/ucr/05cius/data/table_01.html; D. K. Gilliard, *Bureau of Justice Statistics Bulletin: Prison and jail inmates at midyear 1998*, NCJ 173414 (Washington, DC: U.S. Department of Justice, Office of Justice Programs, 1999); Federal Bureau of Investigation, *Crime in the United States, 2004*, 2006, retrieved December 5, 2006, http://www.fbi.gov/ucr/04cius/arrests/index.html.

24. Bureau of Justice Statistics, *Criminal sentencing statistics: Summary findings*, August 15, 2006, retrieved November 28, 2006, http://www.ojp.usdoj.gov/bjs/sent.htm; Bureau of Justice Statistics, *Felony sentences in state courts, 2002*, December 21, 2004, retrieved December 4, 2006, http://www.ojp.usdoj.gov/bjs/abstract/fssc02.htm.

25. CASA, *Behind bars*, 11.

26. CASA, *Criminal neglect*, 7.

27. CASA, *Behind Bars, 123–24*.

28. Sentencing Project, *Drug policy and the criminal justice system* (Washington, DC: Author, 2001).

29. CASA Analysis of U.S. Department of Justice and Office of Justice Programs, "Justice expenditures and employment in the United States, 2003," *Bureau of Justice Statistics Bulletin* (April 2006).

30. Bureau of Justice Statistics, *State prison expenditures, 2001*, 2004, www.ojp.usdoj.gov/bjs/pub/pdf/spe01.pdf.

31. Join Together, *Meth a toothache for prisoners*, April 21, 2005, retrieved April 22, 2005, http://www.jointogether.org/sa/news/summaries.

32. Center for Children of Incarcerated Parents, *CCIP data sheet 3a: How many children of incarcerated parents are there?* June 30, 2004, retrieved July 8, 2005, http://www.e-ccip.org/publication.html.

33. H. Danks, "County will open drug court," *The Oregonian*, West Zoner, March 3, 2005, 1.

34. CASA, *Criminal neglect*, 74–76.

35. Associated Press, "Drug experts urge better prison treatment," *Yahoo!News*, July 24, 2006, retrieved July 24, 2006, http://news.yahoo.com/s/ap/20060724; NIDA, *Principles of drug abuse treatment for criminal justice populations: A research based guide*, NIH Publication No. 06-5316 (Rockville, MD: DHHS, NIH, NIDA, 2006).

36. Miami-Dade Public Defender, *Bennett H. Brummer recognizes retiring drug court judge*, 2005, retrieved November 26, 2006, http://pdmiami.com/retired_judge.htm.

37. C. W. Huddleston, K. Freeman-Wilson, D. B. Marlowe, and A. Roussell, *Painting the current picture: A national report card on drug courts and other problem solving court programs in the United States* (Washington, DC: National Drug Court Institute, 2005).

38. Utah Commission on Criminal and Juvenile Justice, *Drug Offender Reform Act—Pilot program,* 2006, retrieved December 5, 2006, http://www.usaav.utah.gov/Policy/2005DORAreport.pdf.

39. SAMHSA, *Incarceration vs. treatment: Drug courts help substance abusing offenders,* 2005, retrieved December 1, 2006, http://www.samhsa.gov/samhsa_news/VolumeXIV_2/index.htm. National Association of Drug Court Professionals, *Successful parenting for recovery: 2006 national drug court month field kit,* May 2006, retrieved December 5, 2006, http://www.nadcp.org/Field%20Kit2web_final.pdf.

40. J. Gonnerman, "New York's drug-law debacle," *Village Voice,* May 6, 1998, retrieved November 26, 2006, http://www.villagevoice.com/generic/show_print.php?.

41. R. L. Hubbard, M. E. Marsden, H. J. Harwood, E. R. Cavanaugh, and H. M. Ginzburg, *Drug abuse treatment: A national study of effectiveness* (Chapel Hill: University of North Carolina Press, 1989).

42. H. E. Sung, "Rehabilitating felony drug offenders through job development: A look into a prosecutor-led diversion program," *Prison Journal* 81(2001, 2): 271–286.

43. J. Seyfer, "Drug treatment option failing, grand jury says; proposition 36 lacks accountability, hasn't reduce crime, report finds," *San Jose Mercury News,* June 21, 2005, 4A.

44. F. Byrne, S. M. Carey, D. Crumpton, M. W. Finigan, and M. Waller, *California drug courts: A methodology for determining costs and benefits: Phase II Testing the methodology: Final report* (Sacramento: Judicial Council of California, Administrative Office of the Courts, 2005).

45. Washington State Institute for Public Policy, *Washington state's drug courts for adult defendants: Outcome evaluation and cost-benefit analysis: Executive summary,* March 2003, retrieved December 5, 2006, http://www.wsipp.wa.gov/rptfiles/drugcourtMar2003ES.pdf.

46. CASA, *Behind bars,* 19.

47. CASA, *Criminal neglect,* 5.

48. CASA, *Behind bars,* 20.

49. B. R. Johnson, D. B. Larson, and T. C. Pitts, "Religious programs, institutional adjustment, and recidivism among former inmates in prison fellowship programs," *Justice Quarterly* 14 (1997, 1): 145–166.

50. J. Sterngold, "Illinois prison program a model for state? Schwarzenegger seeks to emulate therapeutic approach to rehabilitation," *San Francisco Chronicle,* August 7, 2006, A1.

51. National Institute of Justice, *Stress among probation and parole officers and what can be done about it* (Washington, DC: U.S. Department of Justice, Office of Justice Programs, 2005).

52. Federal Bureau of Investigation, *Uniform Crime Reporting Program: Crime in the United States, 2005,* 2006, retrieved December 21, 2006, http://www.fbi.gov/ucr/05cius/.

53. Bureau of Justice Statistics. (January 11, 2007). *Key facts at a glance: Direct expenditures by criminal justice function, 1982–2004.* Retrieved January 24, 2007, http://www.ojp.usdoj.gov/bjs/glance/tables/exptyptab.htm.

54. Join Together, "Panel recommends treatment, other steps to cut recidivism," February 1, 2005, retrieved February 2, 2005, http://www.jointogether .org/sa/news/summaries/reader.

55. Oklahoma Governor's and Attorney General's Blue Ribbon Task Force, *Task force recommendations: Mental health, substance abuse and domestic violence in Oklahoma,* February 17, 2005, retrieved December 5, 2006, http://www.odmhsas .org/web%20page%20publications/BR.pdf.

56. *Washington Times,* "Study shows support for drug treatment," June 5, 2006, retrieved November 26, 2006, http://www.washtimes.com/functions/ print.php?StoryID=20060604.

CHAPTER 7

1. CASA, *Shoveling up: The impact of substance abuse on state budgets* (New York: 2001), 2.

2. J. J. Collins and P. M. Messerschmidt, "Epidemiology of alcohol-related violence," *Alcohol Health and Research World* 17 (1993, 2): 93–100.

3. B. C. Alleyne, P. Stuart, and R. Copes, "Alcohol and other drug use in occupational fatalities," *Journal of Occupational Medicine* 33 (1991, 4): 496–500; D. B. Kandel and M. Davies, "Labor force experiences of a national sample of young adult men: The role of drug involvement," ERIC No. EJ411296, *Youth and Society* 21 (1990, 4): 411–445; R. Cook and W. Schlenger, "Prevention of substance abuse in the workplace: Review of research on the delivery of services," *Journal of Primary Prevention* 23 (2004, 1): 115–142.

4. *NationMaster.com,* "People statistics: Divorce rate by country," November 27, 2006, retrieved November 27, 2006, http://nationmaster.com.

5. U.S. Census Bureau, Selected Social Characteristics, *2004 American Community Survey,* 2004, retrieved November 27, 2006, http://factfinder.census.gov.

6. D. Schramm, *The costly consequences of divorce in Utah: The impact on couples, communities, and government,* press release, June 25, 2003, retrieved November 27, 2006, http://www.utahmarriage.org.

7. L. S. Neher and J. L. Short, "Risk and protective factors for children's substance use and antisocial behavior following parental divorce," *American Journal of Orthopsychiatry* 68 (1998, 1): 154–161.

8. M. P. Marshal, "For better or for worse? The effects of alcohol use on marital functioning," *Clinical Psychology Review* 23 (2003, 7): 959–997.

9. C. M. Murphy, J. Winters, T. J. O'Farrell, W. Fals-Stewart, and M. Murphy, "Alcohol consumption and intimate partner violence by alcoholic men:

Comparing violent and nonviolent conflicts," *Psychology of Addictive Behaviors* 19 (2005, 1): 35–42.

10. CASA, *Women under the influence* (Baltimore, MD: Johns Hopkins University Press, 2006), 65.

11. DHHS, CDC, National Center for Injury Prevention and Control, *Costs of intimate partner violence against women in the United States* (Atlanta, GA: DHHS, 2003).

12. DHHS, Administration on Children, Youth and Families, *Child Maltreatment 2003: Chapter Five: Perpetrators*, 2005, retrieved November 27, 2006, http://www.acf.hhs.gov/programs/cb/pubs/cm03/chapterfive.htm; Children's Defense Fund, *Child abuse and neglect fact sheet.* (Washington, DC: 2005).

13. Child Welfare Information Gateway, *Substance abuse and child maltreatment* (Washington, DC: DHHS, Administration for Children and Families, 2003).

14. CASA, *No safe haven: Children of substance-abusing parents* (New York: 1999), 23.

15. National Criminal Justice Reference Service, *Characteristics of child abuse reported by NIBRS*, 2001, retrieved November 29, 2006, http://www.ncjrs.gov.

16. B. Farrington, *Missing girl case stings Jeb Bush*, May 8, 2002, retrieved November 28, 2006, http://www.findarticles.com.

17. L. Kaufman, "In child abuse battle, New York scrambles to add workers on front lines," *New York Times*, February 12, 2006, retrieved November 28, 2006, http://www.nytimes.com.

18. R. L. Jones, "Insiders say Corzine plans new unit for child welfare," *New York Times*, March 19, 2006, retrieved November 27, 2006, http://www.nytimes.com.

19. Michigan Supreme Court, Office of Public Information, "Courts located 79 percent of missing foster children in 2004," press release, January 20, 2005, retrieved November 10, 2006, http://www.michigan.gov.

20. CASA, *No safe haven*, 25.

21. Child Welfare League of America, *National fact sheet 2005*, retrieved December 4, 2006, http://www.cwla.org.

22. A. J. Sedlak and D. D. Broadhurst, *Third national incidence study of child abuse and neglect, NIS-3* (Washington, DC: DHHS, Administration for Children and Families, Administration on Children, Youth and Families, National Center on Child Abuse and Neglect, 1996).

23. CASA, *No safe haven*, 5.

24. DHHS, *Child maltreatment 2003*.

25. M. Behnke, F. D. Eyler, N. S. Woods, K. Wobie, and M. Conlon, "Rural pregnant cocaine users: An in-depth socio-demographic comparison," *Journal of Drug Issues* 27 (1997, 3): 501–524; D. Boundy, *Profile: Project SAFE: Reaching out with hope to women*, 2006, retrieved November 28, 2006, http://www.pbs.org/wnet/closetohome/treatment/html/safe.html.

homeless individuals with psychiatric and/or substance misuse disorders? A randomized controlled trial," *Medical Care* 43 (2005, 8): 763–768.

53. National Coalition for Homeless Veterans, *HUD announces 1.4 billion in homeless assistance grants*, January 26, 2005, retrieved December 4, 2006, http://www.nchv.org.

CHAPTER 8

1. NIDA, *Marijuana and medicine: The need for a science-based approach: Testimony before the Committee on Government Reform, Subcommittee on Criminal Justice, Drug Policy and Resources, United States House of Representatives: Nora D. Volkow*, 2004, retrieved December 1, 2006, http://www.nida.nih.gov/testimony/ 4-1-04aTestimony.html; OAS, *National Household Survey on Drug Abuse: Main Findings 1996: Table 4A. Estimated numbers (in thousands) of past year users of illicit drugs, alcohol, and tobacco in the U.S. population aged 12 and older: 1979–1996*, 2006, retrieved December 5, 2006, http//oas.samhsa.gov/nhsda/PE1996/artab 008.htm.

2. L. M. Eubanks, C. J. Rogers, A. E. Beuscher, G. F. Koob, A. J Olson, T. J.Dickerson, et al., "A molecular link between the active component of marijuana and Alzheimer's disease pathology," *Molecular Pharmaceutics*, 3(2006, 6), 773–777.

3. National Drug Intelligence Center and U.S. Department of Justice, *National drug threat assessment 2006*, 2006, retrieved November 20, 2006, http://www.usdoj.gov/ndic/pubs11/18862/18862p.pdf.

4. Office of National Drug Control Policy, *Marijuana myths and facts: The truth behind 10 popular misperceptions*, 2006, retrieved January 10, 2002, http:// www.whitehousedrugpolicy.gov/publications/marijuana_myths_facts/marijuana _myths_facts.pdf.

5. United Nations, Office of Drugs and Crime, press release, June 26, 2006.

6. B. Carey, "Marijuana use is pulling teens into treatment," *Los Angeles Times*, April 26, 2004, http://www.drugstory.org/feature/LATimesArticle.asp.

7. OAS, SAMHSA, *National Household Survey on Drug Abuse: Main findings 1993*, DHHS Publication No. SMA 95–3020 (Rockville, MD: DHHS, SAMHSA, OAS, 1995), 41; OAS, *Treatment episode data set (TEDS): Highlights—2004: National admissions to substance abuse treatment services* (Rockville, MD: SAMHSA, OAS, 2005); OAS, *Drug abuse warning network, 2004: National estimates of drug-related emergency department visits: DAWN series D–28*, 2006, retrieved November 18, 2006, http://DAWNinfo.samhsa.gov.

8. OAS, TEDS.

9. R. A. Roffman and R. R. Stephens, *Cannabis dependence: Its nature, consequences, and treatment* (New York: Cambridge University Press, 2006), xx.

10. OAS, SAMHSA, *Results from the 2005 National Survey.*

11. OAS, SAMHSA, *Results from the 2003 National Survey of Drug Use and Health: National findings,* DHHS Pub. No. SMA 04–3964 (Rockville, MD: DHHS, SAMHSA, OAS, 2004).

12. OAS, SAMHSA, *Results from the 2001 National Household Survey on Drug Abuse: Volume 1: Summary of national findings,* NHSDA Series H–17, DHHS Publication No. SMA 02–3758 (Rockville, MD: DHHS, SAMHSA, OAS, 2002).

13. F. R. De Fonesca, M. R. A. Carrera, M. Navarro, G. F. Koob, and F. Weiss, "Activation of the corticotropin-releasing factor in the limbic system during cannabinoid withdrawal," *Science, 276*(1997, 5321), 2050–2054.

14. I. Wickelgreen, "Marijuana: Harder than thought?" *Science* 276 (1997, 5321): 1967–1968.

15. M. Smith, APA: *Cannabis withdrawal syndrome no pot dream,* April 26, 2006, retrieved November 13, 2006, http://www.medpagetoday.com.

16. CASA, *Non-medical marijuana II: Rite of passage or Russian roulette? A CASA white paper* (New York: 2004), 10.

17. Office of National Drug Control Policy, *What Americans need to know about marijuana: Important facts about our nation's most misunderstood illegal drug,* 2006, retrieved November 21, 2006, http://www.whitehousedrugpolicy .gov/publications/pdf/mj_rev.pdf.

18. M. T. Lynskey, A. C. Heath, K. K. Bucholz, W. S. Slutske, P. A. F. Madden, E. C. Nelson, et al., "Escalation of drug use in early-onset cannabis users vs co-twin controls," *Journal of the American Medical Association* 289 (2003): 427–433.

19. Institute of Medicine, Division of Neuroscience and Behavioral Health, *Marijuana and medicine: Assessing the science base* (Washington, DC: National Academy Press, 1999); A. R. Morral, D. F. McCaffrey, and S. M. Paddock, "Reassessing the marijuana gateway effect," *Addiction* 97 (2006, 12): 1493–1504.

20. U.S. Federal Bureau of Investigation, *Crime in the United States, 2005,* 2006, retrieved December 5, 2006, http://www.fbi.gov/ucr/05cius/arrests/index.html.

21. CASA and American Legacy Foundation, *Report on teen cigarette smoking and marijuana use* (New York: 2003).

22. CASA, *National surveys X and XI* (New York: 2005, 2006).

23. CASA, *Non-medical marijuana,* 46–47.

24. J. A. Califano, "The wrong way to stay slim," *New England Journal of Medicine* 333 (1995, 18): 1214–1216.

25. S. E. Foster, R. D. Vaughan, W. H. Foster, and J. A. Califano, "Estimate of the commercial value of underage drinking and adult abusive and dependent drinking to the alcohol industry," *Archives of Pediatrics and Adolescent Medicine* 160 (2006, 5): 473–478.

26. CASA, *Cigarettes, alcohol, marijuana: Gateways to illicit drug use* (New York: 1994), 17.

27. CASA, *Legalization: Panacea or Pandora's box* (New York: 1995), 14.

28. CASA, Legalization: Panacea or Pandora's Box, 17.

29. OAS, SAMHSA, *Results from the 2005 National Survey of Drug Use and Health: National findings*, DHHS Pub. No. SMA 06–4194 (Rockville, MD: DHHS, SAMHSA, OAS, 2006).

30. BJS, *Drugs and crime facts: Drug use and crime*, 2006, retrieved November 15, 2006, http://www.ojp.usdoj.gov/bjs/dcf/duc.htm.

31. Public Agenda, *Illegal drugs: Overview*, 2006, retrieved November 15, 2006, http://www.publicagenda.org.

32. A. S. Trebach and J. Inciardi, *Legalize it? Debating American drug policy* (Washington, DC: American University Press, 1993). H.D. Kleber, J.A. Califano, and J.C. Demers, "Clinical and societal implications of drug legalization," in J. H. Lowinson, P. Ruiz, R. B. Millman, and J. G. Langrod (Eds.), *Substance abuse: A comprehensive textbook* (Baltimore, MD: Williams and Wilkins, 1997), 855–864.

33. P. Aaron and D. Musto, "Temperance and prohibition in America: A historical overview," in M. Moore, D. R. Gerstein, Assembly of Behavioral and Social Sciences, and Panel on Alternative Policies Affecting the Prevention of Alcohol (Eds.), *Alcohol and public policy: Beyond the shadow of prohibition* (Washington, DC: National Academy Press, 1981), 127–181.

34. CASA, *Legalization*, 32.

35. Aaron and Musto.

36. H. D. Kleber, J. A. Califano, and J. C. Demers, "Clinical and societal implications of drug legalization," in J. H. Lowinson, P. Ruiz, R. B. Millman, and J. G. Langrod (Eds.), *Substance abuse: A comprehensive textbook* (Baltimore: Williams & Wilkins, 1997), 855–864.

37. Ibid.

38. Ministero Della Solidarieta' Sociale. (2006). *Tossicodipendenze: Relazione annuale parlamento sullo stato delle tossicodipendenze in Italia 2005*. Rome, Italy: Ministero Della Solidarieta' Sociale; European Monitoring Centre for Drugs and Drug Addiction. (2006). *The state of the drugs problem in Europe: Annual report 2006*. Lisbon, Portugal: European Monitoring Centre for Drugs and Drug Addiction.

39. United Nations Office on Drugs and Crime. (January 25, 2007). *Extent of HIV/AIDS and intravenous drug use across the globe: Western Europe*. Retrieved January 25, 2007 from the World Wide Web: http://www.unodc.org/unodc/en/drug_demand_hiv_aids_extend.html.

40. United Nations Office on Drugs and Crime. (2006). *UN drugs chief praises Swedish drug control model*. Retrieved November 28, 2006, http://www.unodc.org/unodc/press_release_2006-09-06.html; United Nations Office on Drugs and Crime. (September 7, 2006). *Sweden's successful drug policy: A review of the evidence*. Retrieved January 25, 2007, http://www.unodc.org/pdf/research/Swedish_drug_control.pdf.

41. The number of marijuana users in 1979 was at 25.4 million—OAS, SAMHSA, *Preliminary Results from the 1997 National Household Survey*. It was at 14.6 million in 2005—DHHS, SAMHSA, OAS, *Results from the 2005 National Survey* 13; National Household Survey/CASA analysis; OAS, *Summary of findings from the 1998 National Household Survey on Drug Abuse*, 1999, retrieved October 11, 2006, http://www.oas.samhsa.gov/nhsda/98SummHtml/NHSDA98 Summ-03.htm.

42. OAS, SAMHSA, *Results from the 2005 National Survey*.

43. The White House, *Remarks by the president in announcement of the director of the Office of Drug Control Policy*, 2001, retrieved November 15, 2006, http://www.whitehouse.gov.

44. OAS, SAMHSA, *Results from the 2005 National Survey*.

45. J. S. Mill, *On liberty and utilitarianism* (New York: Knopf, 1992).

CHAPTER 9

1. CASA, *National survey of American attitudes on substance abuse X: Teens and parents* (New York: Author, 2005); CASA, *National survey of American attitudes on substance abuse XI: Teens and parents* (New York: Author, 2006).

2. CASA, *Women under the influence* (Baltimore, MD: Johns Hopkins University Press, 2006), 17.

3. Ibid., vii.

4. Ibid., 7–9.

5. CASA, *The formative years: Pathways to substance abuse among girls and young women ages 8–22.* (New York: Author, 2003).

6. CASA, *National survey of American attitudes on substance abuse VIII: Teens and parents* (New York: Author, 2003).

7. CASA, *Women under the influence*, 62, 27.

8. H. S. Klonoff-Cohen, L. Natarajan, and R. V. Chen, "A prospective study of the effects of female and male marijuana use on in vitro fertilization (IVF) and gamete intrafallopian transfer (GIFT) outcomes," *American Journal of Obstetrics and Gynecology* 194 (2006): 369–376

9. CASA, *Women under the influence*, 26–28, 63, 68.

10. C. M. Dresler, "The lung cancer epidemic in women: Why female smokers are at much greater risk than men," *Women's Health in Primary Care* 1 (1998, 1): 85–92.

11. CASA, *Women under the influence*, 73.

12. Ibid., 9–10.

13. Ibid., 33.

14. Ibid., 35.

15. Ibid., 34–35.

16. Ibid., 35.

17. Ibid., 36–37.

18. Ibid., 25.

19. Ibid., 26.

20. CASA, *Women under the influence*, 23.

21. Ibid., 18.

22. Ibid., 28.

23. Ibid., 18.

24. Ibid.

25. Ibid., 30.

26. CASA, *Rethinking rites of passage: Substance abuse on America's campuses* (New York: 1994), 3. L. D. Johnston, P. M. O'Malley, J. G. Bachman, and J. E. Schulenberg (2006). *Monitoring the Future national survey results on drug use, 1975–2005. Volume I: Secondary school students* (NIH Publication No. 06-5883). Bethesda, MD: National Institute on Drug Abuse.

27. CASA, *Wasting the best and the brightest: Substance abuse at America's colleges and universities* (New York: 2007).

28. CASA, *Women under the influence*, 47.

29. Ibid., 53–54.

30. Ibid., 52–53.

31. Ibid., 56.

32. Ibid., 69.

33. CASA, *Substance abuse and the American woman* (New York: 1996), 32.

34. C. S. Widom and S. Hiller-Sturmhofel, "Alcohol abuse as a risk factor for and consequence of child abuse," *Alcohol Research and Health* 25 (2001, 1): 52–57.

35. CASA, *Women under the influence*, 67.

36. Ibid., 67–68.

37. Ibid., 61–62.

38. C. A. Prescott, S. H. Aggen, and K. S. Kendler, "Sex differences in the sources of genetic liability to alcohol abuse and dependence in a population-based sample of U.S. twins," *Alcoholism: Clinical and Experimental Research* 23 (1999, 7): 1136–1144; CASA, *Women under the influence*, 51.

39. J. D. Colliver, L. A. Kroutil, and J. C. Gfroerer, *Misuse of prescription drugs: Data from the 2002, 2003, and 2004 National Surveys on Drug Use and Health*, January 12, 2006, retrieved November 22, 2006, http://oas.samhsa.gov/prescription/Ch2.htm#2.4.2.

40. CASA, *Women under the influence*, 81–82.

41. Ibid., 98.

42. Ibid., 78–79.

43. Ibid., 101.

44. Ibid.

45. Ibid., 82–83.

46. NIDA, *NIDA Notes: Gender matters in drug abuse research*, 2006. retrieved December 4, 2006, http://www.nida.nih.gov/NIDA_Notes/NNVol13N4/Dirrep Vol13N4.html.

CHAPTER 10

1. Center for Responsive Politics, *Tobacco: Long-term contribution trends*, 2006, retrieved December 4, 2006, http://opensecrets.org/industries/indus .asp?Ind=A02&Format=Print; Center for Responsive Politics, *Beer, wine and liquor: Long-term contribution trends*, 2006, retrieved December 4, 2006, http://www.opensecrets.org/industries/indus.asp?Ind=NO2&cycle=2004& Format=Print; Institute on Money in State Politics, *Tobacco 2000–2004*, 2006, retrieved December 4, 2006, http://www.followthemoney.org/database/ PSearch/index.phtml; Institute on Money in State Politics, *Alcohol 2000–2004*, 2006, retrieved December 4, 2006, http://www.followthemoney .org/database/PSearch/index.phtml.

2. C. Lewis and Center for Public Integrity, *The buying of the president 2004* (New York: HarperCollins, 2004), 119.

3. C. Berdik, *Tobacco industry saves on soft money, spends of advertising and lobbyists*, July 28, 2004, retrieved December 4, 2006, http://www.corpwatch.org/ article.php?id=11470.

4. Alcohol Policies Project and Center for Science in the Public Interest, *Washington report*, November 2003, retrieved December 4, 2006, http://www .cspinet.org/booze/WashingtonRpt0311.htm.

5. D. A. Luke and M. Krauss, "Where there's smoke there's money: To-bacco industry campaign contributions and U.S. congressional voting," *American Journal of Preventive Medicine* 27 (2004, 5): 363–372.

6. Tobacco-Free Kids Action Fund and Common Cause, *Buying influence, selling death: Campaign contributions by tobacco interests: Quarterly report* (Washington, DC: Author, 2004).

7. Alcohol Policies Project, and Center for Science in the Public Interest, *Under the influence: A compilation of alcoholic-beverage industry political contributions to members of the Appropriations Committee of the U.S. House of Representatives, 1997–1998*, 2006, retrieved December 27, 2006, http://www.cspinet.org/ booze/underagedrinking.ondcp5.thm.

8. Center for Responsive Politics, *Beer, wine and liquor: Top contributors to federal candidates and parties*, 2006, retrieved December 4, 2006, http://www.open secrets.org/indutries/contrib.asp?Ind=NO2&cycle=2006&Format=Print.

9. Ibid.; M. Massing, *Strong stuff*, March 22, 1998, retrieved December 20, 2006, http://select.nytimes.com; J. H. Birnbaum and R. Newell, "Washington power 25: Fat and happy in D.C.," *Fortune*, May 28, 2001.

10. Center for Responsive Politics, *Beer, wine and liquor.*

11. G. Radanovich and M. Thompson, *Congressional wine caucus,* 2006, retrieved December 4, 2006, http://www.radanovich.house.gov/wine/index.htm.

12. Center for Responsive Politics, *Mike Thompson: Top industries,* 2006, retrieved December 4, 2006, http://www.opensecrets.org/politicians/indus.asp?CID=N00007419&cycle=2006. Center for Responsive Politics, *Beer, wine and liquor: Top 20 members of the house.*

13. Join Together, "Florida lawmakers repeal drink tax," June 13, 2006, retrieved June 14, 2006, http://www.jointogether.org/news/headlines/inthenews/2006/florida-lawmakers-repeal.htm; U.S. Newswire, "Governor Bush signs bill striking alcohol tax: Repeal of tax will boost hospitality/tourism industry, says DISCUS," June 12, 2006, retrieved June 14, 2006, http://global.factiva.com.arugula.

14. S. E. Foster, R. D. Vaughan, W. H. Foster, and J. A. Califano, "Estimate of the commercial value of underage drinking and adult abusive and dependent drinking to the alcohol industry," *Archives of Pediatrics and Adolescent Medicine 160* (2006,5): 473–478.

15. G. A. Hacker, *Stop the beer tax rollback! Reject H.R. 1305,* April 2, 2002, retrieved December 4, 2006, http://www.cspinet.org/booze/HR1305_statement.htm; M. Grossman, *Individual behaviors and substance use: The role of price,* NBER working paper no. 10948 (Cambridge, MA: National Bureau of Economic Research, 2004).

16. R. J. Bonnie and M. E. O'Connell, *Reducing underage drinking: A collective responsibility* (Washington, DC: National Academies Press, 2004).

17. T. Frank, *Beer PAC aims to put Congress under influence,* October 29, 2006, retrieved December 3, 2006, http://www.usatoday.com/news/washington/2006–10–29-beer-lobby_x.htm.

18. Federation of Tax Administrators, *State beer excise tax rates: January 1, 2006,* 2006, retrieved December 4, 2006, http://www.taxadmin.org/fta/rate/beer.html. D. R. Barber and K. Helland, *Passing the bucks: Money games that political parties play* (Helena, MT: Institute on Money in State Politics, 2003).

19. Federation of Tax Administrators, *State wine excise tax rates: January 1, 2005,* 2006, retrieved December 4, 2006, http://www.taxadmin.org/fta/rate/wine.html.

20. L. Richter, R. D. Vaughan, and S. E. Foster, "Public attitudes about underage drinking and policies: Results from a national survey," *Journal of Public Health Policy 25* (2004, 1): 58–77.

21. Alcohol Policies Project and Center for Science in the Public Interest, *Fact sheet about beer taxes: Stop alcohol tax cuts in the 109th Congress! Oppose beer tax rollback bill H.R. 1306/S. 722,* 2006, retrieved December 4, 2006, http://www.csipinet.org/booze/FedBeerTaxTP.htm.

22. American College of Preventive Medicine, *Increasing taxes on alcoholic beverages: Resolution 438,* 2005, retrieved December 4, 2006, http://www.ama-assn.org/meetings/public/annual05/438a05rev.doc.

23. M. L. Alaniz, "Alcohol availability and targeted advertising in racial/ethnic minority communities," *Alcohol Health and Research World* 22 (1998, 4): 286–289; D. P. Hackbarth, B. Silvestri, and W. Cosper, "Tobacco and alcohol billboards in 50 Chicago neighborhoods: Market segmentation to sell dangerous products to the poor," *Journal of Public Health Policy* 16 (1995, 2): 213–230.

24. P. J. Gruenewald, B. Freisthler, L. Remer, E. A. LaScala, and A. Treno, "Ecological models of alcohol outlets and violent assaults: Crime potentials and geospatial analysis," *Addiction* 101 (2006, 5): 666–677.

25. Public Health and Cigarette Smoking Act of 1969, Pub. L. No. 91-222, 84 Stat. 87; CDC and Tobacco Information and Prevention Source, *Chronology of significant developments related to smoking and health*, February 15, 2006, retrieved November 14, 2006, http://www.cdc.gov/tobacco/overview/chron96.htm.

26. D. Kiley, "Brand new day: Thoughts on marketing and advertising," *Business Week*, March 8, 2005, retrieved December 3, 2006, http://www.business week.com/the_thread/brandnewday/archives/2005/03/booze_industrys.html/; Distilled Spirits Council of the United States, *Code of responsible practices for beverage alcohol advertising and marketing*, October 2003, retrieved December 3, 2006, http://www.discus.org/responsibility/code/read.asp; T. Howard, "Liquor ad TV outlets sought," *USA Today*, April 8, 2002, 2B.

27. CAMY, *Still growing after all these years: Youth exposure to alcohol ads on TV*, retrieved, December 20, 2006, http://camy.org/research/tv/206.

28. T. Howard, "Liquor ad TV outlets sought," *USA Today*, April 8, 2002, 2B; B. Condor, "'Alcopop' ads put a twist into teen marketing," *Chicago Tribune*, August 4, 2002, C3.

29. CDC, *Youth exposure to alcohol advertising on radio: United States, June-August 2004*, September 1, 2006, retrieved September 5, 2006, http://www.cdc.gov/mmwr/preview/mmwrhtml/mm5534a3.htm.

30. CBS News, *Alcohol ads run on youth oriented radio*, August 31, 2006, retrieved December 3, 2006, http://www.marininstitute.org/alcohol_industry/digests/old_news/2006/aug_06.htm.

31. E. M. Lewit, D. Coate, and M. Grossman, "The effects of government regulation on teenage smoking," *Journal of Law and Economics* 24 (1981, 3): 543–569.

32. Campaign for Tobacco-Free Kids, *Increasing the federal cigarette tax reduces smoking (and the cigarette companies know it)*, August 28, 2001, retrieved December 4, 2006, http://www.tobaccofreekids.org/research/factsheets/pdf/0021.pdf.

33. Ibid.

34. Tobacco Free Kids, *Tobacco prices and public health*, August 6, 2000, retrieved December 4, 2006, http://www.tobaccofreekids.org/campaign/global/docs/prices.pdf.

35. Lewis and Center for Public Integrity, 119.

36. C. Berdick, *Up in smoke: Tobacco industry saves on soft money, spends on advertising and lobbyists*, July 28, 2006, retrieved December 4, 2006, http://

www.corpwatch.org/article.php?id=11470&printsafe=1; Federation of Tax Administrators, *State excise tax rates on cigarettes*, 2006, retrieved December 26, 2006, http://www.taxadmin.org/.

37. CDC, *State-specific prevalence of cigarette smoking and quitting among adults: United States, 2004*, November 11, 2005, retrieved December 4, 2006, http://www.cdc.gov/mmwr/preview/mmwrhtml/mm5444a3.htm.

38. Gallup Poll, *Tobacco and smoking*, 2006, retrieved December 5, 2006, http://www.galluppoll.com/content/default.aspx?ci=1717&pg=2.

39. Tobacco Free Kids, *Voters across the country support significant increases in state cigarette taxes*, 2006, retrieved December 5, 2006, http://www.tobaccofreekids.org; K. Buckelew, "Maryland voters want taxes on cigarettes for uninsured," *Daily Record*, May 2, 2006.

40. L. A. Talley, *Congressional Research Service report for Congress: Federal excise taxes on tobacco products: Rates and revenues*, 2002, retrieved December 5, 2006, http://www.uky.edu/Ag/TobaccoEcon/publications/womach_rs20343.pdf.

41. City of New York, *Mayor Bloomberg, Health Commissioner Frieden and schools Chancellor Klein announce a 35% decrease in smoking among high school students since 2001*, press release, March 9, 2006, retrieved December 5, 2006, http://www.nyc.gov; R. Perez-Pena, *A city of quitters? In strict New York 11% fewer smokers*, April 12, 2004, retrieved November 18, 2006, http://www.nytimes.com.

42. B. L. Cowgill, "Opinion: Cigarette taxes a year later," *The Courier-Journal*, August 29, 2006, 9A.

43. Federal Trade Commission, *Federal Trade Commission: Cigarette report for 2001*, 2003, retrieved December 6, 2006, http://www.ftc.gov/os/2003/06/2001 cigreport.pdf; N. Zuckerbrod, *Despite marketing, cigarette sales fall*, October 22, 2004, retrieved December 3, 2006, http://www.tobacco.org.

44. K. Day, *40 states seek to limit "little cigar" marketing*, May 19, 2006, retrieved May 23, 2006, http://washingtonpost.com.

45. Reuters News, "Canada, provinces jack up tobacco taxes," June 17, 2006, retrieved December 27, 2006, http://global.factiva.com.

46. J. Doward, *Smuggling claims hit tobacco giant: Fresh allegations rock BAT as six-year investigation by the Mounties leads to publication of secret letters*, January 9, 2005, retrieved December 5, 2006, http://www.politics.guardian.co.uk/smoking/Story/0138622600.html.

47. E. Carson, *Tobacco road (higher cigarette tax rates can encourage smuggling)*, March 1, 1995, retrieved December 27, 2006, http://global.factiva.com.

48. U.S. District Court, Eastern District of New York, *The European Community (plaintiffs) complaint against RJR Nabisco, Inc. (defendants) in the United States District Court Eastern District of New York*, 2006, retrieved December 6, 2006, http://www.nyed.uscourts.gov/coi/02cv5771cmp.pdf, p. 1.

49. Civil RICO Report, *Tobacco litigation*, October 1, 2006, retrieved March 23, 2006, http://web.lexis-nexis.com.

50. Associated Press, *Westin hotel chain to ban smoking indoors*, December 5, 2006, retrieved December 3, 2006, http://www.msnbc.com.

51. Flight Attendant Medical Research Institute, *History: Flight Attendant Medical Research Institute (FAMRI)*, 2006, retrieved December 3, 2006, http://www.famri.org.

52. P. Ling and S. A. Glantz, "Forum on youth smoking: Why and how the tobacco industry sells cigarettes to young adults: Evidence from industry documents," *American Journal of Public Health* 92 (2002, 6): 908–916.

53. Florida Department of Children and Families, *Florida Youth Substance Abuse Survey (FYAS) 2002*, 2002, retrieved December 5, 2006, http://www.dcf.state.fl.us/mentalhealth/publications/fysas; Campaign for Tobacco-Free Kids, *Special report: State tobacco settlement: Florida*, December 6, 2002, retrieved December 28, 2006, http://www.tobaccofreekids.org/reports/settlements/state.php?StateID=FL; M. Ruiz, *White paper: TRUTH campaign drives smoking attitude change in Florida youth* (Sarasota: Florida Public Relations Association, 2000).

54. M. C. Farrelly, K. C. Davis, L. Haviland, P. Messeri, and C. Healton, "Evidence of a dose-response relationship between 'truth' antismoking ads and youth smoking prevalence," *American Journal of Public Health* 95 (2005, 3): 425–431.

55. J. J. Wilson, *Summary of the Attorney General's master tobacco settlement agreement*, 1999, retrieved December 5, 2006, http://academic.udayton.edu/health/syllabi/tobacco/summary.htm.

56. U.S. General Accountability Office, *Tobacco settlement: States' allocation of fiscal year 2004 and expected fiscal year 2005 payments*, 2006, retrieved December 5, 2006, http://www.gao.gov.

57. E. Carvlin, "Michigan working up first tobacco deal," *The Bond Buyer*, April 12, 2006.

58. National Center for Policy Analysis, *Securitization puts tobacco settlement money at risk*, March 11, 2003, retrieved December 26, 2006, http://www.ncpa.org/iss/sta/2003/pd031103a.html.

59. Campaign for Tobacco-Free Kids, *Special report: Big tobacco still targeting kids*, 2006, retrieved January 10, 2007, http://tobaccofreekids.org/reports.

60. C. King and M. Siegel, "The master settlement agreement with the tobacco industry and cigarette advertising in magazines," *New England Journal of Medicine* 345 (2001, 7): 504–511.

61. Join Together, "States sue R. J. Reynolds, charge settlement violations," March 21, 2001, retrieved June 14, 2006, http://www.jointogether.org/news/; California Department of Justice, *Attorney General Lockyer praises $20 million fine against Reynolds for targeting minors with ads: San Diego court ruling marks fourth successful lawsuit against company in two years*, July 6, 2002, retrieved December 3, 2006, http://ag.ca.gov.

62. U.S. Census Bureau, Population Division. (2005). *Census population estimates, 2004*. Retrieved March 18, 2006, http://www.census.gov/popest/

states/files/SC-EST2004-AGESEX_RES.csv and The National Center on Addiction and Substance Abuse at Columbia University. (2006). *CASA analysis of the Youth Risk Behavior Study (YRBS), 2005* [Data File]. Atlanta, GA: U.S. Department of Health and Human Services, Centers for Disease Control and Prevention, National Center for Chronic Disease Prevention and Health Promotion.

63. Campaign for Tobacco-Free Kids, *Toll of tobacco in the United States of America,* 2006, retrieved October 17, 2006, http://www.tobaccofreekids.org; Schneider Institute for Health Policy and Robert Wood Johnson Foundation, *Substance abuse: The nation's number one health problem* (Princeton, NJ: Robert Wood Johnson Foundation, 2001); R. J. Reynolds Tobacco Company, *Quick facts,* 2006, retrieved December 27, 2006, http://www.rjrt.com/legal/taxQuick Facts.asp; Center for Science in the Public Interest, *Alcohol tax hikes prove popular in new poll,* 2005, retrieved December 27, 2006, http://www.cspinet.org/new/200512071.html.

CHAPTER 11

1. OAS, *Summary of findings from the 1998 National Household Survey on Drug Abuse,* 1999, retrieved October 11, 2006, http://www.oas.samhsa.gov/nhsda/98SummHtml/NHSDA98Summ-03.htm.

2. In 1992, the rate of past month's use among youth was 5.3 percent; in 1979, it had been 16.3 percent. Ibid. Applied to the Census, the numbers dropped from approximately 3.3 million to 1.1 million. U.S. Census Bureau. (2007). *Resident population plus armed forces overseas—estimates by age, sex, and race: July 1, 1979.* Retrieved February 1, 2007, http://www.census.gov/popest/archives/pre-1980/PE-11-1979.pdf.; U.S. Census Bureau. (2007). *U.S. population estimates by age, sex, race, and Hispanic origin: 1980 to 1999.* Retrieved February 1, 2007, http://www.census.gov/popest/archives/1990s/nat-detail-layout.txt.

3. Current illicit drug use was at a rate of 9.9 percent. OAS, SAMHSA, Results from the 2005 National Survey of Drug Use and Health: National findings, DHHS Pub. No. SMA 06-4194 (Rockville, MD: DHHS, SAMHSA, OAS, 2006). Applied to the Census, that number is approximately 2.6 million youth. U.S. Census Bureau, & Bureau of Labor Statistics. (2006). *Current Population Survey (CPS): December 2005.* Retrieved February 1, 2007, http://www.census.gov/cps/.

4. CASA teen surveys, 1996 and 2006.

5. CASA, *Under the counter: The diversion and abuse of controlled prescription drugs in the U.S.* (New York: Author, 2005), iii, 4.

6. Ibid., 4, 23.

7. NIAAA, *Alcoholism: Getting the facts*, 2004, retrieved November 17, 2006, http://pubs.niaaa.nih.gov/publications/GettheFacts_HTML/facts.htm.

8. OAS, SAMHSA, *National Household Survey on Drug Abuse: Main findings 1992*, DHHS Publication No. SMA 94-3012 (Rockville, MD: DHHS, SAMHSA, OAS, 1994); OAS, SAMHSA, *Results from the 2005 National Survey*.

9. Teen smokers dropped from 18.5 percent of teens in 1993 to 13 percent in 2001—OAS, SAMHSA, *National Household Survey on Drug Abuse: Main findings 1993*, DHHS Publication No. SMA 95-3020 (Rockville, MD: DHHS, SAMHSA, OAS, 1995); OAS, *Results from the 2001 National Household Survey on Drug Abuse: Volume 1: Summary of national findings*, NHSDA Series H-17, DHHS Publication No. SMA 02–3758 (Rockville, MD: DHHS, SAMHSA, OAS, 2002).

10. Teen marijuana use jumped from 4 percent in 1993 to 8 percent in 2001—OAS, SAMHSA, *National Household Survey on Drug Abuse: Main Findings 1993*; U.S. Census Bureau. (2007). *U.S. population estimates by age, sex, race, and Hispanic origin: 1980 to 1999*. Retrieved February 1, 2007, http://www.census.gov/popest/archives/1990s/nat-detail-layout.txt.U.S. Census Bureau, & Bureau of Labor Statistics. (2006). *Current Population Survey (CPS): December 2001*. Retrieved February 1, 2007, http://www.census.gov/cps/.

11. CASA, *Wasting the best and the brightest: Substance abuse at America's colleges and universities* (New York: 2007). Associated Press. (June 8, 2006). *Officials: Air support for drug war must remain*. Retrieved October 17, 2006, http://www.msnbc.com.

12. Schenck v. U.S., 249 U.S. 47 (1919).

13. C. Anderson, "Rumsfeld proposes pullout on drug effort," *Associated Press*, 2006, retrieved June 15, 2006, http://www.yahoo.com.

14. There are currently three UN conventions: Single Convention on Narcotics Drugs (1961 amended 1972), Convention on Psychotropic Substances (1971), and Convention against the Illicit Traffic in Narcotic Drugs and Psychotropic Substances (1988). The United States has ratified only the last two—United Nations, *Single convention on narcotic drugs, 1961: As amended by the 1972 protocol amending the single convention on narcotic drugs, 1961*, 1972, retrieved December 5, 2006, http://www.unodc.org/pdf/convention_1961_en.pdf.; United Nations, *Convention on psychotropic substances, 1971*, 1971, retrieved December 5, 2006, http://www.unodc.org/pdf/convention_1971; United Nations, *United Nations convention against illicit traffic in narcotic drugs and psychotropic substances, 1988*, 1988, retrieved December 5, 2006, http://www.unodc.org/pdf/convention_1988_en.pdf.

15. CASA, *So help me God: Substance abuse, religion and spirituality* (New York: Author, 2001), 1; CASA, *National survey of American attitudes on substance abuse IX: Teen dating practices and sexual activity* (New York: Author, 2004), 23;

CASA, *National survey of American attitudes on substance abuse X: Teens and parents* (New York: Author, 2005), 26; CASA, *National survey of American attitudes on substance abuse XI: Teens and parents* (New York: Author, 2006), 23.

16. Of the clergy surveyed, 94.4 percent considered substance abuse an important issue they face—CASA, *So help me God*, 19.

17. Ibid.

18. H. Siegel, *NYC Cigarette smuggling creates problems*, 2006, retrieved November 13, 2006, http://no-smoking.org/jan04/01-07-04-1.html.

19. R. Perez-Pena, *A city of quitters? In strict New York 11% fewer smokers*, April 12, 2004, retrieved November 18, 2006, http://www.nytimes.com. Perez-Pena, R. (2006, December 21). Mayor's curb on smoking is credited with saving lives. *New York Times*, B4.

20. G. H. Brody, D. L. Flor, N. Hollet-Wright, J. K. McCoy, and J. Donovan, "Parent-child relationships, child temperament profiles and children's alcohol use norms," *Journal of Studies on Alcohol, Supplement 13* (1999): 45–51; L. E. McMaster and M. G. Wintre, "The relations between perceived parental reciprocity, perceived parental approval, and adolescent substance use," *Journal of Adolescent Research 11* (1996, 4): 440–460.

INDEX

use of, during late 1960s and 1970s, 22
wide use of, 119
women, fertility treatments and, 137
Marijuana and Medicine: Assessing the Science Base, 124
Marijuana Tax Act of 1937, 20–21
Marijuana withdrawal syndrome, 123
Marinol, 120
Marketing, 3. *See also* Advertising
Marlboro cigarettes, 158
Martin, John, 88
Maryland, cigarette taxes in, 151
Massachusetts Department of Public Health, 61
Master Settlement Agreement, 157–158
Mayer, Andre, 183
McCain, Cindy, 4
McCain, John, 156, 157
McCall's magazine, cigarette advertising in, 14
McCambridge, Mercedes, 180
McDonough, James, 31
McGwire, Mark, 55
MCI Center, 56
McNamara, Robert, 179, 183
MDMA (ecstasy), 26, 30
Medicaid, 104, 169
    costs of substance abuse and, 6
    incarceration expenses and, 91
Medicaid patients
    health care costs, substance abuse and, 82
    substance abuse treatment for, 73
Medical marijuana, 119
    politicization around issue of, 121
Medical profession
    smoking and, 75
    stigmatization of substance abuse and, 164, 165
    substance abuse in patients and, 73–76

Medicare, 104, 169
    substance abuse-related costs and, 82
Medications, for substance abuse, 70
Medicine, labeling drug content of, 20
Memorial Sloan Kettering Cancer Center, 60
Men
    alcohol metabolization in women vs., 140
    drinking and, 139
Mental Health Association, 169
Mental illness
    co-occurrence of, with substance abuse, 78
    dangers of marijuana use and, 124
    drug and alcohol abuse by students and, 44
    homelessness and substance abuse co-occurring with, 115–116
    multiple drug use among children and adults and, 35–36
    psychotropic drugs and treatment of, 21
Menthol cigarettes, marketing of, 13
Meprobomate, 21
Methadone, 31, 70, 78, 167
Methamphetamine, 1, 5, 26, 29, 133
    child abuse and, 103
    children in foster care and, 7
    child welfare system and, 109
    crime and, 86, 128
    domestic violence and, 105
    HIV epidemic and, 65, 67
    hospital emergency room admissions and abuse of, 83
    multidrug episodes, hospital admissions and, 35
    treatment admission rates for, 30
"Meth mouth," 91
Michigan, Master Settlement Agreement and, 157

ABOUT THE AUTHOR

Joseph A. Califano, Jr., was born on May 15, 1931, in Brooklyn, New York, where he grew up. He received his Bachelor of Arts degree from the College of the Holy Cross in 1952 and his LLB from Harvard Law School in 1955. After service in the U.S. Navy and three years with Governor Thomas Dewey's Wall Street law firm, he joined the Kennedy administration and served in the Pentagon as General Counsel of the Army and as Secretary of Defense Robert McNamara's special assistant and top troubleshooter.

President Lyndon Johnson named Mr. Califano his special assistant for domestic affairs in 1965, and he served in that post until the president left office in January 1969. During his years on the White House staff, Mr. Califano worked on the Medicare and Medicaid programs and helped shape dozens of Great Society bills related to health care, criminal justice, the environment, consumers, and social welfare. The *New York Times* called him "Deputy President for Domestic Affairs." At the end of his term, President Johnson wrote to Mr. Califano, "You were the captain I wanted and you steered the course well."

From 1969 to 1977, Mr. Califano practiced law in Washington, D.C., and served as attorney for the *Washington Post* and its reporters Bob Woodward and Carl Bernstein, *Newsweek*, and others during the Watergate years.

From 1977 to 1979, Mr. Califano was U.S. Secretary of Health, Education, and Welfare and became the first voice to alert the nation to the explosion of health care costs and teenage pregnancy, mounted the first national antismoking campaign, began the computer policing of Medicare and Medicaid to eliminate fraud and abuse, and issued the first Surgeon General's Report on Health Promotion and Disease Prevention, *Healthy People*, to set health goals for the nation.

From 1979 to 1992, Mr. Califano practiced law in Washington, D.C. In 1992, he founded The National Center on Addiction and Substance Abuse (CASA) at Columbia University, where he serves as chairman and president. He has been an adjunct professor of health policy and management at Columbia University's Medical School and School of Public Health. He is a member of the Institute of Medicine of the National Academy of Sciences.

Mr. Califano is the author of ten previous books (two with Howard Simons, former managing editor of the *Washington Post*) and has written articles for the *New York Times*, the *Washington Post*, *Reader's Digest*, the *New Republic*, *America*, the *New England Journal of Medicine*, and other publications. He is married to Hilary Paley Byers and lives in Westport, Connecticut. He has three children, Mark, Joseph III, and Claudia; two stepchildren, Brooke Byers and John F. Byers IV; and seven grandchildren.

PublicAffairs is a publishing house founded in 1997. It is a tribute to the standards, values, and flair of three persons who have served as mentors to countless reporters, writers, editors, and book people of all kinds, including me.

I.F. STONE, proprietor of *I. F. Stone's Weekly*, combined a commitment to the First Amendment with entrepreneurial zeal and reporting skill and became one of the great independent journalists in American history. At the age of eighty, Izzy published *The Trial of Socrates*, which was a national bestseller. He wrote the book after he taught himself ancient Greek.

BENJAMIN C. BRADLEE was for nearly thirty years the charismatic editorial leader of *The Washington Post*. It was Ben who gave the *Post* the range and courage to pursue such historic issues as Watergate. He supported his reporters with a tenacity that made them fearless and it is no accident that so many became authors of influential, best-selling books.

ROBERT L. BERNSTEIN, the chief executive of Random House for more than a quarter century, guided one of the nation's premier publishing houses. Bob was personally responsible for many books of political dissent and argument that challenged tyranny around the globe. He is also the founder and longtime chair of Human Rights Watch, one of the most respected human rights organizations in the world.

For fifty years, the banner of Public Affairs Press was carried by its owner Morris B. Schnapper, who published Gandhi, Nasser, Toynbee, Truman, and about 1,500 other authors. In 1983, Schnapper was described by *The Washington Post* as "a redoubtable gadfly." His legacy will endure in the books to come.

Peter Osnos, *Founder and Editor-at-Large*